D1572725

THE ROMANTIC FRAGMENT POEM

MARJORIE LEVINSON

The Romantic Fragment Poem

A CRITIQUE OF A FORM

The University of North Carolina Press

Chapel Hill and London

© 1986 The University of North Carolina Press

All rights reserved

Manufactured in the United States of America

Library of Congress Cataloging-in-Publication Data

Levinson, Marjorie.

The Romantic fragment poem.

Includes index.

1. English poetry—19th century—History and

criticism. 2. Romanticism—England. 3. Unfinished

books. 4. Poetics. 5. English language—Versification.

I. Title.

PR590.L43   1986   821'.7'09   85-28927

ISBN 0-8078-1684-1

For Jerry, who sees me through

CONTENTS

. . . .

ACKNOWLEDGMENTS

.   .   .   .

When I began this book eight years ago, I conceived it as a modest attempt to elucidate a critical practice that seemed to be governed by largely unconscious assumptions. I knew that the irresolution of Romantic poems registered in our scholarship in ways that were neither idiosyncratic nor uninteresting, and that to explain this particular phenomenon would be necessarily to gain some valuable critical distance. I also knew that while the fragment poems of the period are neither all nor exclusively *about* their irresolution, that feature could not be extrinsic to our critique. By conducting a structuralist inquiry informed by contemporary receptions, I hoped to materialize determinate formal procedures that could be systematically examined and, at the same time, to focus the textually constitutive dimension of reception acts.

Over the years, my own procedures began to betray their complicity with the defensive interests (or interested projections) of the poems themselves. In other words, my essentially structuralist inquiry began to problematize—in this case, historicize—the meaning of its own formal premise: the assumption that irresolution plus Romanticism adds up to something special, motivated, and ideologically telling. My determination not to produce another allegory of the age—another fragment thematics—had made me forget that the poems I collected under a particular, formally descriptive rubric are Romantic before they are fragments, and that they are works of the early nineteenth century in England before they are Romantic. In both cases, "before" names a genetic, ideological, and critical priority.

The problem that began to take shape in this book was the most basic one of all. Why *Romantic* fragment poems? Are these fragments inherently different from those produced by other periods? Are they different only because they are received Romantically, or according to a deeply installed canonical code? Can this code tell us anything about the way these poems were written, why they were written—and in such number, and with such effect?

I have not really answered these questions in this book. It took another project entirely for me to use collectively and in a focussed way the meanings—contradictions, ironies, repetitions, illusions—precipitated out in the course of this study. Somewhere in the first chapter, I describe my readings as attempts to light up directional markers that might encourage others to pursue the kind of work begun here. Anne Janowitz initiated a similar critique in 1981, and this coincidence of interest leads me to think that the subject of my book that was begun so long ago has some salience today.

I wish to thank the American Council of Learned Societies for a year-long research grant; this was my opportunity to rethink the terms and method of my inquiry.

Stuart Curran read this book when it was a dissertation. He gave me a great deal of practical support and provided as well priceless historical instruction. I thank him for the chances he gave and for his contribution to their happy outcome.

Celeste Langan and Steven Goldsmith—exemplary students and friends —helped me to ready this manuscript for publication. I cannot imagine shrewder or more conscientious assistance. My admiration and my gratitude go to them.

Last, I thank Stuart Johnson for his editorial acumen and his sensitivity to the project of this book.

I have dedicated this book to Jerry McGann. This is the most I can do but it is also, in this case, very little. When I name him a complete teacher, scholar, and friend, I speak of nothing more than what he is, and I only repeat the knowledge by which his profession knows him.

. . . .

THE ROMANTIC FRAGMENT POEM

As every age has its own character, manners, and amusements, which are influenced even in their lightest forms by the fundamental features of the time, the moral and political character of the age or nation may be read by an attentive observer even in its lightest literature, how remote soever *prima facie* from morals and politics.

"Essay on Fashionable Literature," in Howard Mills, ed.,
Thomas Love Peacock; Memoirs of Shelley and Other Essays and Reviews
(London: Rupert Hart-Davis, 1920), pp. 264–65.

In the course of [the] transition from one social structure to another, the mental or spiritual life of men becomes more intense because it does not exhaust itself trying to live up to certain models. Man sees himself "condemned to freedom" and thrown beyond himself into a new image, which can take a negative form and which is far from being a symbol of integration capable of realization at some future date. And so this individual or collective spiritual life, which can no longer be expressed or fulfilled within the structures of an already disintegrating society, moves toward the imaginary and the creation of new forms.

JEAN DUVIGNAUD
The Sociology of Art, trans. Timothy Wilson
(New York: Harper and Row, 1967; trans. 1972), p. 59.

To crave and to have are as like as a thing and its shadow. . . . When do our senses ever know anything so utterly, as when we lack it? And here again is a foreshadowing—the world will be made whole. . . . Though we dream and hardly know it, longing, like an angel, fosters us, smooths our hair, and brings us wild strawberries.

MARILYNNE ROBINSON
Housekeeping (New York: Bantam Books, 1982), p. 152.

CHAPTER ONE

PRELIMINARIES

The poetic fragment, while not, of course, unique to the early nineteenth century, is nonetheless a peculiarly Romantic form. Let me clarify that distinction by analogy. Throughout the years, numbers of scholars have argued that the novel assumed determinate form *before* the eighteenth century got underway. As we all know, the novel, which maintained its position throughout the eighteenth century, appreciated exponentially in the popular and critical marketplace from the early nineteenth century to the present. Most of us feel we can safely claim the form as a dominant modern perspective.

I rehearse these commonplaces in order to emphasize that while the novel does not occur exclusively, most prominently, or perhaps even originally in the early eighteenth century, it enjoys in our critical canons a privileged relationship with that interval—or, with the general and literary ideologies whereby we conceive that interval an organized and meaningful span, a "period." For a number of obvious and not so obvious reasons (for example, the number of novels published in the eighteenth century relative to former periods; conditions of literary production and reception in the period; structure and tendency of literary historiography), most of us allow the eighteenth-century novel historical and therefore formal priority. Quite automatically, one tends to describe the practice of Fielding, Richardson, and Defoe when introducing the form to a beginning student of literature. Indeed, those who contend for a pre-eighteenth-century novel typically argue their submission on the basis of its resemblance to the eighteenth-century form.

Although poetic fragments occur in periods other than the Romantic, criticism tacitly assigns them an unusually motivated and expressive condition within the early nineteenth century, or within that age's dominant ideologies of reading and writing. The fragment, like the novel, is felt not merely to reflect but to focus the sensibility of its originary or associated epoch. It figures in our criticism as an *exemplary* Romantic expression. This semantic priority enormously influences our practical criticism, and at a most elementary as well as unconscious level. The sorts of texts that are received as poetic fragments—of strictly historical, documentary interest—in the context of seventeenth- or eighteenth-century studies are, within Romantic scholarship, "autonomized." We critically manipulate these items as *fragment poems*, "achieved by [their] inachievement."[1]

The canonical position of the Romantic fragment poem (RFP) differs from that of the novel in one very important respect. Despite the informal consensus on "the fragment(ary)" as a Romantic theme and technical interest, literary criticism, if it defines the fragment poem at all, does so in an ad hoc fashion in order to talk about some unfinished work which is felt to solicit or typically receives serious literary attention. Such criticism is not, of course, conceptually innocent, or not without assumptions that situate the fragment as a meaningful cultural artifact and event. It is simply unembarrassed by the kinds of formulations that eighteenth-century scholars routinely proliferate in their practical and historical criticism.

This is a surprising state of affairs and one that cannot be explained by an airy "*ça va sans dire*," inasmuch as criticism has been far from reticent in its formal discrimination of a host of epochal productions, many of them more retiring than the novel. One thinks, for example, of inquiries into the seventeenth-century religious meditation and the eighteenth-century local poem. More to the point, Romantic criticism has skillfully interrogated such gestural transparencies as the conversation poem, the lyrical ballad, and the organic, interiorized autobiographical discourse. Only the fragment poem—by its own logic, another artless felicity—has escaped demystification.

What we have are strategies for a formal cognition and the set of assumptions supporting those strategies, the whole apparatus so thoroughly and innocently installed as to render it, its meanings, and many effects of the works on which it is deployed imperceptible. By what logic is it the case, one might ask, that although both "Hero and Leander" and "The Triumph of Life" owe their truncation to a historical accident (the poet's death), critics almost without exception address the irresolution of Shelley's poem as a doctrinal and formal issue, whereas Marlowe's unfinished epyllion provokes no such discussion. The kinds of explanation that spring first to mind (Shelley's idealistic dualism, his theory of aesthetic production, "The Triumph"'s particular mode of anticlosure, the argument or vision of the poem) are, we can see, not explanations at all. They merely rephrase the question and in an equally Romantic language.

Explanation of historically differential textual construction properly begins with the most impressionistic and tautological observation; one intentionalizes the irresolution of one poem and not another from a sense of canonical and historical propriety or expedience. This is to say, one feels that "The Triumph," unlike "Hero and Leander," not only "works" in its fragmentary condition, but that its success would be of a different kind, or greatly diminished, or entirely obstructed were anything added to it. I am describing a critical decision overdetermined by historical and ideological factors. One activates a mechanism that discovers aesthetically usable irresolution in a particular poem because one anticipates a higher yield from the work thus construed: a more precise and/or inclusive experience of meaning. This anticipation is not unrelated to the real and often social conditions that enabled the work's first emergence and that remain inscribed in its strategies and silences, and in those of its early receptions. (The poem's manner of working its materials will, to some extent, reflect its own working by history. Both these processes, and their interdetermination, cannot but condition and *should* condition belated receptions.) If poets, publishers, and readers were, as far as one can ascertain, alert to the aesthetic effects of irresolution in certain poems, it is likely that the cultivation of a comparable alertness—comparable in *degree*, not *kind*—would enhance the modern response to those poems. In other words, while I make no formalist claims for the determinacy of the RFP (nor do I argue the self-consciousness of its production and original reception), I do identify a particular, historically circumscribed configuration. By that I do not mean a consensus virtual image (in the technical sense of that phrase), but a real representation of pragmatic actualities: writing, and the history of readings brought to bear on that writing. To describe such a configuration is not, then, to enumerate formal properties nor to construct the idea that organizes a range of actual works, but to offer a "formalized description of changing historical conventions."[2] More specifically, it is to investigate the ways in which certain works, considered collectively, represent their origins, procedures, and interests, and thereby seek to construct their readers.

Epochally differential constructions arise from certain a priori (with respect to particular reception acts) and historically specific assumptions which are the conditions for knowledge of a certain kind, or constitutive of a certain artifact. Ultimately, explanation of the assumptions that transform a textual condition into a formal convention resides in some particular play of complicities among spheres of determination. Roughly speaking, the RFP owes its epochal specificity to certain stable, empirically available facts (composition, publication, and reception data); to the special social, doctrinal, and psychic purposes realized or intended by the sign of indeterminacy in the early nineteenth century (the Romantic ideology); and to the position of the concept, "the fragmentary," in the critical and artistic discourses of the last fifty years (epistemological legacies of the Romantic ideology).

Before I define my critical object and method, let me describe more fully the kinds of discourse available to students of the RFP. I do this not just to make space for my own inquiry, but because this discourse figures so prominently (and often antithetically) in my own critical procedures. Simply, it is part of the subject I hope to illuminate.

Students of the Enlightenment and the nineteenth century have long remarked the sketch, the torso, the poetic fragment, the beauty, the ruin, and the detached overture or song as cultural illuminations. I suspect that the very frequency and thus the apparent polymorphism of "the fragmentary" in the period in question have discouraged specific inquiry into the emergence and effects of particular works and kinds.[3] What sustained commentary there is can best be described as expressive-essentialist, or zeitgeist critique. (I treat the one striking exception to this rule below.) In practice, this means two things: first, an attempt to divine the self-consistent and seminal idea that rationalizes univocally the diverse production of fragmentary forms in the period; second, the abstraction of this idea from the critical and philosophic discourses of the period. Irresolution is represented by this method as a generic deviation from some generic norm (that is, "perfection") that is assumed to be obvious, timeless, and universal: an uninterpretable and uninteresting given. The particular contexts of the deviation (a poem, a poem by Coleridge, a poem by Coleridge written in 1798 but not printed until 1816 and with provocative revisions), and the meaning of the particular norm projected within those contexts, are not considered. Irresolution is thematized (say, an emblem of Romantic aspiration or despair) and totalized without benefit of analysis as a formal effect and one that is historically and ideologically constituted.

Consider, for example, Thomas McFarland's wonderfully erudite study, *Romanticism and the Forms of Ruin*, the preeminent example of the expressive-essentialist critique. Despite its title, the book has little to do with forms or ruins as those words are commonly—that is, materially—understood. The author addresses "modalities"—phenomena as diverse as poetic lapses, early deaths, Wordsworth's agoraphobia, Coleridge's divorce, and the perception of hallways. One encounters here no readings of fragment poems nor, indeed, systematic explications of any actual works. *Romanticism and the Forms of Ruin* is a meditation on "the fragmentary," a category which McFarland defines at the outset as a "diasparactive trio" ("incompleteness, fragmentation, and ruin").[4] From the range of English, and yet more impressively, Continental Romanticisms, the author assembles a stunning array of statements about and illustrations of imperfection. By bringing to bear on this collection his diasparactive schema, McFarland develops a phenomenology of the fragment: a mapping of an epoch's structure of consciousness. "The fragmentary," at the center of this structure, figures in the book as a symbol in the Coleridgean or interpenetrative sense. As the book jacket says, *"under the concept* of fragmentation, the author correlates and unifies such diverse data as . . ." (my emphasis).

McFarland's engaging confession of his Coleridgean proceedings (by his account, syncretic, esemplastic, and openended) masks the real interest of the work: its abstraction of "the fragmentary"—a semantic value—from a set of historical phenomena, and the postulate of this abstraction as the essence of Romanticism. McFarland takes it for granted that we have all at some point and quite naturally registered the incompletion of Romantic works and have assimilated this fact formally and, to some extent, conceptually. "The disrupted nature of Romanticism" is McFarland's real subject, and "the fragmentary" (one might recall here Wellek's symbol and organism) is said to express the age's consciousness of its epistemological fall into dualism.

As I noted, the zeitgeist critique privileges the intracanonical or sympathetic account of the fragment. It takes as its task the critical repetition of the concept of indeterminacy as this concept occurs in nineteenth-century letters. In that "the fragmentary" enjoys a special eminence in German Romantic criticism (and because it receives relatively little critical attention from the English Romantics), the expressive critic typically explains English practice by way of German aesthetics. This is no place to embark upon a comparative study of English and German Romanticisms. Let me briefly reflect, however, on the differing situations of the fragment within the two discourses by way of defending my parochialism.

Friedrich Schlegel's famous aphorism—"the works of the ancients have become fragments; the works of moderns are fragments at their inception" (*Athenaeum* fragment #24, 1798)—not only describes the situation of "the fragmentary" within German Romantic letters, it discursively reflects that relation. Widely differing in practice and ethos, the German Romantic writers nonetheless knew themselves to be coauthors of a chapter in intellectual history, and "the fragmentary" was an acknowledged theme in that chapter. The peculiarly philosophic situation of that theme gave the artistic production of fragments a programmatic aspect. Each such work was as a phase in a project conceived by a group of writers cognizant of the discursive norms which constituted that body.

The English Romantics enjoyed no such cohesion; they acknowledged no common discourse nor did their philosophic reflections define for them a collective problem or program. Coleridge transplanted to English soil cuttings from the German garden, but these cannot, in all fairness, be said to have taken. Coleridge himself, of course, provided the English a method of philosophizing and the *desideratum* of reuniting poetry with philosophy, but the sort of intellectual and social consolidation evident in the German system simply never emerged in England. As Marilyn Butler has so forcefully demonstrated, the English poets aligned themselves on opposite sides of the great political issues of the day, and these divisions largely concealed from them those social, intellectual, and methodological affinities that might have rendered them a movement in the German sense.[5] I emphasize, it is not that the English *lacked* common knowledges, but that they wanted a self-identification based on the recognition of this collective experience—conditions and responses. Coleridge's fervid and persistent attempts to cultivate a clergy should alone suggest how deeply schismatic the English intellectual community felt to one very astute member of it. I note as well that among those topics and representations which recur throughout and, from our remove, can be seen to organize English Romantic letters, "the fragmentary" does not obtrude itself. Coleridge and Shelley meditate metaphysically upon indeterminacy, but their discussions—neither systematic nor sustained—so nearly approximate the unself-consciousness of the poetry as to render them critically misleading. For us to interpret English poetry by way of the German critical model is not only a historically dubious procedure but, in the absence of an English critical apparatus that might counter the German ideology, downright appropriative.

The English Romantics practiced the fragment; they generated the form naïvely—not in the absence of ideological and material constraints but without benefit of collaboration, perceived precedent, or theoretical apparatus. Whereas the German fragments reflect *upon* contemporary life and thought, the English fragments reflect those realities.[6] All reflections "upon" are, of course, reflections "of" as well; the English fragments, individually and en masse, possess a collective meaning, but a different sort of meaning from that which the German fragments enjoy. One could describe this semiotic difference with reference to the notions overdetermined and predetermined. The English fragment acquires its formal distinctiveness ex post facto, or after it enters the marketplace or tradition and is found to resemble a host of poems located in that same Romantic slot. The English fragment is thus constituted a poetic form by the reader's perception of that work as an element in an epochal set. Or, one poetic fragment does not make a fragment poem; ten do. Quantity, as Engels said, changes quality.

The quiddity of the German fragment is bestowed upon it by its author and from his knowledge that he can best express his individuality through and against a formal mode invented by his contemporaries. Whereas the German fragments structurally address an already formulated problem, the English fragments pose by their form a new, unsuspected problem. To adapt Schlegel's aphorism, the fragments of the German Romantics are fragment poems at their inception; those of the English have become fragment poems.

This binary opposition is admittedly of limited usefulness. Who would deny that the meanings embedded in the German fragment undergo metamorphosis as the work takes its place in a system of similar forms? And surely at some level, the English Romantic fragment is designed precisely to solve that "unsuspected" problem which its form betrays. Despite these equalizing qualifications, the fashion of analogical interpretation seems to me ill-judged. Criticism has learned not to take formal similarity or even identity for functional correspondence, and not to abstract verbal events from their various grammars. This is to say, we should no longer elucidate English practice by German aesthetics.

The privileging of that native English critical discourse on the fragment mentioned above—Coleridge's and Shelley's reflections—seems to me no less reductive in its effects. A Coleridgean explanation of the fragment (representation of the historicity of knowledge and belief, and stimulus to a syncretic, higher critical act) or a Shelleyan reading (reminder of existential dualism and of that noumenal order which presides over and occasionally folds into the flux and ephemera of history) cannot but be an idealizing paraphrase of the object, its derivation circular. The critical value of such explanations is strictly dependent on a removed appraisal which would position them as part of the problem and not the solution.

Above, I mentioned one anomalous study of the RFP; this is Edward Bostetter's *The Romantic Ventriloquists*, published in 1963 and, to date, the only full-scale and systematic inquiry into the unfinished poems of the English Romantics.[7] Bostetter proposes that the poetic fragments of each major Romantic reveal the limits of his genius and the congenital defects of Romantic ideology. Bostetter's work is as impressive today for the intelligence and humanity of its critique as it was when it first appeared, but the author's thesis and his critical conclusions do not easily explain the actual reception of the poems he discusses. In Bostetter's view, irresolution represents incapacity—technical, and far more culpably, intellectual and moral. His readings enact a kind of epochal autopsy; Bostetter reveals the specific pathology responsible for the fatal degeneration of the Romantic movement through examination of its most diseased components, its fragments. From the distance of twenty years, we can see the question that Bostetter's premise and practice implicitly formulate. Poems so damaged (unresolved and incapable of resolution), and for such deep structural reasons, logically should not have become and remained prominent and popular elements in the literary and critical traditions. That the Romantic fragments enjoyed both an immediate popularity and a robust canonical afterlife argues that readers tended—and tend—to experience these poems not as defective essays at one excellence but as successful examples of another. And this means that we have for a long time been structuring these anomalous texts in such a way as to deliver them to consciousness as achieved and determinate forms. This reception activity, which so neatly complements-compensates the "defects" of the texts, must surely illuminate the production of those texts, or of their particular defects.

Because Bostetter locates the causes of textual irresolution in the realm of ideology—a realm he conceives as extrinsic to the work proper—he must read the feature as aesthetically unmotivated. That is, because the poem's miscarriage is perceived as *at variance with* its formal intention, it is not made immanent in the author's critical discussion. Thus, while

Bostetter investigates the ideological conditions of irresolution in Romantic poetry, his conceptual framework obstructs a critical implementation of his findings. More specifically, his critique defines the need for a reciprocal explanation of reception and composition acts.

To postulate the RFP is not to claim that the unfinished poem was necessarily so conceived and executed by its authors: that is, as a poem "finished" in and by its imperfection. Bostetter's general interpretation of the genesis of the fragments he discusses is, I believe, perfectly just, but I would put a different inflection on the matter. In the truncation of these works, we might read the writer's collision with that contradiction which enables and informs his art—a contradiction at once too seminal and too assimilated into individual historical consciousness to permit formal resolution or transcendence. I would emphasize, in other words, the ideological provenance of that self-thwarting formal intention, whereas Bostetter assumes a blindness-insight, ideology-enlightenment ratio. That is, Bostetter implicitly sets the RFP at the ideological edge, and characterizes its relation to the center as (incompletely) adversarial. I put the form at the heart of Romantic knowledge, and explain its critical power by reference to that axial stress. Genetically speaking, the particular formal (and social) realization of the fragment poem is its *dis*integration. Moreover, the conflicts which Bostetter locates in a strictly conceptual universe more often than not take the form of the structural or technical dilemma. While these binds contain and reflect ideological tensions, they cannot be directly translated into a thematic discourse without a real loss of particular meaning. In an unfashionable and terribly useful way, Bostetter poses for the RFP questions of origination. By liberating those questions from the exclusively authorial psychic discourse in which Bostetter frames them, we can begin to approach the fragment poem as a site of ideological impasse and thus to appreciate its historical career.

The RFP, understood as a historically specific and therefore structurally distinct artifact—its occurrence and character determined but not inevitable—disappears between the critical poles defined by McFarland and Bostetter. The former develops the fragment as a vehicle for the symbolization of a cultural theme, while the latter represents it as an unfortunate and extrinsically induced deformation of structural intention. The work's unfinishedness is, on the one hand, presented as the source of its poetry, meaning, and value and, on the other, as inimical to the work's formal and conceptual realization. We can surely find some middle way between idealization and disqualification—some method for articulating the irresolution of Romantic poems as a motivated fact that controls but does not create meaning, and whose sphere of operations is the theater of real and social history.

Let me isolate my problematic phrase, "historically specific and therefore structurally distinct," and thus begin to address the reading-writing negotiations that precipitate the RFP. Formal designation and textual construction are, we know, highly private and (theoretically) idiosyncratic affairs. I can call two lines by Sappho a RFP if through that formal concept I can produce a more elegant (explanatory, economical) reading than that which any other concept seems to yield. This kind of license is not what I have in mind when I posit the RFP. Within the idiom of this book, the RFP is an unfinished poem (visibly incomplete or so identified by title or note) written by an English Romantic poet and published during his lifetime or posthumously—a poem whose irresolution invites assimilation as a formal directive and thus functions as a semantic determinant. Or, once again, RFP designates a historically specific and therefore structurally distinct form.

With that phrase, I do not describe an empirically available sign whereby a reader might reliably distinguish the RFP from, say, poetic fragments or non-Romantic fragment poems. I do not propose that all the unfinished poems written in England between 1798 and 1832 possess (or lack) some feature, produce (or fail to produce) some effect, indicate through their presentation (punctuation, lineation, title, placement in volume, preface) a particular rhetorical or formal intention, or originated in a specific authorial determination or through a particular method.

In this context, let me note that I use the term "Romantic" in a frankly mechanical way, thereby designating that group of writers and works generally associated with the period 1798–1832 in England.[8] In the conclusion to this book, I offer a critical reflection on the meanings which this standard usage brings out. Lest my submission to a received dating scheme appear disingenuous, however, let me briefly clarify my epoch-genre deliberations. I do not raise the question of a given fragment's Romantic qualities or lack thereof, so thoroughly do I assume its Romantic *condition*. Rather than postulate a necessary and intrinsic relationship between Romanticism and motivated irresolution (as in the claim that Romantic fragments, by virtue of their Romantic situation, share certain formal characteristics which function as reception imperatives), I propose a necessary but extrinsic relationship, initially derived from an experiential conviction of affinity between "the fragmentary" and widespread Romantic interests and practices, but thereafter automatically invoked for analytic purposes. The reader who adopts this method puts himself in a position to promote certain textual impressions that may not derive from the work proper, without having to argue that all the Romantics reflected on a shared reality in a common and characteristic way, and that their literature betrays this consensus. One need not claim that any one poem per se compels the reader to intentionalize its irresolution. Rather, the decision to construe the unfinishedness of Romantic poems as a motivated feature is informed by one's historical tact, an intelligence gained through the reading of many Romantic poems, fragments and wholes. While the locally arbitrary application of a formal concept is, of course, a dangerous analytic practice, an inductive approach risks historical crudeness. The unprecedented number of poetic fragments written and published by early nineteenth-century English poets imputes a collective meaning to the production of such works, a meaning that may not emerge through isolated, "objective" critical inquiries.

The historical specificity mentioned above describes the conditions of production and reception within which the unfinished poems of the English Romantic poets emerged and flourished. These poems *become* structurally distinct *by virtue of* their historical specificity, having been written and read within a context unique to the early nineteenth century in England. The English RFP may be descriptively indistinguishable from the German Romantic fragment poem or from John Ashbery's fragment, "The Tennis Court Oath"—just as an eighteenth-century British clock may be indistinguishable from an eighteenth-century German clock and from a twentieth-century replica of either clock. Yet as the analogy should suggest, the particular meaning and value of the RFP are determined by its genetic history. (One would not pay for the twentieth-century replica what one might give for the eighteenth-century German clock, nor would the connoisseur include either clock in his collection of eighteenth-century British timepieces.) Moreover, inasmuch as aesthetic production is inseparable from the idea of consumption, the genetic history of that artifact should include an account of real or imagined reception. I refer the reader to a splendidly apropos fantasy, Borges's "Pierre Menard, Author of the *Quixote.*" The trenchant humor of this fiction derives from the narrator's distinction between Cervantes's *Don Quixote* and the pastiche produced by a modern writer. The two texts, excerpts from which are liberally quoted in the story, are physically identical but they are described as immeasurably different in kind, meaning, and value. The pedantic enthusiast responsible for these quixotic and invidious distinctions *is* absurd, and the burlesque of the lit-crit business is well taken. Yet the principle of the narrator's literary analysis is not parodied; the irony of the story hinges on the reader's appreciation of the fantasy of literary replication and (a double irony) on his recognition of his evaluative bias toward the prototext.

The RFP—a work written and read under special historical conditions —offers itself to formal description when that phrase is taken to mean an enactment of the particular social contracts that particular poems seek to establish. Formal description could thus be construed as an attempt to ascertain what people do or did to literature and what that literature does or did to them, the operating assumption being that at any given moment, the two processes are profoundly, *specifically* inter- and overdetermined. Formal description need not, in other words, presuppose an object always already itself, patiently awaiting discursive representations that will leave it serenely unchanged. What I propose by the phrase is a corrective to the concealed and insidious formalism which reifies the conceptual aura surrounding literary works and installs that hypostasis as the essence, cause, or meaning of the work. A formal study can look at the ways in which particular works represent their origins, tactics, and objectives and thereby constitute their readers, among whom we must include ourselves. It can construct its critical object by defining the work's offered intentionality (its representation of its peculiar completeness and autonomy) and revealing the discrepancy between this projection and the discord and disjunctiveness which are the work's truth: the signs of its determinate mode of production.[9] More simply, the exercise is to pry apart the poem's special maneuvers and projections from the totalizing constructs in which criticism, in great good faith and obedient to the rhetoric of the poetry, has framed them.

The RFP is not without its burden of meanings—a certain polemic— but one can best develop those meanings from a position outside the ideology in question and as a critical reflection on it. One begins to secure such a position by refusing the abstract ideas which Romantic fragments generate and offer as their enlightened, self-reflexive logic (for example, the fragment as the form of Romantic becoming, Romantic irony, Romantic autonomy, etc.). By cultivating appreciation of the particular conflicts and defenses which those ideas suppress or displace (and, in any case, postulate by negation)—by examining the particular necessity of the silence that each of these works so prominently installs—we might emancipate the poems from their constraining rubrics and free ourselves from some received ideas of the Romantic. The difference between my ambition and that of the expressive critique described above is partly methodological (a critical and experimental as opposed to deductive, syncretic approach) but the crucial distinction is conceptual. The expressive critic seeks to elaborate the poem's reflective life, its passive location for us of Romantic aspiration and contradiction. I conceive the RFP under a more transformative and aggressive aspect: as a form that works its conditions and conflicts in ways that are neither random, unique, nor disinterested.

I produce my formal object by a genetic inquiry and reconstruction (my point of departure being the poem's own dramatic rehearsal of its provenance and production) and, where possible, by an exploration of the differential obtaining between modern commentary on the poems and contemporary appreciations. My methods and my selection of study texts are explained by my interests. My chief commitment is to the poetry; by reclassifying a range of poems in such a way as to foreground a particular effect, I hope to refocus some familiar and problematic works, and to bring into our visual field some works thus far excluded.

Second, I hope to elucidate the anomalous critical situation mentioned above: the discrepancy between what is said and not said about the RFP and what is done with it. Since criticism agrees to acknowledge the literariness of Romantic fragments, it should define the assumptions that govern this consensus and the readings it facilitates. The immediate question is not whether the fragment was intended as a distinct literary form or whether we have appropriated or should appropriate it as such. Since we *do* intentionalize Romantic fragments, we should acknowledge and explain the principles and the effects of that construction if our conclusions are to be worth anything.

The RFP occurred within what has come to seem a tradition of formal innovation, an innovation tending toward enlarged freedom of literary expression and response. The indeterminacy of the fragment poem, conceived within this context, figures a display of authorial autonomy and an invitation to participatory reading.[10] Quite designedly, it seems, "the law of sufficient information is broken and darkness which has become expressive gains a poetic function."[11] I rehearse these critical truisms by way of introducing the special case presented by the "accidental" Romantic fragments: poems left unfinished, apparently not intended for publication in that condition, and printed posthumously through the intervention of an editor whose motivations may have been bibliographical, biographical, hagiographic, or commercial. The irresolution of these drafts and notebook remains cannot be described as historically intentional nor read as an authorial affirmation. It is, however, a motivated feature if it produces in its readers the appearance of authorial decision or significant function. I suspect this is how most of us construe the accidental RFP. So amenable are these works to the techniques and values of modern criticism, and so accustomed are most Romanticists to intentionalizing the openness of Romantic works, that we absorb these accidental fragments into the genre tacitly established by the "authorized" RFP.

Consider Wordsworth's two-book, 1798–99 *Prelude*—an abbreviated, or rather, arrested epic autobiography. Now that Norton has anthologized the fragment, treating it not as a draft or section, nor as a specimen of the sort of thing found in the finished 1805 and 1850 *Preludes*, but as a self-contained work, it becomes nearly impossible to read this earliest version as one reads the fragments and drafts presented in appendices to standard editions of Wordsworth's poetry. The case is a textbook example of Eliot's "tradition":

> The existing monuments form an ideal order among themselves, which is modified by the introduction of the new (the really new) work of art among them. The existing order is complete before the new work arrives; for order to persist after the supervention of novelty, the *whole* existing order must be . . . altered; and so the relations, proportions, values of each work of art toward the whole are readjusted; and this is conformity between the old and the new.
> —"Tradition and the Individual Talent,"
> in *The Sacred Wood* (London: Methuen, 1920), p. 50.

Once the RFP is established through artistic and/or critical practice, the condition of poetic fragments before and after this catastrophe changes. It becomes possible to read two lines by Alcaeus in *The Greek Anthology* as an achieved (fragment) poem, and it becomes nearly impossible *not* to read Shelley's "The Triumph of Life" as a RFP. This is not to suggest that one does or should read "The Triumph" in the same way one reads Shelley's fragmentary "Vision of the Sea" or Byron's "The Giaour." Knowledge of the work's compositional history cannot but affect—and should affect—one's construction of its irresolution. But just as the authorial prefaces that often accompany the RFP influence interpretation rather than obviate it, so the fortuitous imperfection of some Romantic fragments conditions rather than replaces acts of formal construction. The distinctions that a reader who concedes the literariness and historical specificity of the RFP is likely to make between accidental and authorized fragments produce formal and thematic differences in his textual understanding. These differences are contained and even organized by his concept, the RFP. They do not invalidate that concept.

In chapters three through eleven, I cast the spotlight on a modest collection of poems of varying degrees and kinds of success and ambitiousness, lighting up directional markers that I hope will encourage others to pursue the exploration. I have selected for scrutiny not, generally, the most spectacular RFPs (*Don Juan*, "The Triumph of Life," *The Four Zoas*, *The Recluse*) but those works which seem most instructive in their formal necessity and which have provoked fundamental critical controversies. I also address a few works commonly perceived as so minor as to fall outside the canon altogether (for example, Shelley's *Posthumous Fragments of Margaret Nicholson*). My failure to take on *Don Juan* and "The Triumph" (deliberate fragments, or instances of imitative form) is explained by the fact that these poems have been read brilliantly, exhaustively, and with attention to the particular effects of their particular irresolutions. Kenneth Johnston, for example, has just produced a truly monumental study of Wordsworth's unfinished monument, *The Recluse*. Johnston's astute historical and critical commentary is informed throughout by his sensitivity to the structural peculiarities of the text, one which the reader must assemble and edit before he can perform the most elementary critical act. Frankly, I can add nothing to the existing commentary on *The Recluse* or the above poems.[12]

By way of contextualizing the peculiar situation of the fragment poem in the early nineteenth century, let me describe the categories of poetic fragments available to the pre- (that is, prior, not proto) Romantic reader, and their dominant styles of reception. Most of the imperfect poetic texts known to the eighteenth-century reader can be described as substantial, coherent, and internally finished fragments which, according to the generic parameters they establish, lack one or more terminal units. *The Faerie Queene* and *The Canterbury Tales* are the two outstanding examples of such works. No doubt, critical understanding of *The Faerie Queene* would be altered and enlarged were one to discover the projected cantos.

But the poem as it is, consisting of finished units lacking only their full complement of such units, has not produced cognitive or interpretive confusion in any generation of readers. Similarly, readers of *The Canterbury Tales* are not now, nor were they ever noticeably hampered (or helped) in their response by the fact that Chaucer did not bring the sequence to the particular perfection he projected for it. Each tale appears to realize the author's intentions for that tale; one does not feel that the discovery of additional tales would modify one's reception of the extant units.

The other classes of poetic fragments available to pre-Romantic readers include: (1) specimens of the classical lyric poets published in translation or in the original in the various editions of the *Greek* and *Palatine Anthology* and in individual collections of the Greek and Latin poets; (2) fragments published in posthumous editions as part of the author's literary remains; (3) fragments translated and/or edited (that is, written) by the so-called hoax poets, Macpherson and Chatterton.

Unlike *The Faerie Queene* and *The Canterbury Tales*, these texts potentially cast the reader upon his resources as a reader—a maker of meanings and decipherer of signs. As is the case with the RFP, they enable a participatory or constructive reading. To belabor a point, however, let me reiterate that mine is not a formalist study; I am not curious to compare morphologies. My interest is in contextual configurations and the historically specific meaning of those structures. Each category of fragment enumerated above originally invited (and received) an appreciation best described as historical (biographical, bibliographical, philological, anthropological, sociological). One cannot, of course, deny that some precocious readers conducted a literary redemption of these damaged texts, governed by an assumption of "achieved inachievement." One may infer, however, from the work done on classical scholarship and education in the eighteenth century as well as from the available commentary on pre-Romantic fragments that these works did not stimulate the kind of response common with respect to the RFP. In the early eighteenth century—an age renowned for the moral and pragmatic disposition of its pedagogy and for its zeal in the practice of textual ascription and reconstruction—one would not expect the lyric fragments of Sappho and Alcaeus, for example, to cut a significantly literary figure. First, the texts were typically too meagre and shattered for the procedures of textual reconstruction, and the lives and canons of the poets too dubious for ascription studies. Second, the slight, beautifully nuanced lyric fragments about love and loss, women and wine, would not strikingly appeal to an age whose pedagogical enthusiasms ran to "the didactic poems of Hesiod, Aratus, Lucretius, and Manilius" and whose literary pleasures centered on the Latin poets and satirists.[13] While the lyric fragments pleased by their natural and simple language, personal voice, and direct description of both the tender and martial feelings, they seem to have been absorbed as instances of psychological or domestic documentation: curious insights into the sensibility of their times. Many eighteenth-century translators, seeking to approximate "the spirit and fancy of the poet, not the words or thought literally," expressed not merely a principle of translation but a categorial (and normative) discrimination.[14] It was not until the Longinian revival in the middle to late eighteenth century that the pre-eminence of those lyrics dealing with gods and heroes, and the relatively degraded position of the lesser love lyric (a classification that contained most of the available Greek and Latin poetic fragments) began to be questioned.[15]

Further, styles of presentation have a great deal to do with the way readers are likely to experience the closure of any poem and especially any obviously incomplete one. Generally, editors and translators rendered the classical fragments in strong metrical and determinate stanzaic form. They were made musical: versified and "Englished." The editors thus spared their readers the discomfort of structural irresolution and perhaps inadvertently discouraged them from improvising a literary satisfaction, if these distinctions are not too anachronistic. Regarded as archaeological relics attesting to the universality of fundamental human emotions and experience (much as one might regard some primitive but functionally familiar household item), the classical fragments did not manifest their irresolution as a literary feature. As the visible stamp of antiquity, the imperfection, like the missing nose on an antique bust, lacked artistic implication.

Fragments printed in eighteenth-century "collected remains" or "life and literary remains" editions almost invariably appear in a preface or memoir section and are offered by way of biographical or possibly technical insight rather than as works presumed capable of eliciting and satisfying certain aesthetic expectations. One also finds editors explaining their decision to suppress available "workshop" fragments, citing as justification their admiration for the poet—that is to say, for his sanctioned, or greatest and most polished (finished) achievement. While Dr. Johnson, for example, expresses interest in the "sketches and rough drafts" that Edmund Smith left behind, he defends their suppression: "It cannot be supposed they [those now in possession of Smith's manuscripts] would suppress any thing that was his, but out of respect to his memory, and for want of proper hands to finish what so great a genius had begun." This caution despite Johnson's avowed enjoyment:

> the fable, structure, and connexion, the images, incidents, moral, episodes, and a great variety of ornaments, were so finely laid out, so well fitted to the rules of art, and squared so exactly to the precedents of the ancients, that I have often looked on these poetical elements with the same concern, with which curious men are affected at the sight of the most entertaining remains and ruins of an antique figure or building. Those fragments of the learned, which some men have been so proud of their pains in collecting, are useless rarities, without form and without life, when compared with these embryos which wanted not spirit enough to preserve them; so that I cannot help thinking, that, if some of them were to come abroad, they might be as highly valued as the sketches of Julio and Titian are by the painters; though there is nothing in them but a few outlines, as to the design and proportion.[16]

To publish such fragments would be to expose one's author half-dressed, as it were.

The "collected remains" fragments and the *Greek Anthology* selections are all, of course, eminently susceptible to literary appraisal. Most modern readers probably seize this option automatically and without entertaining alternative modes of reception. But because these works were neither written nor read by people likely to make or perhaps even capable of making this kind of response (and because the meaning of their production differs entirely from that of the RFP), I do not open my study with these specimens, would-be forerunners in a natural evolution of the fragment form.[17]

The hoax poems are another matter. In the controversy which these spurious antiquities stimulated, one may study a set of assumptions (cognitive, critical, canonical) in transition. The completion of this transition, or the replacement of one ideology of reading by another, was the precondition for the production of the RFP. I take up this topic in chapter two.

In 1798, *Lyrical Ballads* presented a new kind of fragment, inaugurating the historical phenomenon we are calling the RFP. The volume contained two fragment poems, both by Coleridge. One poem includes the word "fragment" in its subtitle ("The Foster-Mother's Tale: A Dramatic Fragment") and the other ("The Dungeon"), by its marked and numerous allusions to and dependence on a missing dramatic context, similarly identifies itself as an excerpt from a longer work. Both poems are extracts from Coleridge's play, "Osorio," written in 1797 and performed in 1813 under the new title, "Remorse." Wordsworth added two fragments of his own to the 1800 edition of *Lyrical Ballads*: "A Fragment" (poem # 35, retitled "The Danish Boy" in 1836) and "Nutting," a work which begins on a hemistich, thereby suggesting its divorce from an antecedent (meditative, dramatic) context, and which ends, inconclusively, with a gesture toward the implied listener conjured in the opening lines.

All four fragments are situated squarely in the body of the volume, in the company of newly composed works; they are presented without benefit of authorial introduction, annotation, or apology. They are not relegated to a preface, memoir, appendix, juvenilia, or fragment section. Nor are they identified as prologue, epilogue, extract, or soliloquy. These fragments are neither mood pieces nor detached beauties; their organization is narrative rather than lyric. Coleridge's fragments contain little in the way of imagery or suggestive atmosphere; they fail to yield a unified emotional effect or to engender a certain "tone." Through their offhand and confident presentation, Wordsworth and Coleridge claim for their fragment poems the same degree—though not the same kind—of autonomy as that projected by the rest of the lyrical ballads.

Lyrical Ballads—herald and manifesto of the English Romantic movement—predicts what was to become a convention in the publication of poetic collections. Almost every volume of poetry produced by major and minor Romantic poets includes at least one fragment, either so designated by title or indicated by typographical signs of unfinishedness. Both the placement of these poems and their lack of contextualization (or their strangely uninformative prefaces) are, in effect, rhetorical instructions. The poets seemed to expect that their readers would not only negotiate the obvious difficulties posed by the poems but would construe these as essential or at least contributive to the work's design. That is, the reader is encouraged to consider the fragment as an intentionally unfinished (that is, formally achieved) work, or as a work approved by the poet in and for its accidental unfinishedness.[18] Although a number of poets, by attaching to their fragments explanatory prefaces and/or notes, might seem to have doubted their readers' fragment competence, the nature of the evidence tends to discredit that conjecture. The prefatory accounts are typically inconclusive, nonsystematic, and rhetorically marked. The relation of this commentary to the poetry it introduces is most generously described as asymptotic, and probably most accurately characterized as a repetition. In other words, the explanations have a distinctly conventional character and are more on a par with the poetry proper than they are reflections upon that material. Criticism should find these explanations useful for their elaboration of formal and rhetorical intentions that are more subtly, obscurely, or indirectly inscribed in the fragment itself. To read these accounts as an authentic critical discourse (to be imitated rather than explained by the modern scholar) is to mistake their textual situation.

While one cannot obtain from the nineteenth-century review the kind of self-conscious methodological articulations that would confirm a reception analysis, one does find practical evidence of a certain kind and degree of expertise. The early reviews of *Lyrical Ballads*, for instance, show that despite some seemingly crippling obstacles to appreciation, "The Foster-Mother's Tale" and "The Dungeon" were either praised or passed over, their strangeness not remarked. This is a speaking silence. What it tells us is that the poems were not received as juvenilian exercises, passages from plays, insights into the poet's mode of composition, nor as workshop debris. The visible or advertised irresolution of these poems apparently signified to the Romantic reader not the absence, distortion, or transcendence of form but its presence and determinate identity.[19]

The emergence of a form must, to some extent, indicate a collaboration between writers and readers. The RFP, like all other literary forms, contains a latent imagination of a reader, one who is capable of a particular response to the work's irresolution. Although one cannot, without conducting extensive and careful sociological research, isolate and profile the readers of fragment poems, one can investigate the private representations that are made of the audience in the discourse of artist and critic. While the distinction between real and imagined readers is an important one, it might also be observed that "readers are made by what makes the book."[20] The distinct and even opposed purposes and processes of these makings need not, I think, overly disturb us. In fact, the vexed relationship between the two moments and fields (production, consumption) is our best access to their separate and corporate truths. The activity and imagination that the fragment prescribes for its readership are, to the critic, indices to the poem's productively limited knowledge of itself, and to its distinctive (and interested) representation of this partial knowledge. If we can determine how a particular fragment poem constructs its reader (which is to say, how it seeks to make a reader construct *it*) we can interpret the poem's own mode of production.

Before proceeding, let me confess to a few silent premises. First, readers want an experience of resolution from poetry, and where this is withheld (and if they persist in assuming a literary phenomenon) they will develop a closural effect from the materials and principles at hand. "At hand" means, in order of exegetical recourse, in the poem, on the page, in the volume, in the canon, and in the life or legend. Second, incompletion and disunity are felt only against a background or an imagination of completion and unity. Third, there is a limited number of ways to make literary wholes out of parts, or fragment poems out of poetic fragments.

I present these assumptions so as to indicate the source of some further statements about fragment forms. I use the plural, "forms," advisedly and in order to suggest that RFPs are not all imperfect in the same ways. Each of the poems treated in this book presents a particular kind of irresolution or creates a distinct impression of imperfection. The RFP is the generic construct that contains—is composed of—these various impressions and transactions.

The fragment's formal specificity derives from the model which the work projects as its peculiar and ideal perfection. Irresolution—a feature dialectically dependent on an idea of completion—naturally varies in accordance with the *particular* idea of resolution felt to be relevant. The fragment insinuates in its reader a normative and an extrinsic model of determinate scope and coherence. The work's irresolution is experienced as against this ideal integrity and extensiveness that it presumably could, would, or should have realized. The poem's irresolution is thus discovered by the reader as a determinate or shaped absence. The conceptual model to which the fragment alludes may be embodied as a visual configuration: the concrete spatial form which the fragment, if complete, would describe. Then again, the fragment's ideal and abstract model may be projected as a process or generative law: a dynamic and temporal principle. I take up these figurations and their meaning in some detail in the conclusion.

It seems probable that readers mentally complete/construct such poems by generating the missing parts: the difference between the form on the page and the extrinsic concept of wholeness with reference to which the text identifies its imperfection. In other words, one first ascertains the spatial logic or generative principle that organizes the fragment's discourse. Then, using that template and by way of rather fundamental cognitive acts, one imagines the missing text or context.

The criticism to result from such a reading risks confusing its object of inquiry with its interpretive devices. (The object of the RFP is, as I argue in the conclusion, precisely this confusion—effectively, the substitution of a reading for a writing.) The critic, if he is careful and self-critical, may distinguish the fragment from its ghostly perfection. He may decide, for example, to eliminate from his critique the reconstructive process (a sort of scaffolding) which he performs by way of initial cognition, and to entertain critically the "pure form" of the fragment—its adequate intentionality. Nonetheless, his initial perception of the fragment as an organized discourse (a form), and therefore his entire interpretive superstructure, are based on a dialectical knowing of part through whole and presence through absence. For a critic to free himself altogether from this epistemological involvement would mean reading a torso, for example, not as a meaningful isolation of material from a familiar semantic unit but as an autonomously meaningful construction: not as an abstraction from a known quantity but rather as an approximation to a glimpsed unknown. This kind of freedom—in effect, an undoing of metaphysical closures— was not, I would hazard, available to Romantic readers, nor was it the originary, genetic impulse of the RFP. Moreover, contemporary (that is, Romanticist) criticism perpetuates the organic or Aristotelian dialectics originally activated by the RFP. For these reasons, I explore those part-whole, presence-absence negotiations rather than take up the RFP under the aspect of the avant garde.[21]

The special dynamic engendered by the RFP is a creative but controlled act of cognition/completion. This reception hypothesis is based on the observation of a certain consensus in the criticism of RFPs and on an examination of my own reactions to these works. Although many RFPs are hardly distinguished for their formal clarity, much of the criticism is governed by remarkably similar formal notions. The problem is that while the scholarship tends to exhibit consistent responses to the RFP, it rarely discovers the assumptions and activities that would explain this consensus. Critics tend to blend, confuse, or reverse the fragment and its holistic projection, figure and ground. They offer completions by way of explanation, whereas the proper analytic object is the very act of completion and its product. The reader whom I postulate above knows that his perception of the fragment as a form springs from his recognition of a mismatch between the text proper and the idea in his—and perhaps in the poet's—

mind. What this ideally self-conscious reader explains, then, is the marginal difference between those two structures. The differential which the poem presents as its appointed limit—the condition of its formal achievement—will be seen to express the work's internal divisiveness and contradiction, and to mark the site where its self-thwarting (which is its self-realization) takes place.

By attempting to describe the ideal (abstract and extrinsic) wholes which the RFP projects (and which criticism reflects), one may begin to see how the fragment characterizes its disorder, or what it claims to be. This, of course, is to gain a more authentic, more removed knowledge. To this end, each of chapters three through eleven takes as its task the description of a fragment form. Each brings out a particular conjunction between a form of writing and a form of reading, a conjunction that produces for the RFP that idealized range of appearances and meanings which may ultimately be studied from an antithetical point of view. These elaborations—a rough typology of collisions and collusions—are neither theoretically deduced structures with some a priori legitimacy, nor do they represent an exhaustive analysis of the RFP. But as my remarks should have suggested, neither would I subscribe to a theory allowing, for a particular historical interval, an unlimited number of fragment forms, or as many forms as fragments. One way to conceive the object of chapters three through eleven is as an attempt to express for the RFP its "ideal interlocutor."[22]

Each fragment form details a strategy for closure, a strategy based on an initial and distinct impression of absence and difference. Our competence in executing these strategies has, to a large extent, dulled that first impression. To recover its impact, we can juxtapose against our criticism a more naïve but in some ways a more or differently responsive critical apparatus: the nineteenth-century review. By opposing the Romantic to the modern commentary, and by interposing between those discourses a critical mediation, one begins to fix the subject of all three discourses in its character as both source and product. In discussing fragments that went largely unnoticed (or were not available) in their own day and are not addressed by contemporary criticism, I must rely upon my experience as a reader of Romantic poetry. I try to employ a mode of construction consistent with general principles of Romantic interpretation and with expectations aroused by other and similar fragment poems and by other works of the poet in question.[23]

· ·

CHAPTER TWO

BACKGROUNDS

The literary fragments presented in the various eighteenth- and nine-teenth-century editions of *The Greek Anthology* and *The Palatine Anthology* did not provoke significant philological or philosophical interest among the Romantics, but the sculptural and architectural remains of ancient Greece and Rome spoke forcefully to the Romantic mind. Poetic frag-ments, if discussed, were typically assimilated to the ruins and fragments of the other arts. When Shelley, for example, writes of "those faultless productions whose very fragments are the despair of modern art," does he refer to sculpture, architecture, social institutions, or literature?[1] Given Shelley's holistic vision of the Greeks, one would have to hazard all of them. Romantic classicism was, of course, largely Romantic Hellenism. By way of qualifying that archaeological enthusiasm, we might recall Georg Lukács's trenchant generalization, ". . . every epoch needs its own Greece, its own Middle Ages and its own Renaissance. Every age creates the age it needs."[2] The lyric fragments, along with other remains of Greek and Renaissance culture, were of service in this project of (re)visionary historiography. The second-generation Romantics were, of course, far more intrigued by Hellenic ideals and idylls than the poets of the first generation, and of the second-generation group, Shelley was indisputably the most fluent in Greek and the most familiar with the literature. Peacock was the finer Hellenist but that very superiority in the range, subtlety, and accuracy of his scholarship makes him the less suitable subject for this inquiry. What concerns us here are the more innocently held and ideologi-cally instructive ideas of the Greeks.

Shelley felt an "intense and often avowed admiration for the genius of ancient Greece; an admiration not confined to their work as artists, but embracing the whole of their civilization."[3] Shelley's conviction of the primacy of Greek civilization permeates nearly all of his writing; the main sources for this brief survey are his "Discourse on the Manners of the Antients," the Preface to *Hellas*, and *A Defence of Poetry*. To isolate Shelley's remarks on the Greeks and their achievement from the amassing canonical argument is inevitably to distort and attenuate the sense of those remarks. Plainly, however, even the most economical elaboration of the explanatory context defines a critical project in its own right. Since the purposes of this study neither require nor could accommodate so massive an undertaking, I contextualize the excerpted remarks with reference to some established rubrics of Shelley's thought. In the way of an enabling construct, one might postulate organicism, dialectical idealism, and skeptical philosophy as the three pillars supporting the temple in which Shelley enshrines the Greek fragment. Even as I propose that syncretic metaphor, however, let me undo it a bit by rehearsing a commonplace of our criticism. To the extent that we can characterize Shelley's general philosophical project, we observe that his skeptical orientation predominates over the organicist and dialectical strains of his thought. I repeat the truism so as to account for the nonsystematic and even contradictory representation that follows.

Shelley attributes the "harmony, perfection, and uniform excellence" of classical art to the fact that its makers "lived in a perpetual commerce with Nature and nourished themselves on the spirit of her forms." In a letter to Peacock (November 1818), Shelley describes Raphael's St. Caecilia as a work "of the inspired and ideal kind [which] seems to have been conceived and executed in a similar state of feeling to that which produced among the antients those perfect specimens of poetry and sculpture which are the baffling models of succeeding generations."[4] The observation, made in reference to a Renaissance monument, bears introduction here inasmuch as Shelley not only compares moderns to "antients," but praises the former by reference to the "perfection"—the "models"—that is, the prototypical and normative character of the latter. The juxtaposition of the above remarks suggests that in Shelley's view, the special consonance obtaining in some societies between Nature's animating or formal spirit and the individual's private inspirational resources is the condition for the formal necessity (completeness, integrity, autonomy) of that society's intellectual and institutional expressions. The historical limit-factor on this organic correspondence would seem to be the mediating social dimension itself—its bearing on individual receptivity to noumenal impression. Or, Shelley might be said to account for degrees of necessity evinced by the artworks of various cultures with reference to social constraints upon realization of visionary truth. By "realization," I suggest psychic actualization rather than material embodiment: the artist's primary cognitive response to, and his reflective experience of, ideal existence—a constant. As I noted, Shelley binds this capacity to the character of the moment—we might say, to the dominant ideology, or that which constructs a particular range of private and social experience. In especially fortunate ages, such as that of the early Greeks, ideology effaces (or fulfills) itself to such an extent that human life is as a conscious enactment of the organic dimension. In that coming-to-consciousness, organic life realizes its formal necessity—its telos—as well.

First, and by reference to the rubrics proposed above, we observe that Shelley conceives Greek civilization under the sign of organic perfection: systematic and internally regulated completeness, complexity, integrity, and closure. One impulse, genetically independent of Nature but coextensive with her operations, is seen to inform all aspects and institutions of the ancient world in such a way as to determine each to its own formal necessity. Every cultural expression, from the images in Homer to the state itself, is as a living cell in a vast organism. Nothing produced by such a system (that is, under such an aspect) can be socially superfluous (decorative, obscene) or, in terms of its own formal development, adventitious. The fragments of such products—remnants from the social body and from the subsystem of the original and entire artwork—can be no less formally necessary than any other, however random, division of organic material.

Shelley not only allows the ancient fragments a perfection comparable to that of the larger bodies whence they derive, he sometimes claims for them a formal and philosophic superiority to the originary organic system. (The claim is, we can see, at least superficially inconsistent with a strictly organic model.) To conceive the fragment as that particle which survives the ravages of time is, perforce, to invest it with some saving virtue. Or, the work's manifest, material imperfection—not simply the proof of its antiquity—signifies to the dialectical idealist the presence of an indestructible essence, trace of the work's first cause. By "trace," I mean that noumenal residue which would seem to escape the sociological and organic determinism of Shelley's critique. In the language of today, we might describe this essence as the work's and its culture's genetic code—a teleological construct. This perspective on the fragment derives from Shelley's normative mimetic distinction between essence and substance, inspiration and composition. "Why is that reflection in the canal more beautiful than the object it reflects," Shelley asks in a notebook jotting. I elucidate Shelley's impressionistic answer (". . . the openings from within into the soft and tender colours of the distant wood, and the intersection of the mountain lines, surpass and misrepresent truth") by this commentary from the "Discourse on the Manners of the Ancients":[5] "The wrecks and fragments of those subtle and profound minds, like the ruins of a fine statue, obscurely suggest to us the grandeur and perfection of the whole. Their very language—a type of the understandings of which it was the creation and the image. . . ."[6] One might infer from this observation Shelley's belief that the reflection represents the original as the fragment represents the complete work, by expressing its essential (ideal, formal) nature in a materially uncompromised fashion.[7] Like the reflection in water, the fragment is less constrained by extrinsic conditions than the referential object, which, for the fragment, is, of course, the original representation. Fragment and reflection "obscurely suggest . . . the grandeur and perfection of the whole" by their obviously abstract, discontinuous, and hollowed appearance. Whereas both the natural phenomenon—deceptively adequate embodiment of Nature's formal purposes—and the finished artwork ultimately represent their own false finality, fragment and reflection solicit by their openness those divine visitations that, for Shelley, authenticate and totalize representation. In the "interstices" opened by "the imperfect image," mind (and Mind) engages matter, just as "the imagination moulds and completes the shapes in clouds, or in the fire, into the resemblances of whatever form, animal, building & etc., happens to be present to it."[8] By this corrective and cooperative—that is, redemptive—reception, the fragment may present an accurate image of man and Nature, or of the unitary principles that sustain them both.

By Shelley's lights, then, we may figure the fragment as a random but perfect (internally necessitated) element from an organic whole. Or, we may read it as an uncompromised imaginative expression, dependent for its realization on an imaginative—that is, participatory—reception. "When composition begins, inspiration is already on the decline, and the most glorious poetry that has ever been communicated to the world is probably a feeble shadow of the original conception of the Poet."[9] The fragment, construed as a symbol—"type" in the loose sense—of the imagined order which the original work sought to incarnate, enjoys a more intimate, authorized relation to that order than the first and finished work. The usurpation hinges on the fragment's capacity to engage the viewer's imagination—or its refusal of the bad faith of prosaic intertexture. Together, fragment and viewer reproduce the artist's original construct but in finer—more "abstract and ideal"—tone.

One might observe that the readings of the fragment enabled by the two rubrics thus far treated are not entirely compatible. Does the fragment represent an idealized and extinct historical referent, in which case its value—an analogical one—is aligned with its materiality, its physical survival? Or does the fragment have a virtual and operational character, the power to engage the contemporary imagination in such a way as to conjure the futuristic wholeness it prefigures? In this case, its *immateriality* would seem to be the source of its value, a value that could be conceived as antianalogical. Shelley's word, "type," which he uses ambiguously, focuses this contradiction. In its traditional, technical sense, "type" means, of course, a foreshadowing of that ideal order which is history's (that is, sacred history's) telos. Shelley's usage, however, suggests a belated (symbolic and attenuated) representation of an original and historically specific moment. "Type" would, in this context, describe a backward-looking prophecy. One way to negotiate these difficulties and to fix more securely Shelley's reading of the fragment is to propose that the relation of the ancient world to a redeemed future is itself that of type to fulfillment. The fragment, then, in preserving for the moderns its own, which is also their (that is, *our*) genetic past, predicts a collective human future. Moreover, by appealing to the imagination of the reader, or to that psychic agency which provides access to the ideal, the fragment—independent of its social origins—sketches the poetry of the future.

> What is life? . . . We are born, and our birth is unremembered and our infancy remembered but in fragments. We live on, and in living we lose the apprehension of life. How vain it is to think that words can penetrate the mystery of our being. Rightly used, they may make evident our ignorance to ourselves, and this is much.[10]

Finally, we observe in Shelley's thought a tendency toward a more strictly thematic reading of the fragment than we have thus far sketched. By this reading, the fragment is worked as a univocal sign, its form the irreducible expression of existential discontinuity and flux. In assuming this thematic character, the fragment acquires a special rhetorical function as well. It provokes our curiosity as to origins and destiny: what whole gave the fragment birth, what form will the fragment assume a thousand years from now? In recruiting the fragment as a philosophic theme, Shelley effectively discourages particular acts of formal inquiry or even appreciation. He tends either to peer through the fragment to the mind of its creator or epoch (for example, Petrarch's "sublime and chivalrous sensibility") or to characterize the fragment metonymically, as it were, and with reference to the generally disjunctive and evolving state of human knowledge.[11] Like Winckelmann, Shelley focuses the fragment's peculiar virtue as its capacity to become "an object of constant study."[12] In Shelley's phrase, fragments are the "baffling models of succeeding generations."[13] They tease us into and out of thought by never fully surrendering to our understanding—or, never capitulating to the agencies that enable that understanding ("Ozymandias" aptly illustrates this line of thought: see p. 208).

My object in assembling some of Shelley's perspectives on the fragment is to suggest that the conceptual universe in which the Romantics situated those classical and Renaissance fragments available to them was as nonliterary as that which served the first half of the eighteenth century as its frame of reference. To the neoclassical mind, the formal condition of the fragment was no more than that: the effect of a purely circumstantial intervention, devoid of critical implication. Quite at the other extreme, Shelley develops an epistemological, symbolic, and metaphysical dimension for the condition of irresolution, a condition materialized primarily in the remains of Greek civilization. By Shelley's readings, the imperfections of the ancient fragments signify a lost and anticipated perfection—spiritual, social, and intellectual. Irresolution—a valorizing sign—confers upon the fragmentary work the character of the infinite, inexhaustible semiotic event.

Neither the neoclassical nor the Romantic perspective on the ruins of the ancient world constructs the fragment as a form, capable of generating *a particular range of meanings*. By that phrase, I describe a semantic set determined by the materials and methods historically available to the writer at a given moment and by the more general ideological conditions of invention and reception. Shelley's ardent response to the relics of the classical world did, however, serve an important function. By critically articulating the irresolution of these works and semantically working it, Shelley helped present to his age the compositional and hermeneutic opportunities afforded by this formal condition. He helped, that is, to motivate the feature. Moreover, Shelley's frankly metaphysical and sociohistorical reflections bring into the open certain ideological themes informing, as we shall see, the literary situation of the Romantic fragments.

Ironically, the authentic classical fragments were less instrumental in cultivating reader responsiveness to the aesthetic potential of irresolution than the dubious fragments of Macpherson and Chatterton. The Ossian and Rowley poems and all the furor they excited not only highlighted the relationship of textual imperfection to literary meaning and value, but seem to have increased general self-consciousness about literary reception.

The hoax poems, so-called, looked like and were introduced as ancient texts or textual fragments, but the circumstances of their appearance opened the "editors'" explanations to question. The astonishing passion, prolixity, and longevity of the controversy over the poems' authenticity suggest that these works posed fundamental category problems for their early readers.[14] Before the poems could be assimilated in even the most rudimentary conceptual fashion, these problems, which were formulated as a binary opposition, had to be solved (actually, *dis*solved). The reader who hoped to motivate these works on any level was obliged to commit himself to one of two cognitive (interpretive, evaluative) protocols. He could read the poems as genuinely archaic works, or he could read them as modern imitations (or facsimiles or reproductions) of such works. By presenting these clear options and forcing a decision between them, the hoax poems undoubtedly increased their readers' awareness that they could choose not just how to interpret but how to read. One would further surmise that the hoaxes, or the controversy they engendered, would have exposed the radical dependence of the literary object—its literariness and within that category, its quiddity—on the particular reading paradigm selected. In their efforts to justify their position (that is, to transcend the categorial problem), readers of Macpherson and Chatterton made explicit the assumptions which led them to interpret the evidence one way or the other. This is to say, the arguments—like most commentaries on the anomalous—investigate the unknown by (re)framing the categorial knowledge that constructs the phenomenon *as* an anomaly in the first place. That knowledge and the binds it engenders—the largely unconscious attitudes that predetermined particular receptions—are the real subject of the hoax controversy.

This study is, of course, concerned with the evidence and interpretations only so far as they illuminate a climate of reading. In that the hoax poems were in many instances fragmented so as to resemble genuinely "found" texts, one might expect this new self-consciousness about critical assumptions to bear upon the Romantic fragments, works that emerged in the (protracted) era of the hoax controversy. Like the hoax poems, the RFP emphasizes its dependence on reception for its generic, formal, and therefore semantic determinacy. Without the hoax poems, the fragment might have remained the province of the antiquarian, the metaphysician, and the connoisseur of sensation and sensibility.

As I observed, the hoax poems delivered no literary meaning at all, and certainly no evaluative option to the neutral or "natural" reader (that is to say, to the consciously uncommitted reader). Moreover, by failing quite to satisfy the reading expectations they aroused, the hoaxes effectively challenged the governing assumptions and in so doing, revealed their conventional character. More simply, what I discern in this episode of literary history is a problematizing of reception acts.

In providing a specific date or period of composition, an author (that is, authorial biography), and information about the canon's operative conventions, Macpherson and Chatterton specified those expectations which would produce for their readers the formal determinacy of individual works in the canon, the condition for local semiotic and evaluative activity. Because, however, the "editors" overreached themselves with their excessive contextualization (and because the poems were curiously sophisticated for, respectively, third- and fifteenth-century works), suspicions sprung up.

Once it seemed possible that the "editors" had actually written their found material, this material could not be read spontaneously; it had to be read critically. If the poems were not *exactly* what Macpherson and Chatterton said they were, they could not be received as literature at all.

Barbara Herrnstein Smith's distinction between natural and fictive discourse helps to explain this phenomenon more clearly. Smith, in *On the Margins of Discourse*, defines natural discourse as a functional category including "all utterances, spoken or inscribed, that . . . are understood to be the verbal acts of particular persons on, and in response to, particular occasions. Such utterances are designed to secure more or less practical ends, which they can perform, usually, without the knowing consent of an audience."[15]

Fictive discourse, conversely, is explained as "ahistorical, contextual verbal structures, *possible utterances*, but not actual ones," designed to provoke the reader's exploration of those structures simply for the pleasure of the cognitive activity thereby initiated. Of course, most texts (and oral utterances) can be processed either way, or by means of either apparatus. The reader can choose to honor or ignore the work's internal cues—or, by failing to understand the cues, he may mistake the author's categorial intentions. But the freedom to choose a reading option, and a literature that cultivates this freedom, were not so familiar to most eighteenth- and nineteenth-century readers as they are to us. To decide to take a work in a certain way—that is, to take it as a certain kind of thing—aware that alternative receptions are available, is a sophisticated talent involving a recognition that reading is a kind of learned attention rather than a spontaneous, objective, and absolute perception of a stable object.

For early readers of the hoax poems, there could be no such thing as a "both-at-once" or "either-or" reading. If the poems were not relics of an ancient or medieval literature, they could not be literature at all.[16] The reception history of the hoax poems shows that many readers did, in time, learn to attend aesthetically to works which they knew to have been written for more or less practical or extraliterary purposes and "as the verbal act[s] of a particular person on, and in response to particular occasions." This is to say that some readers developed a generic concept of "the hoax poem" and/or that the most generally operative ideology of reading had changed.

While the reception history of the RFP is not nearly so dramatic as that of the hoax poems, the fragment raised many similar problems for its readers.[17] The acceptance of the fragment qua fragment—its constitution *as* a literary form—argues that readers solved these problems by developing expectations peculiar to these works and by modifying general and prevailing reception practices accordingly.

Like the hoax poem, the RFP originally occupied an anomalous position on the border between natural and fictive discourse. Although clearly intended as fictive discourse, the fragment's apparent failure to realize its aesthetic intention or to materialize its design put its categorial status at risk. Moreover, the poet's publication of his own fragment implied a compositional history which the reader—if he were to appreciate the text as a poem—had both to believe and to acknowledge as a legitimate mode of literary production. One way to focus the RFP is as a found text—its author the editor of a discourse which came to him disjointedly and/or partially, and who refrains from extending or integrating his windfall in the interests of genetic authenticity. Just as many readers of the hoax poems learned to focus in a single field both the instrumentality and the literariness of the doubtful texts, so many readers of Romantic fragments came to receive implicit and explicit "historical" data (compositional, canonical, biographical) as literary material, to be textually worked rather than read as a privileged extrinsic commentary. Before considering the expectations and subsequent constructive activities productive of particular fragment forms in the early nineteenth century, I ask how it is that Romantic readers were able to take the fragment as literature at all.

The hoax poems not only impressed upon their readers the knowledge that reading is more than and different from the verbalizing of an inscribed content or the discovery of an authorizing authorial interest, they highlighted the fact that literary meaning is profoundly determined by the contexts within which a reader situates a work. The defenders of Macpherson and Chatterton and their detractors brought to their readings two very different contextual universes. The conflict alone isolated the assumptions underlying both contextual systems, revealing those systems as contexts adduced to works rather than meanings deduced from them. Romantic readers of the hoaxes profited by this exposure; they used the insight to develop a reading paradigm whereby any text, however produced and presented, might be naturalized under the sign of Literature. The hoaxes were, eventually, found to be modern (or "essentially" antique), deceptive (that is, profoundly true), complete (by requiring of the reader participatory or "writerly" endeavor), and entirely legitimate literary texts. The RFP was, to some extent, a byproduct of this triumph of ironic apperception.

Almost every edition of Macpherson's and Chatterton's work was prefaced with essays intended to validate or discredit the historical authenticity of the poems.[18] The arguments of both sympathizers and skeptics form a record of reading practices, deriving from some uninterpretable, original propensity to believe or disbelieve the "editors'" explanations. To the believing reader, Macpherson's and Chatterton's poems were, respectively, third- and fifteenth-century works. The author of Chatterton's Rowley poems was, by the fiction, a priest favored with a humanist education; as the titles of his poems indicate, Rowley is a writer familiar with the classical kinds. Macpherson identifies his author as a Scottish blind bard whose poems, the Ossian fragments, derive from a pre-Christian oral tradition. In these poems, Fingal's son recounts the heroic exploits of his father; the collected works document the noblest events and the values of a particular civilization at a particular moment. To most eighteenth-century readers, Ossian—the legendary last Highland bard—was a familiar figure, although the poems were, of course, novel and exotic. For the benefit of those readers ignorant of the existing Ossianic lore, Macpherson emphasizes a Homeric analogy. Moreover, he locates Ossian's poems within a firm generic tradition: "*Fingal* was strongly recommended to the public as a perfect work of its kind, answering to and fulfilling all the intention of epic poetry."[19]

Construed as authentic literary relics, the hoax poems manifest their textual difficulties as the effects on a contemporary consciousness of primitive modes of thought and expression. The belated reader naturally refers the work's interpretive resistance to his own ignorance of the relevant linguistic and historical material, and of the social conventions and sensibility of a remote culture. Plainly, the governing assumption here is that the greater one's literary-historical erudition, the more simple, sensuous, and passionate the alien literature becomes.

The modern provenance of the antique texts meant that a comparison of the hoaxes to works of roughly the same period would find the former superior in sensibility as in technique. By "superior," of course, one must read "more consistent with contemporary literary values." The poems pleased, then, not only by their simplicity, a function of their apparent antiquity, but by their gratification of certain modern interests as well (for example, the taste for the sublime, for conventionalized paraphrastic locution, for sharp alternations between metrical smoothness and violence).

By their prefaces and subtitles, Macpherson and Chatterton alert their readers to the operative formal categories. Chatterton's later editors often arranged his poems accordingly, beginning with eclogue and ending with epic. Readers found inscribed in this information directions for the structural manipulation of textual lacunae and terminal imperfection. Thus were these features naturalized; or, thus was their formally disruptive impact neutralized, their semantic dimension reinforced. By introducing "Aella" as a "fragment of a tragedy," for example, Chatterton increases the likelihood that his isolated two acts will be submitted to a literary (*and* archaeological or antiquarian) appraisal. The reader who heeds Chatterton's formal advice might usefully establish correspondences between the baffling, disjunctive text and the familiar conventional constituents of a tragic action. With the help of these parallels and their complement of historical associations—formal and semantic—the reader might effectively "realize" the fragment by reference to its putative original whole. Moreover, by this part-whole, belated-original dynamic, the reader could enjoy two distinct poetic experiences or objects, as it were, as well as their critical and historical ratios.

Read according to editorial instructions, the hoax poems bring with them a biographical context as well as cultural and generic paradigms. Both Macpherson and Chatterton include in their editions material concerning the lives and personalities of their poets, material that conforms to established authorial types. The confirmation of this "typical" figure seems to have been as important to the editors and readers as the poetry itself. One might even conjecture from Chatterton's oeuvre that the poetry was largely instrumental to the construction of an authorial persona. The poems attributed to Rowley were, of course, offered by Chatterton for their literary interest, but they also function in the overall project as historical documents—no different from the maps, heraldic charts, coins, and chronicles that Chatterton produces by way of authenticating his persona. To put a slightly different slant on the matter, we might remember that without the fiction of a Rowley and his world, Chatterton had no voice, no form of literary address at all, ex post facto comments about his literary genius notwithstanding.

The three contexts—epoch, genre, and author—by means of which the sympathetic reader processed and approved the hoaxes encoded some fundamental assumptions. Chief among these is the notion that these three contexts, fully developed, must fully and finally explain—deliver— the poems to the modern mind. To paraphrase one of Chatterton's editors, inconsistencies point not to forgery but to insufficient information concerning Rowley's life and times.[20]

By providing the reader with an organized body of contextual material, Macpherson and Chatterton structured their readers' imaginations in such a way as to make the retrieval of this material and its application to textual cruxes seem like simple and inevitable discoveries rather than authorially guided maneuvers. I do not suggest that the process of shuttling between text and context was a conscious one for most readers. Quite the contrary, the editorial material was probably enjoined automatically, solving the literary problems before they could be consciously experienced as problems.

The primary assumption isolated above—the reader's perfect confidence in extrinsic canonical models as removers of textual difficulty— inscribes an array of related ideas. We can see, for example, that the authorial type which at once "explains" the poems (their occurrence, devices, character, motive, meaning), and is both realized and ratified by those poems, is an a priori construct rather than an inference drawn from the sum of the voices and manners assumed in different poems. Sympathetic readers seem not to have entertained the possibility that a poet might produce psychologically inconsistent—that is, atypical—expressions, nor that such inconsistency might imply the very limited usefulness of conventional authorial-psychological models with respect to questions of attribution and interpretation. Readers convinced of the authenticity of Chatterton's hoaxes argued that the boy who wrote "scurrilous satires" could not have struck off the high moral tone of the Rowley poems. These readers did not question Chatterton's technical expertise, they simply assumed a persona far more logical (internally consistent) than many real personalities. It is important to see that the regulating (and normative) concept here is not, as I said, literary expertise, but literary character, understood as a postulated continuum linking the personae of all the poems in a particular canon. Readers appear to have formed an estimate of the poet's maximum capability and his characteristic moves; although they allowed a certain latitude within these norms, they seem to have had trouble admitting a voice that seemed qualitatively different.[21]

A similar harmony was seen to govern the relationship of ethical to aesthetic integrity, and here the issue *is* expressed in terms of literary skill. According to one argument popular with Chatterton's supporters, Chatterton could not have produced so expert an oeuvre as the Rowley poems and at the same time have been so debased as to deceive his readers.[22] We observe here a familiar assumption: good poetry can only be written by good men. While readers who argued from this premise pointed out the substantive discrepancy between the piety of the Rowley poems and the notion of a literary hoax, the more compelling defense juxtaposed the technical happiness of the Rowley poems against the hypothesis of a con-artist. Naturally, the two images were found to be utterly incompatible. The manifest excellence of the poetry thus conquered the necessarily inferential attack upon Chatterton's character.

To readers who reasoned along the lines sketched above, the distinction of fiction (aesthetic lie) from falsehood (historical deception or inaccuracy) was, of course, central not only to the general defense of poetry but to the business of particular textual experience. By marking those fictions located outside the work proper with some conventional designation (for example, Letter to the Printer), a writer could safely extend his invention. Direct and sincere—uninflected—editorial or authorial commentary was not, in most cases or by most readers, consciously brought into the fictive construct. Those Romantic readers who penetrated Chatterton's hoax, yet regarded the "editorial" commentary as a means of realizing a special and structurally integrated poetic effect, demonstrated a markedly new kind of reception.

Those who defended the authenticity of Chatterton's poems offered as evidence the many misinterpretations found in the notes to the poems, errors that only an editor and translator (in this case, as unlearned as belated) would make: ". . . every writer must know his own meaning: and if any person by his glossary, or any other explanation, shews, that he could not arrive at such meaning, he affords convincing proof, that the original was by another hand."[23] The discrepancy between Chatterton's learning and his poetic intelligence was not initially interpreted as a sign of his genius—his transcendence of social fact—but as proof that he honestly, if ineptly, transcribed another man's words. The reasoning here suggests that for this group of readers, poets could *not* write better than they knew. That is, we observe in this logic the assumption that writers cannot divorce their authorial identity from their historically determined social character. Poets may, of course, imitate extinct literary forms, as they may affect the style associated with a type of author or a particular author from the past. They cannot, however, divest themselves of the conditions which their epoch, personality, moral character, chosen genre, and established authorial persona impose upon them. Poets cannot, through sympathy, assume the temper of another age: ". . . though his words should speak the language, they would never convey the sentiments, of a poet writing in the fifteenth century."[24] Edmond Malone, a skeptic who grasped Chatterton's creative and scholarly achievement, turned the sympathizers' assumption on its head. "My objection is not to single words, to lines or half-lines of these compositions (for here the advocates for their authenticity always shift their ground, and plead that any particular exceptionable word or passage was an interpolation of Chatterton); but it is to their whole structure, style, and rhythm"—in Malone's view, the epochal signature of the text. Although the poet was expected to imitate the great precursors and to interpret their achievement through his own, he was neither expected nor allowed to capture the essentials of another writer's or epoch's art. He could not, that is, *reproduce* the original. Within the discourse that sprung up around the hoax poems, "essentials" seems to have meant those contextual factors which, being the least intentional aspects of the work, are also and therefore its most inimitable dimension.

This dimension locates the point at which the past refuses to become contemporary knowledge of the past—the work's bottom line alterity, so to speak.

Readers who denied the historical authenticity of the Ossianic and Rowley poems and who grounded this denial upon the above assumptions, antithetically manipulated, were unable to receive the texts as literature. The poems were, to such readers, forgeries *tout court*: a congeries of poetic devices designed to produce an overall impression entirely unrelated to those devices and effects per se. This discourse, in serving an extrinsic, illegitimate purpose (a strictly selfish praxis: neither didactic nor hedonistic), forfeited its aesthetic status. The features that figured as virtues to the believing reader were disqualifying defects to the skeptic. The exotic simplicity of the poetry was construed as a contrived imitation of simplicity—that is, affectation. The direct and ingenuous expression of feeling was, to the skeptic, a vulgar, mechanical, and sentimental parody. Similarly, in that the skeptic regarded the ostensible matter of the poems as a pseudosubject, disguising the poet's real intention—*mis*representation—he discovered no literary rationale for these productions whatsoever. Inasmuch as the poems were judged devoid of legitimate literary content, they could hardly be received as instances of any of the literary kinds, discriminations based on conventional referential gestures.

Thwarted in his attempts to autonomize the hoaxes by way of such categories as subject, genre, and historical context, the skeptic also foundered when he tried to invoke authorial type as an aid to (literary) understanding. Where was the precedent for "an illiterate charity-boy of the present age" who acknowledges his inferior work and disavows his greater, who produces phony manuscripts of a pious nature, and who prefers the minor glory of editorial competence to the recognition accorded the expert imitator and promising 'imaginator'?[25]

The poems were rejected "with disdain or indignation, as a palpable and most impudent forgery."[26] Their beauty could not "support them, independent of their authenticity," because to recognize this beauty—to receive the forgeries as poetry—required that the skeptic reconstitute his grounds of literary legitimacy. It is, of course, mad to patronize those readers who banished poet and poems from the literary universe, effectively short-circuiting the questions which their reading raised. The retreat from these questions was not, clearly, a decision to maintain the dominant assumptions at the cost of the poetry, but the result of an inability to grasp the conventional character of the enabling ideology.

I cannot account for the fact that a number of prominent nineteenth-century poets and critics, fully aware of the duplicity involved in the hoaxes, were capable of a thoroughly aesthetic reception. "The slur of forgery no longer applied,"[27] as statements made by Southey, Coleridge, Browning, and Scott attest.[28] Certainly one cannot credit the provocation offered by the hoaxes as having radically altered the dominant set of literary expectations. It would require a wide-ranging sociological inquiry to ascertain why and how a group of poems that had so severely violated the reception norms as to be judged not bad poetry but *not* poetry could have suddenly come to enjoy a fully literary appreciation. My object here is simply to use the hoax controversy to describe the new cognitive paradigm—assumptions about the literary tradition, the poet, and the text—that enabled Romantic readers to distinguish authorial and historical intention from poetic intention. This critical discrimination was essential to the aestheticization of the poetic fragment.

Those Romantics who read Chatterton's Rowley poems as the finished (that is, intentionally unfinished) productions of a near-contemporary approved the poems not as imitations of fifteenth-century verse but as a modern expression of the sensibility which engendered and informed the prototype verse. It was not, of course, the imitation per se that had offended the early skeptics, but rather the attempt at counterfeit. The Romantics turned the tables by praising Chatterton for his *recreation* of the medieval mode. Thus did they sidestep the whole business of mimesis—its scope and proprieties. In the Romantic view, Chatterton's claim that his poems were medieval was no more than the assertion of an imaginative truth. According to one student of the controversy, "Blake and Keats . . . insisted on an essential genuineness, a *poetic* truth in Rowley that rendered irrelevant disputes about historical evidence."[29] Whereas the skeptics had conceived poetic "essentials" as those historically specific and therefore inimitable textual elements, Romantic readers seemed to define as essential the trans- or omnihistorical dimension of the work that waits for its meaning upon recurrent and redemptive reproductions in time. According to Romantic usage, the work's essentials (not, of course, to be confused with a mimetic universality) are synonymous with its soul or genius: that ideal and imaginative truth independent of but only realized in particular representations, and often located in what were traditionally considered the ornamental parts of the composition (tone, trope, aside, introductory material). Shelley's familiar assertion of historical determinism —"Poets . . . are in one sense, the creators and in another the creations of their age. From this subjection the loftiest do not escape" (Preface to *Prometheus Unbound*)—need not contradict his earlier pronouncement: "Sophocles and Shakespeare can be produced and reproduced forever."[30] I juxtapose these remarks not to illuminate the equivocal "creators"-"creations" logic but to isolate a line of thought that runs through the entire *Defence*. Although the poet's expressive potential is limited by the conditions of his epoch (roughly, the dominant ideology), the various productions of poets in time are all, if they are truly poetry, approximations to the same ideal order and therefore *essentially* identical. When the social conditions of two historical intervals coincide significantly, the poetry of these ages reveals its essential affinities. At such moments, "Rowley" will reproduce the voice of the fifteenth century.

Chatterton's Romantic supporters attributed his transcendence of historically imposed, experiential fact to his preternatural sympathy. And of course, the Romantics' own imaginative embrace of Chatterton's world and its referential—or rather, expressive—original, marks *their* serviceable sympathy as well.[31] We further observe that Chatterton's failure to produce an exact facsimile of medieval poetry was not judged by these readers as a defect, evidence of a lapse in sympathy. To the contrary, Chatterton's faults were construed as the conditions of his sympathy. This is to say, the discrepancies authenticated that sympathy and were consequently valorized. In the Romantic view, it was Chatterton's belatedness—all that he was and knew as a man of the late eighteenth century—that enabled him to reproduce the essentials of another century's verse. This redemptive reading of mediation, estrangement, and noncoincidence—historical and psychic—is, of course, a familiar and distinctively Romantic move. One might recall in this context Abrams's topos of the spiral. As the gyre of history revolves, it returns to the same point it had reached perhaps three centuries earlier, but because the point is now located on a higher (or lower) plane, it does not coincide with the original point. Literary history is not a linear advance (or regression) but an ascending descent back to first things: to an early innocence won by hard experience, or to antiquity repossessed by the modern mind, a mind that gives up none of its self-consciousness—its modernity—in its achievement. Far from implying the depravity of the present age, Macpherson's and Chatterton's hoaxes proved to the Romantics that the eighteenth century had not been so barren as had been supposed.

The notional interdependence of private and poetic morality (according to which Chatterton's falsehood invalidated the poetry) was not dissolved by the Romantics so much as transvalued. Although Wordsworth condemns Macpherson roundly, he takes issue with the affective and procedural inauthenticity of the verse, and not with the author's extrinsic or private fraudulence. In his "Essay, Supplementary to the Preface," 1815, Wordsworth criticizes Macpherson's failure to sympathize wholeheartedly with his subject. In representing Nature and psyche in a formulaic, unimpassioned, and detached fashion, Macpherson opposes Wordsworth's emphasis on the epistemological and existential primacy of the literary event. We can see that the grounds of Wordsworth's critique are entirely different from those which supported earlier hostile assessments. The business of the hoax—the practical as opposed to discursive insincerity—does not enter into Wordsworth's consideration.[32]

The early skeptics judged Macpherson's poems devoid of authentic subject matter. In that the poems were not about the mighty warriors, passions, and values they presented but were instead imitations of heroic representations, the Ossian poems were condemned as one sustained mannerism. While the Romantics agreed that the poetic intention was not the honorific representation of specific characters, emotions, and mores, they located Macpherson's true subject in his expression of a modern longing for a lost world. To these readers, the poetic intention was what we might call, unpejoratively, escapist. The poems were felt to address and to satisfy the desire to experience a heroic sublime every now and then. This is to say, Chatterton's and Macpherson's poems were read more according to lyric expectations than narrative; the events were construed as subordinate to the feeling and as serving primarily to evoke and to structure that feeling. Read in this manner—as it were, a lyrical ballad reception—the hoaxes facilitated a new and privileged temporal experience. Like the spot of time, these works were felt to deliver prospects of a renovating past and redemptive future without falsifying the contingency-ridden present.

In repudiating the offered intentionality of the hoaxes, the skeptics had seriously compromised generic and formal recognition, since traditional genre distinctions were so deeply informed by mimetic values. Dr. Gregory, a reader of the Romantic temper, finds the poetry to be spurious with respect to its professed origins, yet he insists that "the thoughts and images are all truly pastoral; and it is impossible to read it without experiencing those lively, yet melancholy feelings, which a true delineation of nature alone can inspire."[33] The remark points up a new emphasis in generic discrimination. Gregory identifies Chatterton's work as pastoral because it expresses and, more importantly, *inspires* a certain kind and intensity of feeling. Gregory implies that generic or formal adequacy—resolution—depends upon the success of the poem's affective dimension rather than upon its mimetic and conventionally determined approximation to the represented object. Moreover, complete emotional expression in a poem need not result from the cumulative, *seriatim* effects of its constituent parts or phases. Affective resolution may be realized within individual stanzas, extended metaphors, songs, or any other division of the work, and identified synecdochically with the whole. This means that a reader might exert different kinds of formal attention in response to different parts of a poem. Or, he might focus his reaction to a work by way of specific generic ideas and yet conclude that the work as a whole escapes existing taxonomies. Further, the closural impressions produced by the individual parts of a work might combine to yield an overall impression of wholeness. Conceivably, a reader could respond to a fragment consisting of such parts as if it were a conventionally complete poem.

The Romantic shift from a mimetic to an affective basis with respect to generic and formal classification meant that poetry could assume the same otherness and ontological primacy associated with all representable objects. The poem, once it escapes the compositional orbit, acquires an autonomy that renders irrelevant the reader's knowledge of the poet's life, personality, and even his canon. These factual contexts can be used, of course; the point is, they lose their authoritative evidentiary status. Whereas Gregory's forerunners in the great debate had subjected the evidence of Chatterton's disparate voices to the critical standard of available authorial types (and, finding no correspondence, posited two distinct canons and authors), Gregory and others interpreted the data inductively (insofar as we can use that term). They constructed an authorial persona from the diverse and contradictory evidence produced by the entire collection of poems, presumed to be the elements of a single canon. Quite literally, they imagined what they knew. To see this is to feel that the whole notion and use of context had begun to change and with it, the formerly comfortable distinction of extrinsic fact (History, Nature) to intrinsic or textual fact. For Chatterton's and Macpherson's Romantic readers, context did not precede text; context was what the capable and sympathetic imagination extrapolated from a text in order to make literary sense of its anomalies, its antinomies, its special truths.

In thus conflating or making coextensive text and context, and thereby liberating literary production and reception from historical imperatives, readers effectively deconstructed the notion of privileged authorial interpretation. As they demonstrated, the autonomy assumed by the text once it enters the literary marketplace limits the poet's prerogative; his words become no more transparent to him than to any other reader. Morever, according to certain Romantic views aired in the controversies, the poet is as ignorant of what he intended as of what he produced. If the poet happens to explain his utterance in a preface or note, the reader is bound to receive the commentary as critically as he treats any other interpretive voice. Of course, the very subjectivity of the poet's explanation, inscribed in its rhetorical inflections—its textual gestures—assumes a special value for the reader insofar as it is seen to extend and elaborate the poetic impulse. In other words, rather than defer to or quarrel with authorial commentary (in either case acknowledging its evidentiary priority), the reader learns to enlist this material as a reception guide. The functional element is not the poet's assessment per se, but what the reader perceives as his unconscious or intentional emphases. *Whatever* a poet says about his poem is thus situated as a fiction and mined for its rhetorical clues. As with one *trompe l'oeil* device popular in nineteenth-century painting, where the frame is painted directly on the canvas, the viewer-reader acknowledges both the fiction and the art almost simultaneously. The frame —the editorial "lie"—is not only part of the painting's meaning, it is the way the painting produces its meaning and is therefore as innocent as the central painterly or poetic lie.

The more or less consciously held attitudes I have enumerated and focused by the hoax controversy are, we can see, commonplaces of Romantic and Romanticist criticism. By rehearsing them, I hoped to indicate their dialectical relationship to a set of attitudes and practices that delivered a very different literary object. The hoax poems, ultimately subjected to both varieties of textual construction, provoked a debate that bequeaths to us a record of critical assumptions and reading expectations. These poems posed many of the same problems raised by the RFPs; neither group of texts could be received as literature until one set of assumptions had given way to another or until those commonplaces of Romantic criticism mentioned above had thoroughly insinuated themselves into the mind of the reading public.

Collectively, those commonplaces form an ideology of reading, one that eschews historical (and this includes authorial) authority altogether, thereby and paradoxically producing for poet and poem a remarkable freedom—at the same time, however, narrowing their sphere of operations and undermining their effectiveness even within this sphere. The battle was fought in the name of the writer and text—the intent, to salvage the anomaly—but the real victor was the reader. The liberty he won was the self-determination of textual construction. The Romantics grasped the illusionary character of the hoaxes but in that character, radically interpreted, they read the *virtual* truth (psychic, affective, lyrical, visionary) of the representation. The hoaxes were approved for their irony. They were found to be simple and sophisticated, historically evocative yet timeless in appeal, ancient and modern, personal and impersonal, studied and spontaneous, sincere and capricious, fragmentary and complete. They were seen to demand interpretation yet felt to be ultimately impervious to it and thus eternally vital and inviting.

I have glanced at several features common to the hoax poems and the RFP. More to the point, each of the four fragment forms that I elaborate in the following chapters can be associated with one of the transformations in reading assumptions cited above. This is not to say that they cannot be traced to a point further back or elsewhere. The watershed is nowhere so marked, however, as in the hoax controversy.

For the fragment to figure a literary form, readers had to conceive textual irresolution as a formal fact susceptible to structural and semantic manipulation. The hoaxes, judged to have affected various kinds of irresolution in order to suggest the condition of genuinely antique texts, brought out the rhetorical and thematic uses and thus the potential literariness of the feature. The early skeptics naturally interpreted textual lacunae and general signs of imperfection as intentional devices: by design, a poetic convention rather than a textual condition. All the poems were regarded as complete in that they appeared exactly as they were written, and in that this appearance was intended to produce a specific—albeit nonfictive or practical—effect. If the fundamental imperfection of the hoaxes could be regarded as a sign of achieved intention (formal, not authorial), then the irresolution of the Romantic fragments might be similarly welcomed as an aspect of and avenue into poetic meaning.

As I noted, readers tended increasingly to discount originary historical situation and to become commensurately enterprising in their fabrication of enabling interpretive contexts for the orphaned texts. These imagined contexts, largely determined by editorial commentary but responsive to internal cues as well, figured in the reception as integral textual elements. Instead of explaining textual gaps, obscurities, and contradictions with reference to dynamics of textual transmission—theories of historical change—readers motivated these features in such a way as to assemble not just interpretive (that is, secondary) contexts but primary cognitive paradigms. Obviously, what I sketch here and associate with Romantic reception is a curiously circular procedure.

In the opening chapter of this book, I mentioned a range of fragment forms—reading protocols—that together constitute the RFP a distinct literary-historical event. Let me now observe that only an audience predisposed to the reading tactics I have outlined could have constructed those forms. The true fragment, for example, is a form that suggests both an antecedent and subsequent context of events or description. To organize the fragment, the reader must first extrapolate from the given text the before-and-after from which it appears to have been excerpted. In effect, the reader imaginatively completes the fragment that he may read the meaning of its partiality (that is, that he may motivate that partiality).

Clearly, the initial appreciation of this form required a reader willing and able to generate contexts from internal textual signals as well as from accompanying authorial-editorial commentary. Second, the reader would have to work these contexts no less aggressively than he worked the primary or nuclear textual material. Both these aptitudes were, as we have seen, cultivated by the hoax phenomenon.

The completed fragment impresses itself as the result of the poet's effort to finish his fragment some time after it was first written and from an antithetical and remedial position. Such poems foreground the breach between early and later writings by counterpointing various moods and modes, much as the hoaxes effectively presented binary historical and stylistic perspectives. The completed fragment yields an experience of closure to the reader who can revise the poem into a unity. By interpreting the discrepancy between the two moments and positions, he effectively cancels it, healing the breach, as it were, with his own hermeneutic resources and activities. As with the hoaxes, the completed fragment is formally intentionalized by a reader who can discriminate within a text mutually exclusive styles, values, and voices, and then rationalize these polarities through an interpretive act.

The propensity to intentionalize irresolution was crucial to the emergence of the deliberate fragment, a form which presents its imperfection as a semantic determination—roughly, a theme. In order to motivate such fragments, the reader must read them as instances of imitative form. One formulates that particular poetic argument which will present the work's irresolution as the precise and uniquely appropriate expression of its doctrine.

The dependent fragment presents itself as an episode or exercise in the poet's career. As with the true fragment, the incompletion displayed by this fragment form appears to be (and often truly is) fortuitous. However, whereas the true fragment invites the reader to tease out of the truncated form an essentially autonomous or text-specific context, the dependent fragment conjures the canonical development within which the fragment at hand performs some particular function. Before assessing the nature and meaning of the poem's irresolution, one must ascertain the nature of the poem's original insertion in this evolutionary field. The perceived form of the fragment depends upon the perceived function of the exercise in advancing the poet's thought and improving his craft. One observes that for the contemporary reader, the canonical construct is a highly speculative affair, inasmuch as the corpus is, and is felt to be, incomplete and evolving. In effect, then, the readers of dependent fragments were compelled to invent authorial personae from the readiest materials and, as it were, provisionally. One is reminded of those flexible readers of the hoaxes who, in their eagerness to claim the doubtful texts as literature, ventured to imagine what they (textually) knew: the figure of the capable poet.

The hoax poems elicited a remarkably uniform response from one group of readers and an equally determinate but different response from another and chronologically overlapping group. From this I inferred that a change in reading expectations and critical attitudes had occurred among a discernible, significant portion of the reading public. This is a big leap. How do we know that this transformation was not a response restricted to the hoaxes and inoperative with respect to other works? Can we find evidence that authentic fragments—those, for instance, printed in collected editions of seventeenth-, eighteenth-, and nineteenth-century poets—underwent general changes in reception? As I noted in chapter one, this book is not a study of publication practices, nor does it propose a sociology of reading with respect to literary parts and wholes in the Romantic period. Admittedly, only such an inquiry could tell us that the differential reception of the hoax poems was not a specific response to Macpherson's and Chatterton's performances. And only such a study could indicate whether or not the statements made by the critical or professional public, so to speak, represent an attitudinal consensus within the more general readership.

Although I have not conducted this study, I have looked at a range of eighteenth- and nineteenth-century editions, in quest of noteworthy changes (or allusions to such changes) in publishing practices. It seems sensible to assume that publishing practices reflect general reading tastes and talents. The basic questions I put to the editions which I examined were: (1) when are poetic fragments first published as a matter of course in posthumous editions, and how fragmentary (a qualitative and quantitative question) are these poems? (2) how do editors explain their inclusion or exclusion of available fragments? (3) when do editors cease explaining their decisions about the presentation of fragments and begin to assume that readers will treat these works as legitimate and autonomous poems? (4) when do poets begin publishing their own fragments to any significant degree, and how are these pieces introduced?

The Poetical Works of Sir John Davies, published from a corrected copy and edited by T. Davies, 1773, includes Davies's unfinished "Orchestra," described in the 1622 edition and between stanzas 126 and 127 as follows: "Here are wanting some Stanzaes describing Queene Elizabeth. Then follow these." The 1773 edition offers a prefatory apology for the unfinished text: "It is a great pity, and to be lamented by the poetical world, that so very ingenious a poem should be left unfinished, or what is more likely, that the imperfect part should be lost; for in all probability, he completed it. . . ."[34] Bishop Sprat, editor of Cowley's works, 1668, explicitly excludes fragmentary poems: "I have now set forth his Latin and English Writings, each in a Volume apart; and to that which was before extant in both Languages, I have added all that I could find in his Closet, which he had brought to any manner of perfection."[35] Although Cowley's unfinished "Poem on the Late Civil War" is included in a 1716 edition (*First Part of Miscellany Poems*), the editor takes pains to defend his decision and to provide a frame of reference for the work:

Meeting accidentally with this Poem in Manuscript, and being informed that it was a Piece of the incomparable Mr. Abraham Cowley's, I thought it unjust to hide such a Treasure from the World. I remember'd that our Author, in his Preface to his Works, makes mention of some Poems, written by him on the late Civil War, of which the following is unquestionably a part. In his most imperfect and unfinish'd Pieces, you will discover the Hand of so great a Master. And (whatever his own Modesty might have advised to the contrary) there is not one careless Stroke of his but what should be kept Sacred to all Posterity. He could Write nothing that was not worth the preserving, being habitually a Poet, and always Inspir'd. In this Piece, the Judicious Reader will find the Turn of the Verse to be his; the same Copious and Lively Imagery of Fancy, the same Warmth of Passion and Delicacy of Wit that sparkles in all his Writings.[36]

The poem can sustain a reading, the editor suggests, because it is distinguished by the same graces that characterize Cowley's finished work. These virtues are, one observes, local happinesses (phrasing, imagery, feeling, wit). The editor does not praise the conceptual strength or invention evinced by the fragment. The piece is judged "worth the preserving" because it testifies to the ease or naturalness of Cowley's talent. His genius was not something got up for a particular occasion but the basic and determining quality of the man's character. The "Judicious Reader" is not asked to approve the fragment as an independently pleasing poem, but as a historically and psychologically interesting document—interesting, that is, to the connoisseur of Cowley's finished works. The same interest might well extend to other "treasures": diaries, marginalia, letters, notebook entries. But one would not, of course, on that basis identify these items as poems, however poetical their attributes.

As I observed in chapter one, Dr. Johnson expresses an interest in the "sketches and rough drafts" left behind by Edmund Smith. In these, "the fable, structure, and connexion, the images, incidents, moral, episodes, and a great variety of ornaments, were so finely laid out, so well fitted to the rules of art, and squared so exactly to the precedents of the ancients, that I have often looked on these poetical elements with the same concern, with which curious men are affected at the sight of the most entertaining remains and ruins of an antique figure or building. . . ."[37] Unlike Cowley's editor, Johnson approves the substance of the fragments, their intellectual matter. He discovers in these pieces not just the spirit, symptoms, or ornaments of genius but the structural elements of poetical composition. Despite his praise for these works, however, Johnson approves the suppression of imperfect texts: "It cannot be supposed they [those individuals in possession of Smith's manuscripts] would suppress anything that was his, but out of respect to his memory, and for want of proper hands to finish what so great a genius had begun."[38] Johnson implies that publication of the fragments would not only set the reader unwarranted challenges, but that it would violate the editor's primary obligation to his author: the obligation to display the writer in the best possible light. By printing the poet's fragments, the editor would render him vulnerable to public derision and/or misprision.

This sensitivity, an expression of editorial decorum, appears as early as 1598, in Chapman's "Epistle Dedicatory" to Marlowe's "Hero and Leander":

> Sir, we think not ourselves discharged of the duty we owe to our friend, when we have brought the breathles bodie to the earth: for albeit the eye there taketh his ever farewell of that beloved object, yet the impression of the man, that hath been deare unto us, living an after life in our memorie, there putteth us in minde of farther obsequies due unto the deceased. And namely of the performance of whatsoever we may judge shall make to his living credit, and to the effecting of his determinations prevented by the stroke of death. By these meditations (as by an intellectual will) I suppose my selfe executor to the unhappily deceased author of this Poem, upon whom knowing that in his life time you bestowed many kind favours . . . I cannot but see so far into the will of him dead, that whatsoever issue of his braine should chance to come abroad, that the first breath it should take might be the gentle aire of your liking.
>
> At this time seeing that this unfinished Tragedy happens under my hands to be imprinted, of a double duty, to yourself and the deceased, I present it to your allowance.[39]

The apology is, of course, on one level Chapman's gracefully disingenuous defense of his own effort. But the form of the apology—an honorific protest—suggests some real concern to protect Marlowe's fragment from an unjust reception. Chapman assumes (or pretends to assume), that the reader, unable to work out his frustration through a creative reorganization of the fragment, will abuse both the poem and its author. This is not to say, of course, that Chapman's apprehensions were justified, only that to some extent they dictated, or were exhibited as dictating his editorial policy and presentation. One *might* conjecture that for want of exposure to poetic fragments, due to the editorial scruples of editors such as Chapman and Johnson, readers *were* unduly nonplussed by—and thus unduly critical of—fragments that came their way.

Eighteenth-century editors of contemporary and of earlier poets seem generally to adopt one of three attitudes toward the fragment. They might publish fragments and justify their practice by locating some not strictly literary value or interest in the piece, print self-contained and completed units of works intended to be longer, or explain their failure to print available fragments by citing accepted editorial principles.

The 1716 edition of Cowley, cited above, exemplifies works of the first kind. Charles Churchill's "Fragment of a Journey" illustrates the second case.[40] The fragment ends, "I on my Journey all Alone proceed." The "journey" is, of course, the rest of Churchill's poetic progress, a progress initiated with the volume that ends on this open and generous note. The journey metaphor, by characterizing the relation of fragment poem to volume as that of envoi to argument, effectively completes the fragment— that is, assimilates it to another discursive form. Moreover, within the volume, "The Journey" functions as a closural reflection on the author's poetic career, and chiefly on his compulsion to versify. The unfinished "Journey" is at once Churchill's confession and repetition of his vice. These internal facts would seem to identify this work as a rather exceptional fragment poem. Within its volume and in its textual aspect as envoi and reflection, "The Journey" describes a self-contained, achieved, and determinate form.

Joseph Cottle's introduction to his poem, "War: A Fragment," 1795, evinces what seems to be a typical eighteenth-century attitude toward textual irresolution: "It may not be amiss to inform the reader, that WAR A FRAGMENT was extracted from a didactic Poem of some extent on HAPPINESS. If the specimen given should be approved of, the remainder of the piece will probably appear in a second edition."[41] The fragment ends with a full stop and this couplet: "Compassion draws a veil, and leaves their wrongs / With Heav'n, to whom decision's right belong." (lines 351–52). The sound as well as the sense of the couplet close the fragment conclusively; one reads the text as a complete, intentional form —a discrete unit of a more extensive work, not unlike one of Dryden's detachable dramatic prologues. We notice as well that Cottle had his fragment published on 14 July 1795, and, for those readers who might miss the resonance, he offers the following commentary, a defense of his selective procedures:

> A conviction that a detailed account of one murder, occurring either on the high-road, or on the field of battle, more interests the heart, and leaves on it a longer impression, than the general account of slaughtered thousands, occasioned the Author to introduce the Tale of Orlando and Henry in WAR A FRAGMENT; and while the reader sighs over individual destruction, he should remember that War is but another name for destruction in the vast. . . .[42]

Cottle suggests by this passage a particular thematic motive for the formal condition of his poem. The relation of individual to general destruction illuminates the synecdochic relation of fragment to complete poem.

A more interesting aspect of Cottle's introductory note is its expression of authorial obedience to reader response. Of course, Cottle may never have intended to produce the "didactic Poem of some extent. . . ." He may only have wished to print his fragment, but, hesitant to entrust the partial work to the cold appraisal of an unprepared public, he presents the piece as a sample of the alleged whole, and therefore as a legitimately imperfect text.

Byron employs the same device at the end of Canto two, *Don Juan*, and again at the end of Canto five. There is a world of difference, however, between Cottle's earnest apology and Byron's broadly facetious one. Byron's remarks are asides to the reader, instances of the many authorial intrusions that constitute one major plot line and theme of the poem. We know perfectly well (and Byron's archness reassures us) that his modesty is a costume he can put on and take off at will. "This work is epic, . . ." and it is epic, Byron insists, not in conception alone and/or once completed, but as it stands. Further, who would believe, despite Byron's pitch in Cantos two and five, that the sprawling *Don Juan*—its tone, that of assured indifference to the nicer tastes and distastes of its audience—represents a trial by which to determine critical response? In that Byron prominently dramatizes throughout the poem his improvisational method, the piecemeal construction would, to the most naïve reader, seem to reflect an epistemological imperative. Attentive servility to reading appetites would be the last explanation advanced for Byron's discontinuous procedures. Moreover, it is clear that the irresolution which characterizes *Don Juan* describes neither the relationship of one canto to its successor, nor the terminal condition of the work as a whole. The poem's (in)famous irresolution occurs within each canto and through the author's digressions and his disruptive posturings. The subject of *Don Juan* is, we see, its method: acts of interpretation and uses of context. One does not care about the completed whole Byron has, or pretends he has, or promises. One cannot even believe in such wholes by the end of the poem.

William Mason, in his *Memoirs of the Life and Writings of Mr. Gray*, 1775, can be taken to represent those editors who defend their decision to publish or not to publish available fragments by reference to conventional editorial practice and values. Mason not only prints Gray's fragments, he situates them in a "Poems" section at the end of the *Memoirs*.[43] We do find in another section of this edition a fragment of an Ode, a work which Mason himself "finishes" ("elucidates") in the endnotes. The most interesting aspect of Mason's edition is his determination to defend the propriety of fragment presentation even in a Memoir. Mason's anxiety on this score extends to his treatment of all material not intended for publication. One is reminded of the "preface to the second part of Mr. Waller's poems," 1690: "It will perhaps be contended after all, that some of these ought not to have been Publish'd: and Mr. Cowly's decision will be urg'd, that a neat Tomb of Marble is a better Monument, than a great Pile of Rubbish . . . so 'twas thought a greater piece of kindness to the Author, to put 'em out; whilst they continue genuine and unmix'd; and such, as he himself, were he alive might own."[44] Mason, in his edition of Gray, clearly anticipates criticism for his boldness in exposing his author's unfinished work; he averts this censure by protesting the extraordinary perfection to which Gray brought all his poetry. By polishing each unit of writing as he composed it and before proceeding to the next unit, Gray bequeathed to posterity a collection of highly finished fragments in no way capable of embarrassing the poet's finest achievements. I quote in full from his Preface:

> Mr. Gray intimates, in the foregoing letter, that he had two or three more lyrical ideas in his head: One of these was "The Bard," the exordium of which was at this time finished; I say finished, because his conceptions, as well as his manner of disposing them, were so singularly exact, that he had seldom occasion to make many, except verbal emendations, after he had first committed his lines to paper. It was never his method to sketch his general design in careless verse,

he always finished as he proceeded; this, tho' it made his execution slow, made his compositions more perfect. I think, however, that this method was only calculated to produce such short works as generally employed his poetical pen; and that from pursuing it, he grew tired of his larger designs before he had completed them. The fact seems to justify my opinion. But my principal reason for mentioning this at present, is to explain the cause *why I have not been scrupulous in publishing so many of his fragments in the course of these memoirs. It would have been unpardonable in me to have taken this liberty with a deceased friend, had I not found his lines, as far as they went, nearly as highly finished as they would have been, when completed*: if I am mistaken in this, I hope the reader will rather impute it to a defect in my own Judgment, than a want of respect to Mr. Gray's Memory.

This consideration, however, *emboldens me to print the following fragment of an Ode in this place.* . . . I print this careless note, in order that the reader may conceive the intended arrangement of the whole; who, I doubt not, will, on perusing the following beautiful stanzas, lament with me that he left it incomplete; nor will it console him for the loss, if I tell him that I have had the boldness to attempt to finish it myself, making use of some other lines and broken stanzas which he had written: But as my aim in undertaking this difficult task was merely to elucidate the Poet's general meaning, I do not think that my additions are worthy to be inserted in this place; they will find a more fit situation if thrown amongst those notes which I shall put at the end of his Poems. (my emphases)[45]

Forty years after the appearance of Mason's edition, the Reverend J. Mitford includes in his table of contents to Gray's poetry a section entitled "Posthumous Poems and Fragments."[46] Although Mitford includes a biographical section in his edition, he does not feel constrained to insert the fragments there. Mitford accounts the fragments legitimate poems, albeit of a special kind, and he positions them in his volume accordingly. One might introduce in this context the Waller edition cited above. Robert Bell, Waller's editor, defends the propriety of his gathering "everything of Mr. Waller's that is not put into the former collection; so that between both the reader may make the set complete."

The range of nineteenth-century editions I have surveyed shows, first, that as time went on, more and more fragments were published. The label, "eighteenth century," is useless, of course, when speaking of editions that were in effect all products of the 1790s—the same general milieu as Southey's, Wordsworth's and Coleridge's. One can, however, observe the coexistence of what we might call a neoclassical and a Romantic attitude toward fragments during this transitional period, and as the nineteenth century advanced, the gradual disappearance of the kinds of justification that were typical of many eighteenth-century editions. While the biographical and historical interest in fragments did not disappear, poetic fragments tended increasingly to be appreciated for whatever intrinsic literary interest they might provide. Third, there seems to have been a marked increase in the number of poets who published their own fragments after 1798. Modest demurrals still not infrequently accompany these works, but the general effect of these statements tends to differ significantly from the sort of thing one finds in eighteenth-century apologies. John Merivale, for example, introduces one of his imperfect pieces with this note: "several unconnected fragments of verse which are here brought together as component parts of a larger poem, were actually written, as may be inferred from what has already been stated in the Preface, without any such design."[47] Merivale not only goes out of his way to deny the compositional—that is, conceptual—integrity of his fragments, he pointedly refrains from connecting the pieces which he "brought together as component parts of a larger poem." The poet collects, the reader connects. Merivale's confidence in this context, however, is offset by his "completion," à la Chapman, of Beattie's *The Minstrel*, as it is by the "diffidence" or ambivalence he exhibits in his Preface: "Notwithstanding the encouragement given him by his friends, he is very diffident of success with the public; he therefore offers his poem in its present unfinished state, not as a pledge for its completion, but that he may find, in the manner of its reception, a touchstone by which to ascertain its real merit, and judge whether it will be expedient for him to pursue his design any farther, or to relinquish it altogether."[48] It is hard to know how to read this disclaimer; one wonders how seriously to take Merivale's representation of his fragment as an experiment in reception. What kind of reception does Merivale project for a piece lacking in independent literary merit? If the reception is to be worth anything in predictive value, then it must approximate, on a smaller scale, the reception possibilities for the finished work. And if this is the case, what distinguishes the fragment from the whole but the poet's experimental design?

An easier case can be made for increasing fragment confidence on the part of writers (from which we infer some competence on the part of readers) on the strength of Alexander Boswell's note to his "Clan Alpin's Vow: A Fragment," 1811: "It is not my wish to give an air of importance to a trifle which owed its existence to the sudden impression created by the perusal of that narrative which I have subjoined, and which was written with corresponding precipitancy. But. . . ."[49] Boswell's preface is not an apology but a clarification of a literary device. He explains his construction of a fragmentary form with reference to affective decorum, or stylistic sincerity. The form of the fragment is intended to communicate to the reader the spontaneity and excitement of Boswell's initial response to the narrative which he "subjoins." In that Boswell's reaction to the tale takes the form of a particular literary response, he naturally seeks to represent his formal impetus in the work's actual devices. Hence the (highly intentional) production of a fragment poem.

I have not, of course, in any way proved that some time between the early eighteenth century and the early nineteenth century certain widely shared assumptions about poetic closure changed, and changed so radically that poems which no rightminded editor nor poet would have "obtruded" on the public began to appear in number and to enjoy a notable popularity. I have merely outlined and reflected on a single episode in reception history—the Macpherson and Chatterton controversy and the surprising legitimization of the hoaxes in the Romantic period—and compiled a small range of editorial statements suggesting some increase in fragment consciousness among poets and editors. There are undoubtedly examples, and important ones, of fragment publication by sixteenth-, seventeenth-, and early eighteenth-century poets and editors, as there are certainly instances of Romantic readers, editors, and poets unable to conceive the fragment as a poetic form. Still, one would have to characterize each of these bodies of evidence as exceptional if one is to begin appreciating more concretely certain modifications in literary ideology—modifications that most of us accept, but that we find hard to demonstrate. How can we explain a statement such as the following unless we allow some fundamental and consistently realized revision of the literary system with respect to the nature and status of the poetic fragment? "Among the contents of this volume [Shelley's *Posthumous Poems*, 1824] we have to remark "The Triumph of Life" as one of the most elaborate of the finished poems of Mr. Shelley."[50] Such a comment makes no sense in the absence of some hypothesis about the special relationship obtaining between Romantic readers and Romantic fragments.

CHAPTER THREE

THE TRUE FRAGMENT

"Nutting"

In a letter to Coleridge, Dorothy introduces "Nutting" as "the conclusion of a poem of which the beginning is not written."[1] The text as it appears in the 1800 edition of *Lyrical Ballads* and all of Wordsworth's subsequent publications opens on a hemistich, thus implying the existence of some antecedent context. That context, a fifty-two-line passage addressed to Lucy, can be found in *Poetical Works*, ii, 504–506.

Wordsworth's entire canon includes only six poems that begin on a half-line, four of them ("A Night-Piece," "Airey-Force Valley," "Nutting," and "The Simplon Pass") grouped among the first seven Poems of the Imagination in the 1845 edition. ("A Night-Piece" and "Nutting" appear in the 1815 edition; the two remaining works were added in 1845.) There are arguments to be made for the doctrinal affinities shared by these poems and conceivably responsible for Wordsworth's arrangement. These need not disconfirm, however, the simpler and more obvious explanation: that the concentration of these works under a single rubric indicates Wordsworth's interest in emphasizing a common procedural character and in soliciting a distinctive reception. Insofar as the half-line opening, the mark of a truncation, pronounces the discourse's integral relationship with a missing body of writing, these poems invite us to organize the presented text with reference to that putative material. Morever, and more generally, Wordsworth's celebrated comparison of his canon to a gothic church, composed of "little cells, oratories, and sepulchral recesses," encourages us to locate the existing discursive matrix within which these fragments might realize their distinct formal character. While it is possible that Wordsworth figured *The Excursion* for this role (that architectural meta-

phor appears in the Preface to the 1814 edition), a number of compositional and structural facts would suggest *The Prelude* as the likelier, specific interpretive framework. "Nutting," we know, was originally destined
for *The Prelude* and is clearly of a piece with the earliest (1798–99) version of that poem.[2] Indeed, some of "Nutting"'s surrounding manuscript
material makes its way into the later versions of *The Prelude.* "The Simplon Pass" defines, of course, a critical moment in the 1805 and 1850
Preludes, and "There Was a Boy," the first Poem of the Imagination and
one that opens conventionally on a whole line, appears almost verbatim in
the *Preludes.* "Airey-Force Valley" and "A Night-Piece," while they remind
us of "I Wandered Lonely as a Cloud" and "The Solitary Reaper," so
exceed even those works in semiotic-discursive (meditative-descriptive)
integration as to refuse doctrinally, as it were, a secondary, abstracted
critique. In their reflexivity, these poems conform more closely to the style
and interests of *The Prelude* than to the more public, didactic, and politically composed *Excursion.*

One is hard put not to subordinate these fragmentary lyrics—"minor
Pieces"—to the "main Work" which, for modern readers, is more often
than not *The Prelude.* Rather than develop independently the structural
determinacy of "Nutting," for example, one tends to read the poem with
reference to its probable position and function in *The Prelude.* To do this
is, of course, to lose the impact of the opening hemistich; more generally,
it is to efface the fragmentary gestures which the poem, situated within its
actual context, sketches.

One might conjecture that Wordsworth intended the half-line—a sort
of open link—to provoke just such an interpolative reception. In binding
together the minor pieces and subordinating them to the main, and presumably ongoing work, the reader would effectively annul the "absolute,
independent singleness" of the individual poems.

We observe, however, and somewhat paradoxically, that the insertion of
these fragments into an existing composition tends to insulate them and
to subject their protean potentiality to the exigencies and impulses of that
main work. "Nutting," imaginatively situated in *The Prelude,* assumes the
look of a spot of time. The passage impresses itself as a discrete, independently perspicuous narration which concentrates diverse impressions and
emotions—past and present—into an experiential unity, thereby enabling
the poet to proceed more profoundly and surely with the business of
writing and living. The disconcerting effect of the hemistich is lost; the
typographical indentation is construed as the beginning of a new para-

graph, thus reinforcing the formal and narrative isolation of the passage. What was a fragment becomes as it were a perfect part: a little cell, oratory, or sepulchral recess.

To read "Nutting" along the lines sketched out for the Wordsworthian meditative poem is to produce a rather special critical awkwardness. David Perkins has described the Wordsworthian meditative poem as follows: ". . . [the] attention fixes itself on some object or memory. . . . The mind goes on a journey, wandering from the present object and returning to it. . . . Finally there is a moment of discovery. Some new insight dawns, or some old truth is recaptured with clarity and force."[3] Given this protocol—a popular interpretive model for "Nutting"—Wordsworth's didactic conclusion introduces a serious flaw. Indeed, the three lines have generated almost as much critical commotion as the pious retraction with which Coleridge concludes "The Eolian Harp."

> Then, dearest Maiden, move along these shades
> In gentleness of heart; with gentle hand
> Touch—for there is a spirit in the woods.

If "Nutting" is read as a spot of time or a meditative poem (or anything but a fragment poem), these lines must vitiate the entire poetic effect. In that the conclusion misrepresents and trivializes by abstracting the experience reported and enacted in the course of the poem, it marks a moment of evasion or repression rather than "a moment of discovery." Neither a "new insight" nor "an old truth recaptured with clarity and force," the conclusion seems the product of an irritable reaching after certainty. Moreover, the sudden word to the wise—or the stylistic discrepancy between this instruction and the preceding narrative mode—corks the poem in a painfully mechanical way, contravening its procedural logic and confusing its discursive effect. The rhetoric of sincerity that colors these lines throws the self-conscious, even mannered quality of the body of the poem into relief, installing a conflict that must be addressed.

By putting oneself in the position of a reader of *Lyrical Ballads* in 1800 —a reader who knew neither *The Prelude*, with its memorable definition and examples of the spot of time, nor *The Excursion*, nor Wordsworth's directives as delivered in the 1814 Preface to that work—one gains a fresh formal perspective. A reader who lacked these important aids to understanding would probably attend more closely to questions of causation than consequence. Rather than ask of "Nutting" as one does of the spot of time, "what action does it facilitate, what knowledge does it produce" (that is, what purpose does it serve in the psychic, philosophical, and narrative development which the poem unfolds), the 1800 reader might well have remarked the curiously abrupt opening line. An impression of this kind could not but modify the perceived form of the work. Whereas modern criticism tends to interrogate the effects of the poem within its assumed, autobiographical context—that of *The Prelude*—the poem's early readers would have focussed the work as *itself* the effect of a particular history, and one they would have to invent.

Although Dorothy describes "Nutting" as the conclusion to an as yet unwritten poem, "Nutting"'s own conclusion—an address to a figure nowhere mentioned in the poem—opens the work rather than closes it. By reading the "dearest Maiden" lines figuratively, or by treating them as an informal but conventional coda, one may produce for the poem a terminal closure. But "Nutting" is, throughout, quite literal. Not only are its figures self-consciously "poeticized," thus establishing the narrator's matter-of-fact remove from his inventions, but the bold rhetorical address of those closing lines militates against a figural reading.

I take up that curious conclusion in some detail below. For now, let me suggest that we honor the incongruity of the address to the Maiden, and read in that mild violence an anti-closural gesture. To see this is to observe that the openness indicated by the initial hemistich is duplicated or paralleled in the concluding movement. "Nutting," thus organized, figures an excerpt from some completed or continuing work, and it urges upon the reader a reconstruction of this originary matrix. To designate "Nutting" a true fragment is to suggest that it authorizes a method of textual construction that would formally contour the given text by reference to that particular before-and-after which would explain its truncation.

Moreover, by construing the text as a fragment from a discourse stretching away from it in either direction, we establish a rhetorical and dramatic context that alters the values, even the identity of the work's constitutive elements. The content of the moral injunction in the last three lines remains inadequate, but this inadequacy, read as a gestural seme, properly concludes the discursive and dramatic argument developed in lines 1–53. In other words, the conclusion may be logically wrong and yet formally and psychically sound, given a context that brings out the dialogic dimension of the utterance.

By context, I mean to suggest a speaker, a listener, and an occasion. While the first or final circuit naturally involves poet and reader, we can see that the represented discourse features a particular speaker and an equally distinct auditor, the dearest Maiden. The occasion might be a ramble through some countryside familiar to the narrator and his companion. That is, the couple either happens upon the original scene to which "Nutting" refers, or some association triggers the memory, or we have some combination of these promptings. Then again, speaker and Maiden may be sitting at home, in which case the closing admonition would refer to the indefinite future when the Maiden might find herself on some woodland excursion.

To acknowledge the conversational situation of the poem is to obviate a certain kind of rationalization. Once we conceive the concluding lines as a dramatic address, contained by the poetic fiction (and not an application of it), we solve—or dissolve—the problem of our natural resistance to a doctrine Wordsworth compels us to take at face value. That is, "we" are not directly compelled in the least. It is the Maiden who gets instructed. Moreover, by construing the closing utterance as a gesture to the Maiden —loosely, a speech act—we find that the mental action therein represented follows naturally from the speaker's efforts throughout the poem, as I shall illustrate below. As the culmination of a syllogistic structure—an inference drawn from the perceptions and syntheses developed in the course of the poem—the lines *are* a mistake. They are nonetheless—and by virtue of this wrongness—formally, dramatically, and psychically appropriate. One is reminded of other complexly appropriate Romantic oversimplifications, such as the Mariner's doctrinal synopsis, "He prayeth best, who loveth best / All things both great and small. . . ."

The concluding disclosure that the discourse is not a mute and solitary meditation but represents an episode in an ongoing human relationship implies that the motivation behind the verbal structure and its delivery lies elsewhere than in the desire to exemplify the final lines. Something in the speaker-listener, I-dearest Maiden relationship at once brings this particular memory to consciousness and to speech, and at the same time prevents the speaker from making the authoritative moral summation he strains for. Further, the implied presence of a companion adds rhetorical conditions that complicate the lyric or meditative impulse—that is, the drive to produce an internally necessitated form. These conditions offer us a means of elucidating the speaker's otherwise baffling failure to organize the elements of his discourse into a coherent whole. The concluding gesture—or more precisely, the dramatic information it encodes—explains why the affective and intellectual resolution one is led to expect fails to occur in the poem. The narrator in effect saves his discourse by letting it go. He delivers the discursive experience, not its intellectual precipitate, to the Maiden —and, mediated by her and the conditions she figures, to the reader.

This emphasis on a mere three lines may seem more deserved if we compare these lines to those that conclude "The Solitary Reaper." The conclusions are identical in rhetorical function, opposite in dramatic effect; both are designed to reorganize radically and startlingly the reader's perception of form. In the conclusion to "The Solitary Reaper," one learns that the speaker is alone and has been throughout his narration. Despite his imperatives, injunctions, and interrogations, we find that he is neither addressing a passerby, looking at a vale, listening to a voice, nor beholding a living reaper. The conclusion tells us that the material which the poem works was detached from its historical origins some time before the poem was even conceived. The revelation characterizes the work as a tertiary transformation—that is, a discursive representation of memory-digested, or ideologically processed material.

In "Nutting," one learns that the speaker *has* a listener, has had one from the start of the poem, and that his words have an immediate rhetorical dimension. On one level, of course, the poem delivers internalized and fictive material; the ultimate referential object—the nutting excursion—is a memory. But working alongside, against, and finally through this material is the story enacted within the immediate discursive context and by the two participants, one silent, one vocal, in this conversation poem. Whereas the tense switch at the end of "The Solitary Reaper" directs interpretation toward abstract and epistemological issues, the conclusion to "Nutting" invites a more literal and located reading than the poem would otherwise suggest. "Nutting," while it remains a poem about the "emergence of a modern [adult] imagination," comes into sharper focus as an exploration of the particular conflicts surrounding that emergence— conflicts involving memory, its referents, and its own existential immediacies.

Once we conceive "Nutting" as a dramatically located and rhetorically controlled utterance upon which we eavesdrop—a dramatic monologue scenario—the opening hemistich acquires a fairly specific significance. The phrase, ". . . It seems a day / (I speak of one from many singled out) / One of those heavenly days that cannot die," sounds less like a stale, sentimental poeticism or simply a way to begin. It evokes a once-upon-a-time formula and implies that the speaker is about to tell a story to a familiar and receptive listener, presumably the Maiden. We notice that he ends in typical fable fashion, by verbalizing the moral of his tale. What we deduce from this analogy is that the story is told and the moral articulated not, or not only, for their intrinsic or general truth value but on account of their immediate and situational function. In narrating the nutting memory, the speaker effectively distinguishes the present occasion. He marks the discursive moment with a shared semantic and verbal experience as one might inscribe a legend on a wayside stone, thus commemorating both the moment of inscription and the human history which informs and precipitates that moment. The meaning of the narration should thus be sought in the communicative context conjured by the last three lines.

We see that the narrator's impulse to signify, or to constitute a specifically serviceable discursive moment, coincides with an interest in existential continuities. In relating to his companion this particular memory, the narrator seems concerned to interrelate past and present structures of feeling—that is, to achieve a certain psychic consolidation. At the same time, he works to integrate another and alien presence, the Maiden, into his history of associations and affections. The discourse consists of a series of efforts to "single out" a memory in such a way as to realize these integrative interests. By these efforts—each one the assumption of a new narrative perspective on the nutting memory—the narrator effectively brings to bear his present, adult sensibility upon the childhood events.

Let me roughly plot the sequence. From lines 1–13, the narrator assumes a pose of bemused detachment. He refers to himself, pedantically, as a "Figure quaint" who sallies forth "Tricked out in proud disguise of cast-off weeds." He describes his outfit and his actions with arch but affectionate hyperbole; the narration luxuriates in its excesses and in the breach they figure between original experience and mannered narration. With lines 14–24, the mock heroics grow more obtrusive and decidedly leaden. The censorious edge to these lines suggests an interest in tempering the self-indulgence of the preceding passage. The corrective movement, however, introduces a threatening tone. The narration is clearly "forcing [its] way" and we feel the resistance. Line 25 marks the assumption of a new orientation toward the childhood memory; the narrator sentimentalizes the remembered scene, depicting his boyhood self as a grateful intimate of Nature, blessed by a sort of sensory grace. The superficial distortions of Fancy lead into a more properly imaginative representation; in lines 35–42, the narrator authentically subjectivizes both his former, objectified self and the remembered action. Still, the representation veers toward the factitious (marked by a kind of inscrutably circular generality in lines 39–40), and again, in a stylistically corrective move, the narration shifts gear. Lines 43–48 report an action sequence in direct and assertive prose. The organization is paratactic—an implicit critique of the nicer discursive and conceptual connections featured above. Stylistically, then, these lines articulate the self-reproach hinted throughout the poem.

I anatomize the narration not to claim some particular significance for the sequence or for its components. What I isolate is the sheer diversity of positions assumed; what I infer from this narrational discontinuity is the speaker's sense of the deficiency of any one position. None of the perspectives is found capable of "singling out" the memory in such a way as to make it presently appropriate—that is, apt for experiential inscription.

The local failures seem to derive from a primary conceptual error, an error repeated and exposed in the substance of the memory selected for this discursive occasion. The speaker seeks, in effect, to raise a particular memory into a spot of time, "which with distinct pre-eminence retain[s] / A renovating virtue. . . ." What he forgets or does not understand is that the spot of time has no essential difference from any other moment. What distinguishes it is its position within the continuum of times it is (found to be) not. What makes the spot of time profound, determinate, infinitely self-reflexive and suggestive is its serendipity. The mind discovers by accident, as it were, a hidden organization which, *by that manner of emergence*, assumes a providential virtue. The mental material and the encounter with it cannot be willed into being or compelled to assume a "distinct pre-eminence." They must both be experienced with a wise passiveness.

In seeking to isolate and heighten the nutting memory and to claim for it an intrinsic distinction, the narrator foregrounds some elements of that memory and suppresses others, repeatedly fracturing the original (or putative) existential unity of the event and the memory. The narrator's impulse to distinguish is tantamount to an impulse of appropriation toward the "quiet being" of the memory, of the present moment, and of his companion. By "appropriation," I mean an interest in turning mind and Nature to advantage. The narrator of "Nutting" addresses his own memory in such a way as to compel it to perform a particular function, necessarily extraneous to its original or mnemonically acquired character. This is where the violence lies, and this is what precipitates the strangely sexualized representation of the event—in effect, an adult displacement of the inscribed aggression.

How might we locate this displacement, restricted as we are to the temporal and psychic perspective afforded by the monologic narration? First, we find in that single narrative voice two points of view—one the perspective of innocence, the other that of experience. Lines 48 and 49— ". . . unless I now / Confound my present feelings with the past"—must be one of Wordsworth's most ironic understatements, for the poem interweaves, transposes, and superimposes past and present feelings throughout. "I came to one dear nook / Unvisited," the narrator tells us, and as if to reinforce that curious "unvisited," compares his mood to that of those who "after long / And weary expectation, have been blest / With sudden happiness beyond all hope." In other words, the narrator represents the boy's purposeful quest for a clearly conceived object ("one dear nook"— that is, endeared by prior knowledge) as a fortuitous discovery. Moreover, it is hard to believe that the boy who set off eagerly, intelligently equipped for his journey, "Forcing [his] way" through difficult terrain, "eyed / The banquet" with "wise restraint / Voluptuous." Surely this is the dalliance of an adult, who knows to savor the anticipation of a pleasure, or who knows that gratification is the end and the end*point* of pleasure. The "sense of pain," as well as the language that specifies it ("deformed and sullied," "mutilated bower"), belong to the adult narrator who confounds his present feelings with the past. The explicit sexuality of the imagery here and above (lines 19–26, 40–43) suggests that the boy's original recoil from his own aggression has been brought into the service of the narrator's current emotional needs. The narrator has emptied his memory of its own quiet being and has made it the vehicle for another tenor.

We must wonder what it is about the dramatic context that suggests the nutting memory to the narrator and then distorts it. Or, why might the speaker describe a "heavenly day" in terms so overtly erotic that every reader of the poem remarks them, and then offer this dubious discursive posy to a "dearest Maiden"?

The discourse itself would lead us to guess that the narrator fears more for his own despoliations, past and possible, than for the Maiden's aggressiveness, and given the structural facts of the fragment, we might associate these fears with the Maiden's presence. This is not to say that "Nutting" is a kind of antiseduction poem, but that the impulse to isolate and idealize a memory (like the impulse to claim for oneself the quiet being of another person) is represented in the poem as an existential violation. It is the *conjunction* of epistemological, verbal, and erotic desires that precipitates the anxieties which shape the narration.

In his concluding exhortation to the Maiden, the narrator effectively offers her not only his memory of the nutting excursion but the perverse and self-contradictory version of it he has just produced. Through the gesture of address, the narrator owns the association responsible for those structural, stylistic, and tonal distortions enumerated above: an association of direct object-desire with more displaced and sophisticated forms of aggression. "Nutting'"s conclusion, then, figures a genuine dramatic recognition; the lines are simple, perspicuous, and general, and they move us far more than the histrionic chronicle which calls them forth. By articulating the initially unacknowledged—unsuspected—occasion of his utterance, the narrator ironically achieves his ambition to "single out." What he distinguishes, however, is not the memory of the nutting outing but rather his *present* experience, which will live in his memory, steeping in its meanings, growing ripe for some future realization. A beneficent unconsciousness working through language and association leads the narrator to the goal he had so fervently, wrongheadedly sought.

Geoffrey Hartman characterizes "Nutting" as "close to a turning-point in English poetry." In "Nutting," we can trace "the emergence of a modern imagination from the toils and temptations of the old." Wordsworth's "sketch" develops the insight that "poetry cannot exist without Romance, yet modern poetry cannot subsist on Romance."[4] The general argument of Hartman's great study suggests that "Nutting" chronicles in a wonderfully concentrated way the Romantic war between Nature and the imagination—its outcome here, the emergence of the aggressive ego, separate from and even hostile to Nature. In his discussion of the romance dimension of the poem, Hartman emphasizes that while the action of "Nutting" is "almost purely psychological. . . . The scene . . . remains English, the hero a boy, the wood a wood."[5] The one reality Hartman omits is the Maiden. Why should she be a literary fixture, an allegorical emblem, or a nympholeptic vision when the scene, the hero, and the wood are insistently literal?

Perhaps Hartman felt that unless he implicitly characterized the Maiden as an abstraction, the action could not be "almost purely psychological." It would have to be characterized as almost purely dramatic and rhetorical, and the poem would lean more toward a human and historically situated meaning than a literary and metaphysical one.

I see no real conflict here. By supplying "Nutting" with the surrounding and formally controlling context of an oral, a dialogic discourse, one puts in sharper focus the themes that Hartman enumerates. One locates a motivation for the articulation of these themes—a motivation that illuminates the stylistic and structural properties of that articulation.

I would like to expand a bit upon an observation offered above. I noted in passing that the desire to signify—to distinguish dialectically figure from ground, a formal truncation—is, on one level, a desire to appropriate. Fully indulged, this desire describes an existential violence. The reference for these remarks is, of course, the verbal drama played out in "Nutting"—a poem very much about "singling out" and about cognitive, mnemonic, verbal, and erotic expressions of that act.

To define-distinguish an object by desire is to abrogate the "quiet being" of that object. "Affection" is, of course, a different case. By that word, Wordsworth describes a holistic and humane, or integrative relational mode, and Wordsworth's concern to define this (contrastive) mode in itself suggests the specificity with which he conceives desiring acts and interests. To single out is to focus certain qualities and suppress others, thus shattering the integrity—formal and environmental—of the object in question. These acts of designation and the concomitant sensory and semiotic occlusions or exclusions eventuate in an annexation of the object— effectively, a reduction of its autonomy. We kill the things we love not so much because one extreme precipitates its obverse (one explanation of the boy's sudden violence in "Nutting") but because of the selective and appropriative nature of desire—and recognition, and representation.

The Lucy poems, written in Germany during the same period as "Nutting"'s composition, are a sustained investigation of these ideas. In order to structure and/or strengthen his memory (in this way reviving/preserving a former self), Wordsworth consecrates various remembered landscapes profoundly associated with his evolving identity. His consecrating (he might say, "humanizing") method is personification. Thus does he conjure a range of vital, indwelling *figurae*—that is, *genius loci* and *mentis*. Personification is, of course, not merely *an* act of selection and idealization, but probably *the* such act, and it comes as no surprise that the aggression we witness in "Nutting" surfaces so murderously in the Lucy poems. By a happy economy, however, Lucy's extinction—clearly associated with the narrator's acts of distinction—restores her to the continuity of the landscape, quite literally her ground of being. By thus replacing the loved figure in Nature's continuities ("Rolled round in earth's diurnal course . . ."), the narrator produces a relatively guiltless semiosis.

David Simpson's *Wordsworth and the Figurings of the Real*, a careful and penetrating study of these issues, brings out the creative potential of the figure, or of figured perception and representation. He emphasizes the social and cognitive relational functions of the figure—its capacity to generate "companionable forms" and thus to emancipate poet and reader both from their own psychic isolation and from the alien indifferences of the real.

My reading of "Nutting" develops the de-creative aspects of the figure, or of the perceptual and conceptual activity that produces reality by undoing it. To emphasize Wordsworth's sensitivity to the violence implied in our most passive significations, is not, of course, to deny his commitment to the figuring activity. I quote Simpson's balanced appraisal of the matter: "Wordsworth's idea of the mind, looked at as a whole, allows for the interplay of antithetical drives and dispositions, discouraging the ultimate replacement of any one by any other. There are, then, two versions of world-construction or figurative attribution, or rather two poles of a coherent process, one of which aims at fluidity and the other at fixity."[6] Let me juxtapose two familiar passages. One is from Wordsworth's letter to Lady Beaumont, 1807, and the other, part of a critique of Macpherson's poetry, from the Essay, Supplementary to the Preface:

> . . . the mind can have no rest among a multitude of objects, of which it either cannot make one whole, or from which it cannot single out one individual, whereupon may be concentrated the attention divided among or distracted by a multitude? After a certain time we must either select one image or object, which must put out of view the rest wholly, or must subordinate them to itself while it stands forth as a Head.

> In nature everything is distinct, yet nothing defined into absolute independent singleness. In Macpherson's work, it is exactly the reverse; everything (that is not stolen) is in this manner defined, insulated, dislocated, deadened,—yet nothing distinct. It will always be so when words are substituted for things.

The first excerpt is part of a commentary on the sonnet, "With Ships the sea was sprinkled far and nigh"—a poem that traces the mind's progress from distraction to fixation and thence to serenity. The narrator characterizes this action, represented in the poem as a perceptual and epistemological motion, erotically.

> This Ship was nought to me, nor I to her,
> Yet I pursued her with a Lover's look;
> This Ship to all the rest did I prefer.

The mechanism whereby the narrator singles out his Ship is simile ("like a giant"), which, in this case, produces a personification. Neither the poem nor the letter which glosses it communicates much anxiety about the psychic imperative to figure or designate, nor about the effects of such actions upon the privately and socially constituted object world. Perhaps Wordsworth's easy acquiescence to the fact that we "must either select one image or object, which must put out of view the rest wholly, or must subordinate them to itself while it stands forth as a Head" reflects the evolution of his political commitment. Mental order, like social, requires a degree of arbitrary—incidentally unjust—authoritarianism.

But Wordsworth does not always or everywhere evince this complacency about perceptual and poetical figuring. The commentary on Macpherson in the second excerpt reflects the ambivalence that emerges so palpably in "Nutting." All speech—and certainly all poetry—not only substitutes words for things, as Wordsworth is well aware, but delineates arbitrarily, wantonly, a circle of significant representations and pretends to discover what it in fact produces by its curtailments. The lyric, of course, draws a tighter circle than most poetic forms. That is, the poet produces the characteristic lyric effects—intensity and depth—by sacrificing the semblance of experiential fullness, integrity, and movement. Perhaps the most comfortably insincere of forms, the lyric singles out with a vengeance, investing its privatized material with all the meaning it steals from the historical and material relations that it excludes. Moreover, the lyric is most successful in its own terms when it makes this theft invisible, thereby implying that its subject is naturally or generally significant—which is to say that its words are the adequate representations of things to which we all have access—its subjectivity a realization of our own inwardness.

As Simpson has usefully noted, the whole impulse of high Romantic language theory is "predominantly nominalist, as part of the movement away from the materialist or realist idea of the world."[7] In other words, the estrangement of world from word—inevitable and pronounced in any signifying act—is intentionalized and intensified in Romantic poetry, for both practical and ideological reasons.

Given Wordsworth's anxieties about designation and its dislocations, why does he isolate "Nutting" when he could easily have included it in *The Prelude*? The presentation of the text as an independent lyric would seem to underline that formal insincerity and authorial willfulness that prompts, in "Nutting," the powerful and determinate backlash we have observed. We might conjecture that the covert rhetorical aspect of the poem discouraged Wordsworth from incorporating it into the introspective *Prelude*. Whereas Coleridge's presence in that poem is a relatively inert semantic and rhetorical factor, the Maiden's presence in "Nutting" strongly distorts the dominant discursive thrust. We might also observe that by the fragmentary gestures sketched in the first and last lines of "Nutting," Wordsworth counteracts the divisive or discontinuous effects we have discussed. That is, by its half-line opening and its gestural (in)-conclusion, "Nutting" creates the illusion that it is still embedded within an experiential continuum and that its figures and meanings are not so contrived as they might otherwise seem. To read "Nutting" as a true fragment is to feel that the poem—or the experiences it records and enacts —is one event randomly selected from a series of historically and onto-logically equivalent events. By this fiction—a reception protocol—we feel that were "Nutting" resituated in that natural sequence of "many such days" (that is, "singled out" modifying "many" rather than "one"), its general and intrinsic meaning would become obvious, just as in isolation, its personal and relational meaning predominates.

The form of the poem thus suggests that the process of literary transformation is reversible; poetry can be restored to its originary condition as natural discourse or experience. "Nutting" formally proposes what Arnold Hauser, quoting Novalis, observes: " 'all the accidents of our life . . . are materials out of which we can make what we like, everything is a link in an unending chain.' " This proposition is, in effect, a "disparagement of both the beginning and the end of the stream of experience, of both the content and form of the finished work of art."[8]

"Nutting," read as a true fragment, is a determinate form that conceals its authoritarian and expedient appropriation of historical material by formally deferring to the existential continuum which ostensibly gives shape and meaning to the discourse. The form of the poem thus reflects the issues that motivate it, but in such a way as to disguise those issues and to present the work as a more singleminded singling out than it actually is. The fragmentary form of the poem is, then, a technical solution to an existential, epistemological, and moral problem: how to designate without "defining, insulating, dislocating, deadening."

"A Night-Piece" and "Airey-Force Valley," both of which begin on a hemistich, similarly explore the double binds of knowledge and representation. Both poems examine the manner in which places and moments are raised to consciousness—formally and conceptually constituted—by the violence of the adventitious event.

As with "Nutting," these lyrics—inscription poems—escape their philosophic and affective dilemma by a formal maneuver. Both poems conclude by implying their own inadequacy, and both begin at a point that, according to the narrative logic of these texts, chronologically succeeds that ending. Beginning and end are both compromised in order that the representation may emerge without appearing to disrupt the natural continuities from which it was drawn.

Both poems feature an observer: one, the narrator ("Airey-Force Valley"), and the other, observed by the narrator, who also observes the scene. In both cases, this figure is represented as obscurely troubled by the visual and aural indistinctness—registered as dullness and stasis—of his environment. He indicates his wish for some sudden contingency—a clear sky, a freshening breeze—to interrupt the scenic continuities and dispel the monotony. He expresses this desire indirectly and by negatives (see lines 1–2 of "Airey-Force Valley," and 6–7 of "A Night-Piece"). By projecting an imagined stimulus, the speaker establishes a perceptual ground that throws into relief—effectively, formulates—certain absences or negatives. This is to say, the description is explicitly dialectical; the narrator represents the actual scene by contrasting it to an ideal or notional figure.

Nature intervenes. The access of light, which produces the outlines that figure the spatial ground, converts a literally uninteresting environment into a composition-for-consciousness. Whereas the description preceding this revelation seeks to interrelate the various landscape elements, we note the analytic character of the description that follows—its careful discrimination of elements and motions.

Although the narrator credits the epiphanic moment (the sudden emergence of figure from ground, action from stasis) with the composition of the traveller's mind, the *narration* indicates that the observer's attention had been riveted to the scene in a highly selective, "composed" manner from the outset of the poem. *Before* the breeze had sprung up, the wanderer's steps were stayed ("Airey-Force Valley").

These poems, disposed in the present tense, try to persuade us that they were composed after the sudden gleam or breeze—the natural figure —had rendered the landscape visible, semantically layered, and representable, and that the purpose of composition is to reconstitute the wholeness of Nature and psyche, fractured by the natural revelation. The discourse itself thus instances a "thought soothing" of the kind mentioned in "Airey-Force Valley." That is, the musings and harmonies that constitute these poems reassemble the scene—the observer's impression of it—following the shattering, form-producing moment. It seems that, unless this restoration is performed, neither the observer nor the poet (nor, presumably, the reader) can proceed. By analogy, we might recall the surmising narration that occupies stanzas 2–4 of "The Solitary Reaper." The speaker cannot "gently pass" until he has reintegrated a disturbingly defined memory into his mnemonic continuum, where it *lived*, before it reached— and died upon—the page.

The narrator of "A Night-Piece" resists the stasis of the cameoed vision by representing an optical illusion as if it were a physical datum independent of an observer. He knows, of course, that it is the motion of the clouds that makes the moon and stars appear to move, but he chooses to represent the phenomenon naïvely, in this way escaping his own cognitive and representational enthrallments. The sequence might remind us of *The Prelude*'s celebrated skating episode.

In "Airey-Force Valley," the ash bough is relieved of its detached, insulated appearance by a synaesthetic representation: "soft eye-music of slow waving boughs," an unusual locution for Wordsworth. The silence of this poem, like the dull sky of "A Night-Piece," is an instance of Wordsworthian mists from which visions emerge. "When they part, they isolate what is seen in some unfamiliar, timeless realm."[9] Wordsworth then offsets or elides the dangerous and, as it were, *systemic* remove of this region by acts of internal textual integration.

The structural climax of both poems occurs when the speaker projects some levelling, unifying energy—motion, music—into the individuated objects revealed to him, bathing them, as it were, in an indifferently subjectivizing medium that subordinates their distinctiveness. This action is linguistically registered in the first half of both poems, the part that *precedes* revelation. Here, the speaker uses his quickened vision to integrate aspects of the landscape. In other words, these inscription poems manage to signify without insulating and dislocating their material by shifting the center of gravity from the spotlighted vision to the integrative framework. Having experienced a disturbing lucidity, the observer is able to register a scene that is in itself unfigurable, and thus nonexistent *as* scene, phenomenal and psychic. By the half-line opening, Wordsworth situates both discourses as determined attempts to amalgamate multiple simple impressions and thus to recover the psychic and perceptual unity that preceded the disruptive vision.

The problem—one of perception and representation—is solved formally and by rendering the work of integration more interesting and structurally more pronounced than the visionary irruption. The poems resist the standard lyric movement from blindness to insight, absence to presence, stasis to motion, and they do so by turning the reader's gaze on the area outside the poem—the traveller's journey.

Although "A Night-Piece" and "Airey-Force Valley" propose the terms of the dialectic worked out in "Nutting," the conflict between Wordsworth's drive to distinguish and his anxieties about thereby disturbing the order of things is not nearly so acute in the lesser works as it is in "Nutting." There, the dramatic situation at once extends, intensifies, and moralizes the narrator's ambivalence. "A Night-Piece" and "Airey-Force Valley" dramatize the imagination's efforts to figure a landscape, but because the speaker's energy is directed toward a relatively unresponsive object—a scene—incapable of rebuking his appropriative interests, the conflict remains submerged and unproductive. The presence of the Maiden in "Nutting" forces the narrator to confront the concrete, lived effects of his polymorphous aggressiveness, and it is this difficult knowledge, stylistically and structurally graphed, that finally subordinates incident to feeling and thus redeems the narration from its bad faith. The irresolution of all three poems marks an attempted solution to the conflict described above —or, less generously, an attempted evasion of the meaning of that conflict. Only by attending to this irresolution and aligning the poems' formal character with their doctrinal or intellectual concerns do we appreciate the project conducted through the cluster of poems that initiates the Poems of Imagination section in Wordsworth's final edition. Only by recognizing this project can we understand the truncated form of these poems.

CHAPTER FOUR

THE TRUE FRAGMENT

"Christabel"

"Christabel" is "not only a fragment, it is a sequence of fragments composed at different times and in different places." E. H. Coleridge's structural description is largely determined by the 1816 Preface to "Christabel," where Coleridge claims to have completed part 1 in 1797 and part 2 three years later. There is reason to believe moreover, that the Conclusion to part 1 was composed after the completion of part 2,[1] a conjecture that further fragments the work.

Surprisingly, "Christabel"'s early readers responded more strongly to the author's advertisement of "three parts yet to come" than to his compositional account. Throughout the reviews, we find substantial narrative guesswork concerning the poem's structurally allusive beginning and end, and relatively little interest in "Christabel"'s internal fissures. The reviews suggest that, by and large, "Christabel" was construed as a "romantic fragment" consisting of two consecutive sections belonging to a five-part composition.[2] Whereas today's reader tends to situate "Christabel"'s significant ruptures between the two parts, and between these and their respective conclusions, the early reader typically figures the poem as a coherent fragment truncated at either end. "Christabel"'s dramatically suggestive opening scene appeared to these readers the effect of a particular narrative sequence, and its conclusion was seen to establish only a principle—albeit a fairly determinate one—of closure. One reviewer remarks of "Christabel" that "the poet's intention is that you should feel and imagine a great deal more than you see."[3] While all the poems treated in this book engaged their readers in a variety of closural activities, "Christabel"'s reception was unusually extreme and explicit in this regard.[4] In many cases, "Christabel"'s reviewers actually "finish" the poem by inventing identities for the most baffling characters, motivations for the ambiguous or inconsistent, explanations for the ominous opening of the poem, and a conclusion to resolve the internal tensions. "Christabel" is compared to "a mutilated statue, the beauty of which can only be appreciated by those who have knowledge or imagination sufficient to complete the idea of the whole composition."[5]

The completions, both earnest and facetious, typically provide a dramatic context for the fragment, and while the inventions vary widely with respect to the events they posit as the probable origin and end of the action, one can generally trace the conjectures to a set of distinct and disturbing textual impressions. From these impressions, which determined the range of critical surmise, one may deduce a single structural principle. To isolate this principle is to glimpse the meaning of "Christabel"'s final resistances. It is, more generally, to define by the understanding of the past the project Coleridge set himself.

One impression registered throughout the reviews (and indirectly in the parodies of the poem) concerns the sexual implications of Geraldine's evening interlude with Christabel.[6] Coleridge's lean but leading description of the midnight tryst prompted some readers to "feel and imagine" a perverse (homosexual, incestuous, exploitative) seduction scene.[7] The outrage vented in the early reviews should and should not puzzle us. Many readers today, for all their sophistication, are at a loss to explain the weird encounter. We notice, however, that the language of the early reviews is far more vivid and concrete than that of our own Coleridge criticism. These stylistic differences indicate more than a differential intensity of response; they suggest a qualitative difference between the kind of attention which the nineteenth-century reviewer exercised and that which, in the main, characterizes twentieth-century criticism. Rather than transpose the narrative fragment into a conceptual key—a practice that describes most of today's scholarship on the poem—"Christabel"'s early readers typically *visualize* the poetic action, construing the fragment by way of dramatic expectations rather than allegorically or conceptually. The nineteenth-century reader appears to have experienced "Christabel" as a sequence of progressively enlightening disclosures occurring before his eyes, the doctrinal and psychological interest of these developments the unmediated issue of their dramatic unfolding.

Here, for example, is Peacock on "Christabel": "The poem is a succession of scenes, and every succession or change presents as many visible or audible circumstances as the fancy can comprehend at once."[8] Lamb similarly admires "Christabel"'s dramatic immediacy; he remarks the poem's *"picturesqueness* . . . which powerfully affects every reader, by placing, as it were, before his eyes a distinct picture of the events narrated, with all their appendages of sight and sound. . . ."[9] Nor is Lamb disturbed by the awkwardness of Coleridge's quantitative accentual metrics. He simply points out that it is not a "new principle" (as Coleridge states in his preface), but "a very old one." The practice would have been familiar, of course, to readers conversant with the early ballad, as to those familiar with classical prosody.

An *Eclectic Review* article refers to a "scene which ensues," and according to E. H. Coleridge's annotated facsimile, "the most wonderful quality or characteristic of this First Part of 'Christabel' is that the action is not that of a drama which is *ex hypothesi* a representation of fact;—nor are we persuaded to reproduce it for ourselves as by a tale that is told, but we behold it, scene after scene, episode by episode, as in a mirror, as the Lady of Shalott saw the knights ride by."[10] This observation, from the early part of this century, reflects structural assumptions that differ to some extent from those of the original reviews. By his mirror simile, Coleridge characterizes the drama as a self-consciously mediated representation, a relatively textualized experience for the reader. In this he approaches a modern response to the poem. Still, his emphasis on "Christabel"'s scenic immediacy, as on its dynamic—as it were, diachronic—character, situates his response within the universe of the nineteenth-century review.

Another feature frequently remarked in the contemporary notices is "Christabel"'s formal impurity: "This Poem . . . is not heroic, neither is there any thing of Dryden or of Goldsmith in it's [sic] composition: little also (though what it does contain includes the *worst* parts of both) either of Scott or Southey. It is, as Lord Byron says of it, '*wildly original:*' his lordship might have added, in some places, 'incoherently unintelligible.' . . ."[11] The author of this comment goes on to dismiss the categorial criteria he initially invokes (the poem "is not, therefore, to be judged of by comparison") and to praise the work for its own distinctive merits: "Its greatest peculiarity exists in the contrariety of its combinations;—its descriptions,—its incidents, are almost all of them made more imposing by the power of contrasted circumstances."

We are not, of course, concerned with these judgments per se but rather with the formal assumptions that seem to promote them—that is, with the expectations "Christabel" disappointed and those it satisfied. The excerpt quoted above indicates an association of "Christabel" with heroic drama and gothic romance. In the end, or by that reader's experience, "Christabel" would not settle comfortably into either modality, the dramatic or exotic romantic. What the above reviewer does not dwell on, but what other less favorable reviews do, is the deeply disconcerting effect of this hybridization. So many critics picked up on Byron's unfortunately worded compliment, *"wildly original,"* because, ungenerously applied, it describes the fragment's anomalous formal status.

Lamb, a flexible critic (and Coleridge's old friend), was also impressed by "Christabel'''s bipolarity, but like the reviewer quoted above, he approves this doubleness. He calls the poem "a work . . . of indisputable originality, forming almost a class by itself," and he refers his evaluation not only to the content of the poem—its "strange and indescribable terrors"—but to the wonderfully realistic effect Coleridge produces from his weird materials. "What we have principally to remark, with respect to the tale, is that wild, and romantic, and visionary as it is, it has a truth of its own, which seizes on and masters the imagination from the beginning to the end."[12]

The comments of some other reviewers reflect a similar understanding: "This poem, however romantic, is entirely domestic."[13] One might recall here Coleridge's avowed aim in his collaboration with Wordsworth on the *Lyrical Ballads*: to write a series of poems in which "the incidents and agents were to be, in part at least, supernatural; and the excellence aimed at was to consist in the interesting of the affections by the dramatic truth of such emotions as would naturally accompany such situations, supposing them real."[14] Judging by both Lamb's response and Peacock's straightforward approach, Coleridge would seem to have succeeded in this direction; it will require some effort to understand how he achieves his formal and rhetorical objective.

"Christabel'''s two Conclusions instigated yet a third flurry of commentary. Although most of the reviewers were thoroughly perplexed as to the relevance of these passages within the poem, a few critics admire the feeling and expression of the Conclusions. G. Mathew, for example, associates the second Conclusion with what he perceives to be the guiding principle of the poem: the "contrariety of its combinations." He implicitly construes the lines, "Perhaps 'tis pretty to force together / Thoughts so all unlike each other" and "At each wild word to feel within / A sweet recoil of love and pity," as an editorial elucidation of methodology—that is, as Coleridge's defense of his narrative method by reference to psychic laws.[15]

Some reviewers read the conclusion to part 2 as an indirect and even inadvertent expression of Coleridge's ambivalence toward Christabel—an oblique explanation of his inability to complete her history. Generally, the conclusion is treated as a device for the introduction of an authorial persona; thus might Coleridge encourage a particular reception by demonstrating it.

To admirers and detractors alike, "Christabel"'s functional structural features were its juxtaposition of various levels and kinds of action, its projection of dramatically linked *tableaux vivants*, its oblique, unintegrated Conclusions, and its combined novelty and antiquity, realism and fantasy.

In translating image into idea, scene into narrative episode, and character into vehicle, today's criticism suppresses that "wild originality" which was, for the early reader, "Christabel"'s salient. In characterizing "Christabel"'s formal mode as that of allegorical psychodrama, gothic romance, or Christian redemptive myth, one explains the "something disgusting at the bottom" of the poem as one event within a providential history, in effect naturalizing what was originally deeply estranging.

Readings based upon any of the formal schemes listed above are bound to concern themselves primarily with the genealogy, attributes, and motivations of Geraldine.[16] Indeed, studies of "Christabel" differ mainly in their interpretation of this figure.[17] Of course, the early reviews and burlesques also make much of Geraldine, but in these it is Geraldine's dramatic effect rather than her thematic dimension that largely engages the critic.

Formulating an identity and function for Geraldine does little to clear up fundamental textual—and largely structural—difficulties. Who is the protagonist; what is the relation between parts 1 and 2 and their conclusions, and between the two conclusions; what set of events might have occasioned the poetic action and what kind of progression might one project to conclude the interrupted action?

Robert Siegel, in an essay entitled "The Serpent and the Dove," offers an analysis centered on Christabel rather than Geraldine. He notes the aura of ill-boding that pervades the first scene, before Geraldine appears. " 'Christabel' opens at a nadir of activity, both natural and human." According to Siegel, Christabel, although "good," has a virtue that is "cloistered and unfruitful." Like Nature itself—autumnal as the poem opens—Christabel suffers a seasonal suspension of life. In order to animate her goodness and thus "bring [her] love to union and the castle to new life," Christabel must assume the weight of her lover's guilt. (Siegel's conjecture of sufficient causality proposes a crusading and erring fiancé.) Siegel calls Christabel's martyrdom a "vicarious suffering," but according to his own reading, the suffering is not wholly vicarious. That is, Siegel attributes a certain complicity, perhaps unconscious, to Christabel. He interprets her furtive reentry to the castle as a sign of her guilt, and he views the entranced hour with Geraldine as a seduction, not a rape. Christabel's "virgin goodness" is, it seems, not only "unfruitful," it is not altogether virginal.[18]

I would like to extend the implications of Siegel's unusual analysis. First, his identification of Geraldine as Christabel's double suggests that Christabel's guilt precedes Geraldine's influence and even in some way engenders it—Christabel, within this scheme, figuring as the dominant term in the binarity. Christabel's suffering would, then, express and effect a direct expiation as well as a vicarious one. Further, if Christabel feels guilty from the outset, her curious compulsion to pray in the woods rather than the Hall associates her guilt with the moribund state of Langland Hall. Sir Leoline's dreary household, then, would not seem to illustrate a natural, recurrent (that is, autumnal) quiescence, as Siegel suggests; its morbidity would instead signify a particular, historically determinate blight.

Leoline's "world of death" and Christabel's initial resignation to "weal or woe" are intelligible with reference to a single dramatic complication: a family curse or crime incurring both direct and vicarious suffering. The foreshadowed reunion of Leoline and Roland, from whose divorce the trouble at Langland Hall appears to have dated, would mark the successful expiation of that crime. Within this frame of action, the reunion of the two noble houses would figure not as the symbol or byproduct of Christabel's rite of passage but as the *object* of her trial. According to this (re)construction, Christabel suffers neither for the sake of her lover nor to atone for some personal error; the object of her ordeal is a familial, social, and institutional good. The destiny imaginable for this character is not the comic denouement of love and marriage but a tragic fulfillment: personal loss, impersonal justice, and social restitution.

Coleridge's contemporaries responded to what we might call the tragic or classical dimension of "Christabel": its visual immediacy, its dramatic procedures, its choral commentary, its stylized and abstract emotional candor, its metrical allusiveness. The reviewers remark the passivity of the characters and the impersonal, ineluctable force that appears to impel them and thus to advance the action. These readers compare the "horror" excited by "Christabel" ("its prevailing sentiment") to the passion that

Collins apostrophizes in his "Ode to Fear." The Ode, of course, celebrates Aristotelian—that is, tragic and ideal—fear.

While the early critics remark the poem's conspicuously gothic apparatus, their response generally figures a narrative principle distinct from that of romance. Whereas today's reader tends to rationalize this means-manner incongruity with reference to the poem's piecemeal mode of composition (the relation of part 1 to part 2), the early critics comfortably observe and, in a special way, intentionalize the principle of diversity operative throughout the poem.[19]

Christabel, though in certain obvious respects a gothic heroine, lacks the characterological purity and the passivity associated with that literary type. Christabel is shown to assimilate the evil impressed upon her and even to generate it. Nor does the author imply that his heroine will recover her innocence once Geraldine is banished or exposed. This is to say, Christabel collaborates in a manner and to an extent unusual in gothic romance.[20] Moreover, in romance, the function typically performed by the evil agent is to unite the lady with her lover by making him aware of her needs.[21] In "Christabel," however, we note that the heroine is betrothed from the outset; her knight need not, then, prove his mettle to win her, nor is he sent for at the critical moment, Christabel's transmogrification. Further, and most tellingly, the rift between Leoline and Roland is extraneous to the romance structure. Its sole purpose would be to generalize the revival effected by Christabel's marriage. Coleridge's preparation is surely too elaborate and portentous for such a negligible service. The reviewers, almost all of whom isolate the passage describing the falling out of the two friends, seem to have sensed the structural centrality of this representation.

"Christabel," a true fragment, invites us to interpret what is there before us with reference to what might precede and follow the truncated text. We best explain the inconsistencies noted above by constructing a before-and-after roughly conforming to the laws of classical tragedy (its narrative and affective material and principles) rather than by reference to ballad, gothic, or romance norms. We might observe that by identifying "Christabel"'s economy of action as that of tragedy, one simply restores the psychoanalytic critique which the poem has engendered to its original poetic context. Or, in that "Christabel"'s narrative themes and leitmotifs point strongly toward Oedipal issues, one might usefully read the form of the fragment across literature's first Oedipal moment. While the attributes of the characters may remind us of folktale, ballad, and romance modes, their functions suggest a different formal principle. Further, gothic romance is itself an eclectic genre. "Early romantic novelists . . . made elaborate and often indiscriminate use of other literature. . . . The effects are apparent in the echoes of lines, imitations of characters, and assimilation of whole episodes, and above all in a sometimes confusing, sometimes liberating, uncertainty of form."[22] Perhaps the "subtle and difficult idea" Coleridge said he hoped to realize through "Christabel" involved the romanticization of a tragic action, and the moralization, so to speak, of romantic elements.[23] By conjoining the subjectivity, fantasy, and sensationalism associated with romance with the impersonal, fatalistic severity of tragedy, Coleridge would effectively naturalize the supernatural—as we know, a persistent aesthetic ambition of his. In addition, the marriage of tragic and romantic strains would mitigate the inexorable contraction of the individual in which classical tragedy culminates, with the corrective of romantic wish-fulfillment. Whereas the gothic novelists seek to offset the "verisimilitude and moral sentiment" inherent in the novel form by importing the "gesture and emotional intensity of drama, the rhythmic and metaphoric possibilities of poetry," Coleridge counterbalances the romantic license inherent in his material with the ethical and impersonal emphasis of classical tragedy, as it were mirroring the novel's structural protocol.[24] In "Christabel," the laws of grammar and psychology are flexible enough to tolerate the gothic intensity and inwardness of the action, but they resist absolutely the gothic unnaturalness and excess that Coleridge deplored. Humphrey House's account of the ice caves in "Kubla Khan" is impressionistically apropos: "ice is shining, crystalline, hard: and here it adds greater strength and austerity to what would be otherwise the lush, soft, even sentimental, core of the poem."[25] The really interesting question, of course, is why Coleridge could not bring off this desirable merger. I take up the matter at the end of this section.

The above description of "Christabel"'s hybrid form is an account of perceived structure, or of a mode of perception. Although authorial intention is always a moot point, Coleridge's promise of "three parts yet to come," his serious experimentation with antique and quantitative prosody, and his multiple conclusions suggest an interest in approximating the five-part structure, the metrical effect, and the choral commentary associated with Greek tragedy. The advantage to us of focussing "Christabel" as a romantic interval within a tragic action is twofold. First, we not only gain a new purchase on the poem and on our traditions of explanation, but we curtail the endless speculation on Geraldine's character and on Coleridge's neuroses.

Second, the formal construct sketched above illuminates the intensity of the outrage expressed in the poem's reviews and indirectly in the burlesques which "Christabel" precipitated. We have observed in the contemporary criticism a tendency to contextualize the "romantic fragment" by way of tragic norms. Insofar as this implied context effectively interrupts the romance discourse without representing itself as a clearly alternative structural model (in which case the doubleness could be construed as a workable opposition), "Christabel" set the reader a critical task so basic as to amount to a cognitive problem. I think we may guess that the poem's most deeply offensive factor was not its suggestion of sexual deviance but its formal monstrosity: its failure to *present* its structural binarity. By keeping the tragic dimension implicit, Coleridge inhibits his reader from adopting contradiction as the work's organizing principle, and thus from naturalizing the poem (and one's response to it) through some notion of irony or dialectic.

The twentieth-century Coleridge is a creature of conflict. Coleridge's conception of genre is, of course, based on the reconciliation or transcendence of opposites, as is his notion of symbol and of figurative knowledge and language in general. Simply, binarity and a higher unity have become the hallmarks of Coleridge's genius. Our indifference to "Christabel"'s impropriety, narrowly conceived, is the result of our textual rather than sexual sophistication.

The early critics were, I believe, keenly responsive to "Christabel"'s textual cues but they were unable to organize their impressions; they had no ready way to think "Christabel"'s form. Paradoxically, the formal, canonical, and biographical concepts that so ably theorize Coleridge for us obstruct the kind of response encoded in the poem's form and demonstrated in those first reviews.

In a very general sense, tragedy always looks or feels like a true fragment. More than any other literary form, tragedy is a passing that directs the observer's attention to what has passed and what is to come. To some extent, of course, all verbal representation figures a before-and-after by means of a here-and-now, but tragedy seems to empty itself into the events that precede the first scene and those that succeed the last in the reader's or spectator's imagination. The formation of a certain history and the manner in which that history is revealed ensure that a certain kind of future will take shape one word or one moment beyond the last line of the play. In this sense, tragedy has no present; it is always looking backward or ahead. Athenian audiences knew the prehistory of their dramas, and their notions of the characters' futures, so to speak, were supplied by other plays, by myth, or by choral summation and prediction. What I remark here is the immediate contextual framework within which the Greek drama existed, and whereby its actions and characters assumed particular forms or produced particular meanings.

"Christabel"—literally a fragment—is a critical though ambiguous transition between two determinate but suppressed states of affairs and of mind. Once we conceive "Christabel" as a true fragment—in this case, two parts from a tragic unity—we can call on our knowledge of tragic heroes, tragic emotions, reversals and recognitions, and use this experience to structure the surmising which the text encourages.

One might observe, for example, that parts 1 and 2 and their respective conclusions structurally resemble the prologue, parode, episode, and stasimon Aristotle includes among tragedy's components. The resemblance suggests that the projected parts, 3, 4, and 5, would have made up the exode, or slow denouement. Typically, the exode demonstrates how the recognitions and reversals undergone in the course of the drama shape the fortunes of the main characters, in turn modifying the conditions that initially defined the characters' range of narrative options. Coleridge forecasts part 3 as Christabel's "song of Desolation"; it makes sense to assume that the rest of the poem would depict the effect of her sorrow on those around her and, chiefly, on her father, her sole companion.[26] *His* "rage and pain, shame and sorrow"—that is, his remorse—rather than Christabel's or Geraldine's, would logically occupy the last two sections. I suggest that we cannot concede the applicability of tragic norms to "Christabel" and continue to read the poem along the lines laid down by modern criticism. It is not so much that tragedy carries with it a set of particular meanings and values as that the structure and associations of tragedy preclude certain critical findings.

To read the poem more or less as we have done for the past forty years—as the fragment of a gothic romance—is to assume Christabel's centrality. Within a romance structure, Geraldine figures an ambiguous but primarily evil agent. Leoline, by this formal logic, serves exclusively to represent and intensify Christabel's suffering (he forsakes his daughter), and to complement her recovery (by his revival: the breaking of that spell which enthralls languishing Langland Hall).

Conversely, when we extrapolate from Coleridge's romantic fragment its controlling tragic context, we cast Leoline in the leading role. Christabel cannot qualify; she lacks the personal stature (attributes), the action potential, and the social resonance to draw the gaze of the gods. Watling's note to Sophocles' "Antigone" is germane: "To see statecraft misdirected into blasphemous defiance is for [Sophocles] (and for the Athenian audience) the greater tragedy; the sacrifice of a well-meaning woman, the less. Thus the king's final humiliation and chastening, through the loss of his son, is of higher dramatic significance than the fate of the woman."[27]

If Leoline is the tragic hero, then Christabel's ordeal must be understood as consequential or instrumental—somehow subordinate—to her father's experience. This is to say that the function of Christabel's suffering in the poem is to precipitate, constitute, or intensify her father's ordeal. Within a tragic narrative economy, the complicity which Siegel remarks in his analysis of Christabel's character would signify the dependence of her involvement with Geraldine on the history of Leoline's interaction with Geraldine and/or her father. By interpreting Christabel's susceptibility to Geraldine's baleful influence as an extension or effect of some action performed by Leoline, the reader perceives Christabel's suffering as the means by which Leoline's destiny is molded. Given the narrative elements provided by the fragment and the expectations associated with classical tragedy, one would infer that the House of Leoline labors beneath a curse originating in some crime or error involving the head of that house, Sir Leoline. Christabel, the last scion ("The one red leaf, the last of its clan"), is the figure who must expiate the wrong. As one reviews the range of narrative possibilities that might have occasioned the fragment's opening scene, the conventional and apparently ornamental gothic motifs begin to assume significant structural function. Why, for example, does the mastiff bitch howl at her mistress's shroud when, according to Christabel, the mother died naturally in childbirth? *Did* Christabel's mother die naturally or was there foul play? Why is Leoline's weak health emphasized? Why does Christabel leave the house to pray? Why is she resigned to weal or woe before we see cause to worry? What portents did her dream contain? Why is Geraldine associated favorably with Christabel's mother? Why does Leoline declare his realm "a world of death"? Why is Bard Bracy possessed of so acute a foreboding? Why did Leoline and Roland separate?

Barbara Herrnstein Smith characterizes any act of literary interpretation as "the construing of a particular set of conditions, a context, that could plausibly occasion an utterance of that form."[28] For "of that form," one might substitute "posing those questions," since the questions raised by a work most persistently within a given audience—lines of textual resistance—demarcate a formal domain. The questions listed above are collectively answered by the hypothesis of some guilt incurred by Sir Leoline. Using this hypothesis, the *dramatis personae*, the actions described in the fragment, and the narrative tendencies associated with classical tragedy as constraints on invention, one can construct an adequate occasioning context for "Christabel." No reader actually elaborates the scenario I will offer, although equally detailed accounts are encountered in the contemporary criticism. I present my completion in order to elucidate the kind of project "Christabel"'s early critics undertook, and which a good deal of modern criticism reproduces, less directly and schematically, of course.

What I consider useful in the following account is not the particular events proposed but the demonstration that Christabel's story is incidental to Leoline's and that this fundamental reevaluation of the work's dramatic structure is inevitable once we conceive the fragment's formal context as that of tragedy. In elucidating Geraldine's actions with reference to Leoline rather than Christabel, one focuses Geraldine as a morally neutral and exclusively instrumental figure—not so much a character as a narrative device. Her "appointed task" is to penetrate the torpor that enfolds Langland Hall—that is, to breach the enchantment. The object of this disruption is not, as we have assumed, Christabel's liberation or metamorphosis, but rather the exorcising of that evil which engendered and sustains the limbo world of the poem's opening. Geraldine herself is as essentially indifferent or unmarked an agent as the albatross in "The Ancient Mariner." But her presence alone "requites" both Leoline and Christabel —or Leoline through Christabel—for the guilt that contaminates them both.

In order to answer the questions listed above, or more generally, in order to assimilate Christabel's tragedy to Leoline's—one would conjecture a triangle of some kind, involving Leoline, his wife, and Roland. The following scenario builds from a certain consensus among the reviewers concerning Leoline's jealousy, the importance of lines 408–26 (wherein the estrangement of Leoline and Roland is described), and the persistent textual allusion to Christabel's dead mother. It also develops the suggestion forcefully presented in the poem, lines 190–213 and 326–31, and elaborated in Coleridge's suppressed annotations: namely, the symbiotic relationship between Geraldine and Christabel's mother.[29]

Let us imagine that Leoline jealously suspects his wife of loving Roland, his best friend, and even perhaps of carrying Roland's child. The wife dies soon after Christabel's birth, feeling betrayed by her husband's suspicions. He in turn is left with his bitterness or, if he realizes his error, with his guilt. Either way, his feelings toward Christabel are bound to be vexed.

Leoline's suspicions (and their effect upon his wife) condemn him and his child to a life-in-death until the arrival of Geraldine, daughter of his former friend. Geraldine appears to Leoline as a replacement for his dead wife; the two figures are, of course, consistently and provocatively linked. Geraldine, thus situated, represents to Leoline a means of atonement for his crime (through the embrace of the enemy's child), and/or of further revenge (by stealing Roland's daughter). By the markedly ambiguous representation of Geraldine's motives, Coleridge brings out the darker side of the association with Christabel's mother; that is, Geraldine as the expression of certain retributive interests. Geraldine's role in the fragment is, then, that of a Fury: as the personified vengeance of Leoline's wife, she is at once terrible and pathetic—no less Christabel's "guardian spirit" than the mother's happier incarnation. Geraldine forces Leoline to repeat his initial sin: as he blindly rejected his wife, so does he reject his daughter, Christabel. Leoline is, by this logic, a composite Othello-Lear. His punishment—the enactment and effect of his enlightenment—must be the loss of Christabel, "the one red leaf, the last of its clan." Indeed, the frequently noted analogy between Christabel and the oak leaf makes sense only if she fails to marry, procreate, and perpetuate the family line. Or, in terms of the context we have established, Christabel's marriage would inevitably add one more generation of infamy to the family chronicle. Only by her death or celibacy might innocence be restored. Sir Leoline's crime must be revealed and redressed at this point.

These narrative inventions are, as I have said, prompted by certain formal principles sketched within the fragment. Part 1 introduces the complication that sets the drama in motion. Christabel's anxiety is clearly evoked, its causes left mysterious. The reader is invited to hypothesize a situation preceding and dramatically generating the opening scene. Through Geraldine, Christabel's anxiety increases, finally spending itself and leaving her calm. "A star has set." The conclusion to part 1 characterizes Christabel's experience as a painfully therapeutic catharsis. Thanks to (not in spite of) her strange bedfellow, Christabel's sleep is the sleep of an innocent. She reposes secure in the knowledge that "saints will aid if men will call: / For the blue sky bends over all." We must surmise that this conviction of cosmic benevolence or fair play comes of Christabel's encounter with Geraldine, the only causal factor at hand.

Leoline's experience parallels that of his daughter. He too is introduced as one who suffers a nameless grief that manifests itself in restless, wasting anxiety. He too is initially shaken by the vision of Geraldine. (He "waxes pale" and stands abstracted.) Leoline's association of Geraldine with Roland, however, not only assuages his anxiety but brings him genuine pleasure, just as Christabel's association of Geraldine with her mother allays the girl's indistinct fears, enabling new happiness.

The dramatic climax of the fragment seems to occur when Christabel involuntarily mimics Geraldine, assuming thereby a character antithetical to her own. The genuine reversal, however, which we grasp as a tragic necessity, takes place when Leoline leads "forth the Lady Geraldine," thereby abandoning his own sweet maid. With this action, Leoline takes an action that was formerly impossible, and so initiates the long process of denouement.

The second conclusion, like the first, offers an authoritative, rather detached interpretation of the action, albeit in a dramatic mode consistent with the formal gestures of the poem. Since the subject of the passage is the psychic vicissitudes of a father, not a child, the conclusion directs the reader's attention to Leoline and deflects it from Christabel.

> A little child, a limber elf,
> Singing, dancing to itself,
> A fairy thing with red round cheeks,
> That always finds, and never seeks,
> Makes such a vision to the sight
> As fills a father's eyes with light;
> And pleasures flow in so thick and fast
> Upon his heart, that he at last
> Must needs express his love's excess
> With words of unmeant bitterness.
> Perhaps 'tis pretty to force together
> Thoughts so all unlike each other;
> To mutter and mock a broken charm,
> To dally with wrong that does no harm.
> Perhaps 'tis tender too and pretty
> At each wild word to feel within
> A sweet recoil of love and pity.

And what, if in a world of sin
(O sorrow and shame should this be true!)
Such giddiness of heart and brain
Comes seldom save from rage and pain,
So talks as it's most used to do.

The passage charts the dynamic activated in a man by his love for his child. We might focus this child figure as a kind of synecdoche for the several primary figures—wife, daughter, friend—that objectify Leoline's actions and passions in the fragment. The passage dramatizes a psychic process whereby a man's love for an object—which, in its apparent self-sufficiency, underlines the fearful potential of object love—prompts in him feelings of "rage and pain." To diminish the tension produced by these feelings, the father-lover reverses the dominance pattern; he victimizes the object of his affection ("he at last / Must needs express his love's excess / With words of unmeant bitterness"). This perversion of affect enables him to "love and pity" the child, wife, or friend—which is to say, he empowers himself to love without feeling dangerously extended.

In general terms, the conclusion describes a process whereby strong paternal love promotes a conflict relieved by an act of aggression. By his false accusation of the loved object, the father produces a sense of superiority, the condition for a compassionate, which is to say, nonthreatening investment. Leoline had once expressed his "giddiness of heart and brain" —his "confusion which cleaved the heart in two"—by injuring both his wife and friend. Now, as Leoline contemplates his daughter, the giddiness "talks as it's most used to do." He repeats the pattern, unjustly accusing Christabel of disloyalty.

The commentary developed by the two conclusions participates in the dramatic economy. Although the voice we hear in these sections betrays a determined psychic perspicacity, the narrational point of view is limited; its knowledge of the action does not exceed that of the reader. Bard Bracy, however, is allowed a certain prescience, a talent textually associated with his excellent memory. He remembers his dream, he remembers legends of sinful sextons, and he persistently reminds his audience how thoroughly the past interpenetrates and determines the present. Bracy is, after all, the bard in the poem, a figure whose traditional function is to remember and recount racial or local history. Due to this highly developed faculty, Bracy's perceptions, unlike those of the other characters, are relatively stable and invulnerable to coercion. Images "live upon" his eye, whereas

Leoline and Christabel are shown to be incapable of retaining simple sensory impressions (as in lines 463–65, 597–609). Geraldine effects her designs by inducing Christabel and Leoline to forget certain critical and, one would think, inalienable facts (lines 268–78). Leoline's climactic lapse, for example, reveals itself in his misinterpretation of Bracy's dream; he incorrectly associates the beauteous dove with Geraldine, forgetting that his daughter is the nearer and apter referent.

Bracy is ignored; he cannot stave off the tragic recognition and ensuing disasters any more than Tiresias can divert Oedipus's investigations or Cassandra save Agamemnon. Bracy's ineffectuality emphasizes the inexorable course of the destiny set in motion long before the chronological frame of the poetic action. He reminds us that, structurally speaking, "Christabel" is tragedy, and any expectations raised by the gothic-romantic features of the text (broken spells, marriage and fruition, the triumph of innocence, naturalistic explanation) must strain against the formal logic of tragedy. He also reminds us that part of our job as readers is to remember: that is, to connect middles with origins and ends.

Let me invoke at this point Victor Weisskopf's useful formulation of a contemporary scientific praxis: "A discontinuity that cannot be explained quantitatively had better be dealt with as a qualitative change—as, in some significant relationship to its parts, a different 'whole.'"[30] By reading "Christabel" as a true fragment and completing it with reference to tragic norms, a reader finds his affections interested "by the dramatic truth of such emotion as would naturally accompany such [supernatural] situations, supposing them real." The early reviews of "Christabel," although a naïve and even clumsy critical discourse as compared to twentieth-century scholarship, usefully sketch for us the fragment's formal determinacy and enable us to relate this pattern to certain aesthetic and moral desiderata habitually invoked by Coleridge.

In "Christabel," as in "Kubla Khan," Coleridge combines a traditional with a fashionable form, an "essential" with an "irregular"—the mode of history with the mode of myth—and thereby expresses the "two-fold nature of the new romantic bard."[31] Coleridge's lifelong respect for things as they are, or the truths of history, and his commitment to things as they should be, or mythological, typological, ideal and philosophic Truth, produce in "Christabel" a poem whose material presences are romantic yet whose determinate absences and formal imperatives are those of classical tragedy. By attending to this doubleness, we appreciate more finely the nature of the poem's escapism. Hartman speaks of the role of surmise in several major Romantic poems. He notes that the "single projections add up to more than their sum: they revive in us the capacity for the virtual, a trembling of the imagined on the brink of the real, a sustained inner freedom in the face of death, disbelief, and fact."[32] "Christabel," like the poems to which Hartman refers, seeks to open that narrow space between the romantic imagined and the classic real, qualifying the freedom of the former with the ethical fatalism of the latter.

Even as I offer these terms, I must severely qualify them. For in what sense are the products of the romantic imagination less real than those of the tragic mind? And conversely, can any literary mode or form, and especially one so ritualized, so confidently conventional as tragedy, be in any practical, much less rigorous sense of the word, "realistic"? Having reconstructed the terms of "Christabel"'s "original" and/or projected discourse, I would like to glance at the meaning of those terms—to deconstruct them a bit. Instead of asking what Coleridge's conception of genre *means*, one might ask what his dialectical or polar procedure *does*—to the reader, to the poem, and for the poet. One might also reflect upon Coleridge's selection of opposites to reconcile and, finally, upon his decision to suppress one term of his opposition by fragmenting the poem.

"Christabel" represents its incompletion as a failure to approximate the fullness of a tragic action. This is the limit it selects for itself. Its more primary and unsuspected restriction, however, consists in its substitution of a romantic idea of reality for some more authentic, more particular, and historically informed understanding of things as they are. That tragedy—classical tragedy—should be enlisted as the antithesis of romance (as the agent through which psychic reality and a social dimension are introduced) tells us something about Coleridge's compositional practice and about the meanings thereby produced.

In "Christabel," Coleridge employs the idea of the tragic as a model of objective reality which, unlike romantic representation, transcends personal and local truth. Thus, whereas Coleridge puts to work the conventional classic-romantic (impersonal-personal, disinterested-interested, naïve-sentimental) binary opposition, his particular formal procedures, or their referential gestures, subvert that antithesis, or at the least restrict it to a very special case. That is, in hybridizing tragedy and romance, Coleridge effectively undoes the traditional formal antithesis of tragedy and comedy, romance and realism. By positioning as *contraries* two *complementary* literary modes—both of them hieratic, self-consciously stylized, abstract, and ideal—Coleridge compromises the stability of those categories and of their mutual relationships.

We know that Coleridge was dissatisfied with the (locally) reductive moralism of "The Ancient Mariner"—the poem formally most akin to "Christabel" as well as its precursor in order of composition. Coleridge need not, of course, have worried about "The Rime"; despite the Mariner's explanation of the poetic action ("he prayeth best who loveth best . . ."), the incommensurability of cause and effect, the unmotivated quality of the narrative transitions, and the plasticity and transitivity of the characters and actions more than offset the authority of the work's moral commentary. Indeed, the foregoing factors roundly criticize that authority, throwing the whole composition into an ironic key.

Coleridge's reluctance to interpret his material is, of course, a reluctance shared by most of the major Romantic poets, for whom the idea of direct and restricted utility conjured the mechanical, with all the degrading associations of that method and of the general praxis felt to sponsor it. The authorial counterpart of negative capability—that dialectically valorized effect restricted to and definitive of aesthetic reception—is the writer's refusal to subordinate his imagination (used here to denote a process and its product) to a particular doctrinal purpose. The winning paradox built into this Romantic equation is that the less deliberate and determinate the poet's extrinsic or practical intentions, the greater his success in realizing them.[33]

The writer's technical problem, given this aesthetic ideology, is how to provide order and intentionality without conclusively fixing the discourse in a moral, epistemological, or philosophic teleology. Or, how might a writer produce poetic structure without thereby establishing a structure of belief, a confining mental form? The writer must somehow prevent his readers from converting sequentiality into causality, and causality into a univocal meaning that would, retroactively as it were, *possess* the work. David Simpson, who observes that "man is compelled to think through cause and effect," helpfully quotes this passage from *The Friend* by way of illuminating his own generalization and Coleridge's linguistic binds.

> But, on the other hand, by the same law he is inevitably tempted to misinterpret a constant precedence into positive causation, and thus to break and scatter the one divine and invisible life of nature into countless idols of the sense; and falling prostrate before lifeless images, the creatures of his own abstraction, is himself sensualized, and

becomes a slave to the things of which he was formed to be the conqueror and sovereign.[34]

The solution represented by "The Ancient Mariner" is a formal one. Metacomment is not only isolated and removed to the margins of the poem, it is given a fictive and historically, temperamentally, ideologically exotic character. This inflected commentary is so conspicuous in its partiality as to highlight the equally, though less manifestly inflected (ideologically enabled and restricted), nature of the central narrative, and of certain authorial interpolations. By foregrounding the operational and historically contained nature of these several, constitutive discourses, Coleridge formally implies that the work as a whole—eclectic and, in conventional terms, disorganized—achieves prophetic lucidity, which is to say, it promotes an infinite and syncretic understanding. Meanwhile, all the explanations included in the poem, however slant and discredited *as* explanation, organize the reader's response and produce a determinacy effect without creating the appearance of a false consciousness.

One could guess that the annotations intended for "Christabel," once completed and attached, would have functioned in much the same manner as the glosses appended to "The Ancient Mariner." Even without these promised marginalia, "Christabel" locates its explanation outside the poem proper and in a mode as specialized and literary as the Catholic and Pagan commentary fringing the Mariner's tale. As we have seen, the "romantic fragment" is situated within the implied context of a tragic unity.

By conjuring this aura, Coleridge could produce in his reader an impression of structural and semiotic determinacy, for tragedy is, above all else, the drama of elucidation, the form of discovery. Everything mysterious, random, and isolated is finally revealed as one moment in a logic—a metaphysics—of necessity. Of course, tragedy's explanations, however necessary, rarely satisfy. In resolving the narrative mystery, they inevitably turn one's attention to ultimate things. *Why* must Antigone see her brother buried, and why must Creon refuse her request; why must Lear formally interrogate his daughters, and why must Cordelia withhold from him the desired answer? Tragedy always makes you wish it would explain its explanations, in that it offers tautology by way of enlightenment. Finally, tragedy mystifies history rather than justifies it. Can anyone focus Oedipus's destiny as history, much less *a* history, in any material sense of that word?

"Christabel"'s irresolution represents a solution to—or, more precisely, an escape from—that quintessential Romantic bind: how to tell one's dream without hypostatizing and privileging one's peculiar, particular narration. In this context, let me quote Michael Cooke's useful assessment of Coleridge's project in Essay IV, *The Friend* ("On The Principle Of Method"). Here, Coleridge "sums up the combination of the casual and the purposive in the 'cultivated' use of fragments."[35] As a solution to the problem of authoritative yet ideologically generous and receptive utterance, "Christabel"'s irresolution is less successful than the formal strategies enacted through "The Ancient Mariner," but the two works are nonetheless, as I have suggested, comparable with respect to formal intention. By intimating the tragic structure from which the romance fragment derives, Coleridge supplies an economy of action which he elucidates without diminishing the poem's apparent infinity, a function of its radical indeterminacy. This is to say, his utterance is as ironic as it is authoritative. At the same time, the two modes—romance and tragedy—enrich and modify each other. The tragic emotions are domesticated; pity and fear are interpreted as instinctual and universal responses to an instinctual and universal psychic Truth. Cruel fathers are internally tyrannized, and their manifest aggressions are only the reflex of their own psychic victimization. Meanwhile, the romantic elements are grounded in psychic fact and social necessity, and thereby rendered humane, affecting, and responsible.

As with so many Romantic poems, "Christabel" expresses through its form a distinction between "surmise and surmise" rather than an opposition of true and false. Coleridge's structural implementation of the tragic economy—situated as a reality principle antithesizing the romantic interests of the fragment—expresses a typically Romantic suspicion not only of absolute, ahistorical explanation but of unmediated, empirically given fact —absolute Nature. It is, after all, to a literary idea of reality that Coleridge refers, and the referent itself is a ghostly presence that each reader and each reading must materialize.

CHAPTER FIVE

. . . .

THE COMPLETED FRAGMENT
"Kubla Khan"

"Christabel"'s two parts and one of its conclusions were composed at
different times, yet the form-producing ruptures come at the beginning
and end of the fragment rather than between the component parts. Ironically, "Kubla Khan," a poem declared to have been conceived and composed in one sitting, locates its irresolution internally, between lines 36
and 37. The poem as first printed in 1816 and in most subsequent editions is a completed fragment—a work apparently begun in one mood
and mode and completed in another.[1] Coleridge creates this effect by
adding a kind of epigraph, the poor-youth lines extracted from his poem
"The Picture; or the Lover's Resolution" (lines 91–100), but not identified as such by the author. This poem, published in *The Morning Post*,
1802, seems not to have provoked any unusual interest, which is to say,
readers of "Kubla Khan," fourteen years after the fact, could not be expected to recognize the source of the headnote extract. Not surprisingly,
at least one reviewer assumes that the passage was composed for and even
as a part of "Kubla Khan": "Still if Mr. Coleridge's two hundred lines
were all of equal merit with the following which he has preserved [the
prefatory extract is quoted], we are ready to admit that he has reason to be
grieved at their loss."[2]
  I quote the passage under discussion:

> Then all the charm
> Is broken—all that phantom-world so fair
> Vanishes, and a thousand circlets spread,
> And each mis-shape['s] the other. Stay awhile,

Poor youth! who scarcely dar'st lift up thine eyes—
The stream will soon renew its smoothness, soon
The visions will return! And lo, he stays,
And soon the fragments dim of lovely forms
Come trembling back, unite, and now once more
The pool becomes a mirror.

By the addition of this passage, Coleridge emphasizes a range of discontinuities—stylistic, thematic, temporal, metrical—that effectively bracket the body of the poem (lines 1–36). The poor youth, lost in a narcissistic revery, prefigures the rhapsode of the concluding section (37–54), he of the "flashing eyes and floating hair." Both images in a general sense represent visionaries—the sort of visionaries who, rather than tell their dreams verbally or materially, enter them. Their enthusiasm stands in pointed contrast to the Khan's cool manipulations, and this thematic opposition is, as we shall see, formally signified, mirrored, and reinforced.

The passage extracted from "The Picture" and prefixed to "Kubla Khan" describes an experience of fading recollection. In its original context, the passage follows the hero's glimpse of his beloved, reflected in a woodland pool. The pool is disturbed, the maiden flees, the image disintegrates then disappears. The youth remains staring at the pool, presumably enthralled by his own reflection now that the captivating external object has vanished. While the headnote lines are clearly intended to illustrate the process explained in the Preface just above the excerpt (that is, the disintegration of Coleridge's "phantom world"), they comment as well on the imagery and development of the poem printed just below. We can see that the "poor youth" passage structurally balances the coda and reflects the same psychic, iconic, and verbal universe. Both sections—cameos rather than narrations—feature a youth who is enamored of his own reflective life. One feels in both the pressure of direct discourse and the immediacy of direct observation. There is a sincerity to the narration, an intimacy and a pathos that are very different from the removed, authoritative, even authoritarian manner that characterizes lines 1–36. The prefatory excerpt and coda surround the unfinished narrative section with a discrete commentary antithetical in method and statement to the body of the work. The internal logic of the poem suggests that the frame was added when the narrative momentum urging on the Xanadu section petered out.

Coleridge separates the extract from the first line of the poem with a few lines of additional prefatory commentary followed by the title, "Kubla

Khan." He thus ensures that the extract not be identified as an epigraph nor through some freak read as the first stanza of the poem. No right-minded reader could fail to understand Coleridge's disposition of parts, nor is it likely that a reader would willfully disregard the author's expressed intentions. The extract, however, recommends itself at once to a reader who is confused by the poem's epic scope and lyric treatment, and frustrated by the striking hiatus occurring between lines 36 and 37—especially a reader lacking the critical and canonical contexts available to today's Coleridgean.

Readers familiar with the higher criticism and with the Continental, aesthetic manifestations of this hermeneutic and historical interest would, I trust, have had no trouble with the compressed and elliptical form of the poem, with Coleridge's account of his spontaneous composition, nor with the lyrical handling of an epic subject. E. S. Shaffer, in her marvellously erudite and exhaustive study, *"Kubla Khan" and The Fall of Jerusalem*, situates "Kubla Khan" within the tradition of the higher criticism—in the period of "Kubla Khan"'s composition and publication, a vigorous intellectual movement that made itself felt in circles to which Coleridge had access. Moreover, we can see that the higher criticism defines an ideology and methodology peculiarly congenial to Coleridge's intellectual and spiritual interests, and wonderfully useful to him as a unifying context for these diverse concerns.

Although both my formal explication of "Kubla Khan" and my representation of its vision or doctrine differ from Shaffer's account, I not only greatly respect her inquiry but I accept her conclusions about the poem.[3] It is not that I hold everything possible to be believed as an image of truth, but that the reader I postulate throughout this book and whose responses I enlist as my point of departure is not the learned, engaged intellectual who figures in Shaffer's critique. My reader is the English reviewer whose voice is heard in *The Edinburgh* and *The Quarterly Reviews* —intelligent, informed men who cannot be expected to have brought to their criticism the scholarly apparatus and the intellectual currency which Shaffer discovers in her circle. The reception construct presented below formulates the experience of readers unfamiliar with the higher criticism and unlikely to turn to philological or philosophical discourses for help with a difficult poem. Shaffer's context for "Kubla Khan" is that of European intellectual history; my context is that of English Romanticism and more narrowly yet, one formal product of the English Romantics, the fragment poem. As for original form and meaning, or Coleridge's relatively conscious intentions for "Kubla Khan," Shaffer is probably closer to the mark than I. With respect to intentions less deliberate, less tractable, and more local in their operation, I believe that mine is the better account, and perhaps this level of intentionality is "original" in a more radical sense. For a full understanding of Coleridge's purposes, we should bring each of these "original" moments to bear on the other.

The initial and impressionistic resemblance obtaining between "Kubla Khan"'s prefatory extract and its coda cannot in themselves support the weight of a formal argument. But the conjecture of a two-stage composition consisting of a vision and revision is reinforced by other factors. First, there is the interval of eighteen or nineteen years between composition and publication. Why would Coleridge publish almost two decades after he wrote it a poem substantially unchanged? Tastes and interests—Coleridge's and/or his public's—could have changed, or Coleridge's sense of his public might have shifted. Neither of these possibilities can be dismissed, but rather than undertake the psychosociological research which alone could confirm those hypotheses, let us take up the matter from a textual perspective. The first question to ask is, of course, *are* the two versions—the Crewe manuscript and the 1816 text—essentially identical? The major discrepancy between the two Prefaces is generally located in their compositional accounts; where the 1816 Preface describes "a profound sleep at least of the external senses," the Crewe manuscript simply cites "a sort of Reverie." The revision implies Coleridge's decision to emphasize the unconsciousness of his composition so as to clear himself of responsibility for the work's imperfections. Of course, the very fact of the prefatory emendation qualifies Coleridge's claim to entire spontaneity.

The formal effects of Coleridge's revision have not greatly exercised us. The internal changes are modest, and they suggest the author's general concern to liberate the poem from its historical and literary sources: Purchas and Milton. The direction of change is from specificity to ambiguity. The bulk of the new Preface with its poetic extract has gone largely unexamined. I locate the significant revisions here and propose that Coleridge's insertion of that extract into a newly revised Preface represents an attempt to modify the form and thereby the statement that he had constructed in 1797–98.

Carl Woodring has observed that Coleridge's verse, after Waterloo, "reflects new concern with distresses in a few original items but especially in minor additions to republished poem." And, we might conjecture, in minor additions to poems long-written but never published. Coleridge's membership in the "Tory humanitarian school" dates from no later than 1802, but his religious and political conservatism grew "especially active in the years after Waterloo."[4] In this, of course, Coleridge was no exception. "Kubla Khan"—a poem about princes and poets—made its debut in a critical year for European history. The timing alone suggests a motivation subsequent to and different from the poem's first rationale (or the poet's initial intention), and it implies the addition of revisionary material, or the reorganization of existing material in such a way as to effect certain ideological retrenchments.

Another suggestive dimension for this study is the scholarly reception of "Kubla Khan" in our own century. Much of the critical literature over the past twenty years reflects a response to the prefatory poetic extract and to other modifications in the 1816 Preface. Although these responses seem to have influenced critical inference concerning the work's intended form and statement, they are rarely acknowledged and addressed. This body of criticism is not wanting in explanatory value so much as lacking in self-consciousness about the means by which it produces its explanations. This deficiency has promoted a phenomenon peculiar to the criticism of Romantic fragments. "Kubla Khan" has precipitated studies proposing radically opposed interpretations based on identical terms. While our scholarship defines the subject of "Kubla Khan" in a fairly uniform way, and while most readers agree that the poem advances one of three arguments, there seems to be no way of discriminating the relative propriety or utility of these arguments. The consensus about the poem's universe of discourse and the extreme, even schematic oppositions over interpretation imply that the poem has imposed certain effective but imperceptible constraints upon reception. Until we examine our practical activities and expose those constraints, criticism must continue to reflect the poem's ambivalences and ambiguities rather than explain them. My object, therefore, in the following section, is not to produce a new formal ingenuity; I hope only to account for "Kubla Khan"'s configuration within our criticism, since this is how the poem delivers the judgments by which we judge it.

Ideally, one would look to the poem's early reviews for a pattern of blindness and insight that might throw into relief our own habitual assumptions and activities. The early reviews of "Kubla Khan," however, are so far from critical, and so very paraphrastic, that they cannot easily serve the purposes of an antithetical inquiry. According to Norman Fruman, "the whole nineteenth century (and most of the twentieth) took 'Kubla Khan' to be a dream."[5] I take issue with Fruman's parenthetical generalization, but the chief proposition seems perfectly sound. By way of Coleridge's own distinction, we might observe that although "Kubla Khan" was received as "poetry," it was not construed as "a poem." The work was regarded as a source of pleasing and exotic imagery and sound, and as a psychological curiosity. The Preface was not, by and large, rhetorically worked. Generally, it seems to have been treated as a sincere, straightforward, historical account of the work's fragmentary condition, a condition that appears to have provoked little cognitive dissonance and therefore little critical interest. We observe in this phenomenon an apparent exception to the rule postulated throughout this book: namely, that Romantic readers manipulated textual irresolution in formally constructive ways. We might illuminate the reception of this particular fragment by remembering that Coleridge's Preface explicitly invites psychological interpretation. One is asked to construe the text as material smuggled out from the unconscious—material fragmented by its difficult passage. By this representation, the poem's internal disjunctions (chiefly, the gap between lines 36 and 37) signify as traces of the work's genetic history and as authentications of that history. One could argue that insofar as these lacunae were assimilated to the dominant structural and compositional model, they *were* formally intentionalized. Thus, although "Kubla Khan"'s early readers practiced an essentially nonliterary reception, their responses to the semantic effects of the work's irresolution were keen, and they motivated these effects with reference to perceived formal intention.

Twentieth-century scholarship has not allowed Coleridge's Preface to deprive it of its critical object. Our most influential studies seek to demonstrate that "Kubla Khan" possesses a special kind of unity and/or/in that it engages its reader in a particular mode of reception, one that mobilizes the poem's scattered parts into a working whole. Even those critics who very sensibly object to the cult of the fragment—the wholesale imposition of coherence upon the most shattered of texts—cannot resist proposing coherent and encompassing explanations of "Kubla Khan." Moreover, many of their findings participate in the interpretive consensus established over the past twenty years, a consensus I outline below.

The critical field was, until Shaffer's landmark study, dominated by three blocs that I designate the partisans, the compromisers, and the syncretists.[6] The first group represents "Kubla Khan" as Coleridge's single-minded presentation of an aesthetic program to which he is entirely committed. Although these critics, the partisans, agree that "Kubla Khan" endorses a consistent aesthetic position, they disagree over the definition of that position, and their differences are extreme and unequivocal.

In the opinion of the compromisers, "Kubla Khan" enacts and ultimately resolves the poet's ambivalence toward the poetic model which the partisans identify (variously) as Coleridge's imaginative ideal. These readers emphasize the poem's internal tensions; they locate "Kubla Khan"'s generative dichotomy—loosely, a dialectic—in the contrasting descriptions of Kubla's empire (lines 1–11) on the one hand, and, on the other, of a less constrained, more imaginative (that is, holistic and unconscious) creative modality, lines 12–36. These readers find that "Kubla Khan" articulates two opposing methods of embodying mental constructs; anachronistically but succinctly, the operative categories are expressionism and formalism, or in Woodring's phrase, "the Romantic and the rationalistic."[7] According to the compromisers, the partisan reading represents an unwarranted imposition of unity upon "Kubla Khan"'s productive antinomies. Right reading, in the view of the compromisers, consists in reconciling the poem's extremes by imagining the artistic ideal cryptically figured in lines 37–54. Here, in the narrator's lament for his lost vision, Coleridge encodes the protocol for combining "Romantic and rationalistic" or affective and philosophic values.

Members of both critical schools find in "Kubla Khan" a beginning and middle but no end. The partisans figure a conclusion wherein Coleridge would articulate his aesthetic ideology, an ideology implicitly but consistently developed in the fragment. The compromisers project for the fragment not a statement but a demonstration of the aesthetic model which Coleridge indirectly and dialectically develops in the text. These readers anticipate the chronicle of Kubla and his empire, narrated in such a way as to objectify Coleridge's syncretic ideal.

"Kubla Khan," as described by both sets of critics, produces a more or less coherent vision and is formally something of a précis or abstract for the ideal, "finished" (that is, projected) work.[8] A third and important segment of critical opinion distinguishes the narrative mode of lines 1–36 from the lyric discourse of the concluding passage, the so-called coda. The coda is interpreted as a metacomment on the narrative body of the poem. Readers of this persuasion—the syncretists—suggest that the act of interpreting the two poetic models occurs in the text but only through the agency of a reader who, instructed by the metacomment, determines the nature of Coleridge's poetic program. "Kubla Khan," therefore, is complete as it stands; it realizes its formal intention—an idealist interest—insofar as it involves the reader in the syncretic act which draws the work's multeity into unity. "For the practical critic ['Kubla Khan'] presents in extreme form a problem which must often greet him in reading romantic poetry—that the total poem may not be readily available in the immediate verbal structure which appears on the page."[9]

I present these critical positions simplistically and schematically because I believe that the principles of critical consensus and disagreement are, in this case, as illuminating as the readings themselves. It seems reasonable to assume that "Kubla Khan" has been read as an endorsement of two widely different aesthetic theories or models not because the poem has been poorly read nor because it fails to make its point effectively, but because it *does* endorse each of these models at different moments, so to speak, of its structural development, as graphed in the printed text.

"Kubla Khan" is a palimpsest; some readers see the original configuration, others see the shape limned over the original. While some focus the *montage* effect—vision and revision—they do not as a rule make this the matter of their critical inquiry. I suggest that we take seriously this doubleness or disjunctiveness and relate it to the poem's genesis: its original composition and its nineteen-year seclusion, followed by publication and recontextualization. In emphasizing these distinctions and thus highlighting formal and doctrinal discontinuities within the poem, I do not suggest that we curtail our efforts to resolve the presented textual contradictions. I merely propose that these efforts inform rather than replace critical explanation.

Earlier, I described a completed fragment as a poem begun in one mood and mode and completed in another. Poems of this kind effectively present to us a beginning and an end; what they lack is that middling continuity which naturalizes the changes productive of those extreme and determinate moments. In order to "narrativize" a work such as this—essentially, a spatial representation—the reader focuses its differentials as engendered by its two-stage genesis. By this manipulation and intentionalization of textual *différance*, the reader weaves an interpretive fabric that integrates original with belated intentions. Simply, one constructs for such works an adequating middle.

"Kubla Khan," construed as a completed fragment, is not about the relative merits of two orders of aesthetic production. Its subject is the impossibility of accomplishing either ideal. To read "Kubla Khan" as a completed fragment is to feel the work's center of gravity shift from the concrete vision of Xanadu and its alternative modes of representation to the vision's effect upon the visionary. The salient question, then, for this poem as for all completed fragments, is why the author himself fails to homogenize his divided utterance; or, why does he retain in the "finished" text traces of the conflict played out through the poem's two-stage composition process? Had Coleridge eliminated from the central section (1– 36) those gestures which he repudiates in the framing passages (prefatory extract and coda), "Kubla Khan" would have generated a single and consistent statement and would have approximated Coleridge's organic, syncretic ideal. We take up this question at the end of the discussion.

In order to establish critically the two moments or achievements which together produce the text that is our "Kubla Khan," we first read the 1797–98 "Kubla Khan" and then address the 1816 version as if these were two different poems yoked by violence together. We recover the original or Crewe manuscript text by disregarding the enlarged Preface with its poetic extract. This is essentially the version read by the compromise readers; it was Coleridge's initial composition and it represents, I believe, his first intention.

The vision of Xanadu (1–36) consists of an antithesis and a third term. Kubla's garden, described in a lofty, commanding, but matter-of-fact tone, is landscaped according to geometrical principles abstracted from the natural phenomena which are their ultimate source. Kubla imposes his forms (dome, rills, towers, walls: parabola, curve, cylinder, rectangle) upon naturally occurring materials whose own properties are thereby modified, appropriated, or eliminated. The garden's perimeter, for example, is not an organically uneven and adaptive line, respecting the earth's contours. Kubla "girdles" his empire with a circular figure, in the process suppressing irregularities that interfere with his idea of order. The organizing spatial and dynamic principle of Kubla's garden is that of ascent or verticality, perhaps a phallic principle: trees, tower, wall, dome. Kubla subdues the profound and generative natural principles figured by the chasm, river, and cavern—yonic and psychic imagery—in the interests of civil and domestic order and by way of asserting his dominance. The garden's physical beauty and its carefully constructed harmonies conceal the violence of its underlying natural—we might say, libidinal—energies. Kubla's empire, a product of will and reason, is fanciful rather than organic, its internal necessity an artifact, its beauty an anti-truth.

Interpreted naturalistically, the "ancestral voices prophesying war" describe the echo produced by the rush of the river through the caves. Or, by way of the narrative and tonal suggestiveness of the poem (lines 2, 6, 12, 14, 16, 21, 29, 30), we might find in the emblem an image of Kubla's empire threatened by the mighty principles he has suppressed. The ominous rumbling issues from the "one Life within us" (the caverns measureless to man) and the one Life "abroad" (the sacred river). These chthonic and creative principles (portrayed as subterranean and/or descending), become treacherous when repressed. The phrasing of the description suggests that the force of the "mighty fountain" is directly proportional to the containment it suffers in its underground course. These impulses constitute the second term in the dialectic: the instinctual and atavistic (that is, romantic) substratum of Kubla's artful garden—its generative ground of being. Although the tone of this description is spirited and filled with a joyous urgency lacking in the stately, measured progression of the first twelve lines, the passage carries ominous overtones, suggesting the need for reconciliation.

Between these two orders lies the shadow of the dome, emblem of their synthesis. Although the shadow lacks the uncompromising material determinacy of the real dome, it asserts its formal coherence in the midst of the turbulent waves. The shadow dome neither ascends nor "sinks"; it "float[s] midway on the waves," maintaining a liminal position between the realms of Nature and culture, instinct and defense. The shadow dome combines formal determinacy with organic and processual energy.

In the eighteen-line coda, the poet solves the equation he has set up.

> A damsel with a dulcimer
> In a vision once I saw:
> It was an Abyssinian maid,
> And on her dulcimer she played,
> Singing of Mount Abora.
> Could I revive within me
> Her symphony and song,
> To such a deep delight 'twould win me,
> That with music loud and long,
> I would build that dome in air,
> That sunny dome! those caves of ice!
> And all who heard should see them there,
> And all should cry, Beware! Beware!
> His flashing eyes, his floating hair!
> Weave a circle round him thrice,

And close your eyes with holy dread,
For he on honey-dew hath fed,
And drunk the milk of Paradise.

Here, Coleridge imagines a mode of artistic production that would draw
upon Nature's "vital entelechy" but that would formally imitate the principles engendering that phenomenal dimension, just as the shadow dome,
composed of natural and mutable water and light, is formally determined
by a geometric law abstracted from and independent of Nature.[10] Such a
composition might incorporate and psychologize factual reality while resisting the tyrannical, material overdeterminations of that content. Moreover, the poet's dome, a palace of art, would transcend even the idealized
shadow dome. Using the watery reflection as a visionary model, the poet
would raise the consummate structure—a dome in air. The maker of this
ideal yet organic form is, by the poetic imagery, the possessed seer into the
life of things, immersed in his fertile visions. His art holds open a rare
space between Nature and imagination; or, in Coleridge's metaphysical
idiom, it sustains an equipoise between centripetal and centrifugal forces
—intelligence and fact. Or again, in the language offered by the poem
itself, the ideal art form situates itself in the territory between Mount
Abora (Amahra, first draft: Amara, Milton's false paradise) and Abyssinia
(authentic Edenic site). The ground thus marked out is not, however,
bordered by truth on the one side and falsehood on the other (that is,
Abyssinia-Amara); it is defined with reference to conflicting but onto-
logically comparable traditions—figurings of the same syncretic and infinite truth. The ideal dome of the coda floats in middle air.

This airy dome is liberated from even the flexible material foundation
that supports the shadow dome. Its formal determinacy is a purely internal
necessity, and its organic assimilation of alien material is perfect. In the
hypostatized dome, Coleridge offers a spatial representation of the negatively capable poem, a form whose necessity might be compared to that of
the Möbius strip. While both these forms realize a clear and distinct idea,
the origin and terminus of that idea, as well as its structural and genetic
divisions (means, manner, end), are indistinguishable.[11]

To produce such a form, the writer must relinquish his conscious arti-
sanal control: his ambition to construct a particular vision in a particular
way cannot but engender the factitiousness evinced by Kubla's empire. At
the same time, however, the organic and negatively capable form requires
a complete interpenetration of form and content. In order to accomplish

this radical simplicity without conscious critical exertion, the poet must remain in continuous contact with his visionary model or governing inspiration. In that model and only there does the poet find the "mingled measure" of form and content, word and thing, imagination and fact, energy and boundary which, in animating his song, at the selfsame moment organizes it.

By introducing the poetical extract into the new Preface, Coleridge alters "Kubla Khan"'s internal relationships. The extract describes a process of vision and revision. The youth initially observes in the stream a "phantom world," presumably a reflection of the surrounding scenery. An externally induced disturbance in the water fractures the reflection; the imaged—but not *imagined*—world disintegrates. The youth, mesmerized first by the vision and then by its sudden evanishment, continues to gaze into the water. As the surface smooths out, a new image takes shape, that of the observer's own face: "The pool becomes a mirror." There is a quiet pathos to these lines, suggested, it seems, by the youth's failure to detach himself from the shadow world. Rather than enhance his pleasure in or knowledge of the surrounding landscape (the object world) and inspire him to projective, fully imaginative activity, the vision enthralls him, drawing him into its field. Transfixed by the medium, the youth forgets the forms of Nature and the beauty of their liquid sublimation. When the reflection fades, he substitutes for its "phantoms" his own no less attenuated image, transferring to that image the interest originally excited by the natural reflection. Within this short passage, the visionary youth undergoes a Narcissean metamorphosis.

The coda describes a nearly identical sequence of events. The narrator recalls a paradisical vision (damsel with a dulcimer) and declares himself presently deprived of this inspiration. Could he revive within himself the charm of that original phantom world, he might actualize the vision in a musical form, or externalize and objectify it so that others might know its treachery: the seductions of vision and the resultant, solipsistic impoverishment. The irony, of course, is that the narrator confesses his need for the vision even to expose it. The discourse sadly exemplifies that dependency which it refuses and deplores.

The coda clearly refers to the preceding poetic material—or, more precisely, to its abrupt cessation. Let us identify the narrative voice of the coda with Coleridge, and the paradisical vision (damsel: symphony and song) with the vision of Xanadu. This vision, like the phantom world of the prefatory extract, was neither a hallucination nor an unimagined representation, but rather a product of mind and fact: or historical chronicle (Purchas's history) perceived through the imagination's felicitous veils (Purchas's, Milton's, and Coleridge's). As with the youth of the Preface, Coleridge's vision is disturbed by an external intervention (man from Porlock), and again, like the youth, the poet is unable to extricate himself from the enthrallment of his revery. Rather than complete the poem ("what had been originally, as it were, given to him") by finishing the narrative—that is, inventing the missing events—Coleridge abandons narrative and substitutes lyric. He inserts himself—his persona—into the vision ("Could I revive within me"), offering images of poets rather than potentates. Instead of finishing the portrait of Kubla, Coleridge frames the sketch with the extract and coda and calls the piece a self-portrait: according to one version, a "vision in a Dream of the fragment of Kubla Khan."

Norman Rudich refers to the implicit "apotheosis of S. T. Coleridge" in "Kubla Khan"—"the victory of the vatic Poet . . . over the Power Principle embodied in the Khan. . . ."[12] We can see, of course, how very equivocal this victory is. For once Coleridge replaces Kubla, empire-builder, with the lyric "I," he is compelled to respect the logic of grammar and psychology. Kubla's fate and the poet's must converge; the holocaust prophesied by the ancestral voices becomes, perforce, the dread destiny of the narrator, just as it looms for Kubla. Hence Coleridge's reluctance to develop the history of Kubla Khan. Given Coleridge's syncretic methodology, one which assimilates all characters and moments to a univocal but infinitely polymorphic principle, Kubla's extinction must signify the defeat of all visionaries, including the poet.[13]

The question, of course, is why Coleridge fails to elaborate objectively, so to speak, his given vision of Xanadu and the Khan through the conscious exercise of his imaginative faculties. The bare but complete history was already available in Purchas; Coleridge need only have imagined what he knew in order to complete his fragment.

According to the aesthetic ideal formulated in the Crewe manuscript version, the genuine artist gives himself and his purposes over to the vision that inspires him, finding in its mingled measure the formal and therefore philosophic necessity that no abstruse research could yield. "The images rose up before [the author] as *things*, with a parallel production of the correspondent expressions, without any sensation or consciousness of effort." Image and word are given simultaneously; by selflessly reproducing this semiotic simplicity, the poet not only produces a full presence, he avoids the bad faith of mechanical, discontinuous, and arbitrary composition. Since, however, this blessed dynamic depends upon the poet's conscious sacrifice of practical consciousness, the unvisioned or dispossessed poet has no recourse but to rehearse the gone dream in strictly private space. He becomes at once his own poetic subject and object; or, as we observe in "Kubla Khan," he lyricizes his epic material.

Although Coleridge refuses the mordant logic of his aesthetic ideal—in practical terms, the self-reflexive representation of the Khan's destruction—the interpolation of the poetic extract establishes a parallel between the Narcissistic youth who opens the work, and the vatic youth ("His flashing eyes, his floating hair!") who closes it. The association characterizes this Dionysian figure, suspended in and by his vision, as one who shall drown in and by that vision.[14] The tragic end which the poem and Purchas promise is, although not realized, rendered; that is, the representation is indirect and displaced.

In the new Preface, the author declares that he woke from his dream and jotted down his "recollection of the whole" or "general purport" in "scattered lines and images." By this claim, he so much as says that the poem is complete; all it wants is a mechanical narrative invention to supply continuity and connect the dots, so to speak.

By abstaining from providing that continuity, Coleridge conceals the circular structure of the poem. His camouflage of the "poor youth" lines and his refusal of the narrative, formal, and imagistic logic to which his artistic ideals and methods commit him, create the illusion that "Kubla Khan" is a poem that is not self-reflexive; we seem to have the beginnings of a truly epic vision in the service of objective knowledge.

In creating this effect, Coleridge turns his initial (Crewe manuscript) disparagement of Kubla's governance inside out. Once we associate the "poor youth" of the extract with the rhapsode of the coda, we find that Kubla's creativity—impersonal, objective, authoritative sublimation —looks very much like a healthy envisioning, defending as it does against both the "charm" of the phantom world and the devouring psyche. In the midst of a wildering sea of unconsciousness—the hiding places of power —Kubla's ordonnance figures a "sunny spot of greenery." His is a dry, serene, and stable world—a place to live and work.

Coleridge's inability to narrate the history he promises is especially ironic in that Kubla is precisely the sort of maker whom Coleridge emulates. The Khan ordains and decrees; he selects the materials and determines in each instance the method and end of his art, maintaining at all times a mediated relationship to the forces he harnesses. Rather than imitate this exemplary creative statecraft, Coleridge embeds the Khan in a lyric context. Within this charmed circle, he ceases to function as an object of imitation. He becomes instead Coleridge's ideal object—his "positive Negation," his double.

"Kubla Khan" is a completed fragment. The first and central movement is as it were the creative thrust, or the recording of an unsolicited vision (1–36). This movement demonstrates the superiority of an organic and visionary aesthetic to what we are meant to construe as the perilous repressions of a ratiocinative, mechanical, and abstractive exercise of creative power. Presumably, the missing narrative material recounts the humbling of the Khan: the destruction of his fragile empire (a folly perched atop a rumbling volcano) and the triumph of the organic unconscious.

The prefatory poetic extract and the coda together form the second or revisionary movement; by introducing the extract, Coleridge seeks to complete his fragment at a later date and from a different position. The extract, by its resonance with the coda, brings out the practical dangers of submission to those profound, organic forces celebrated in the central stanzas. The revisionary statement amounts to a rejection of the "romantic" style idealized in the first (Crewe manuscript) movement, and it figures a longing for the safety zone which is, by the revisionary movement, the meaning of Kubla's empire. The methods of the two movements differ as well as their statements. Whereas the conceptual logic of lines 1–36 is dialectical and the discursive convention is that of detached, reliable, absolute narration, the framing movement—extract and coda—is lyrical and impressionistically descriptive in mode, associative and allusive in method. This section does not affect a disinterested sincerity; it is offered as a deliberate attempt to retreat from an earlier position.

This retreat sounds several depths; the aesthetic statement deepens into a psychic resolve and a political posture. (It may be, of course, that the psychic and/or political dimension is primary.) The poem's final endorsement of a controlled and thoroughly conscious poetics is surely informed by Coleridge's hopeless love for Sara Hutchinson and by his opium addiction—real or, at this point, feared. In both these facts of his life, Coleridge read the mind's annihilation of its own will, its moral control, and its fearful self-delivery into an intense inane, the realm of "sensualities beyond the bestial."[15]

Woodring advances this phrase by way of describing Coleridge's political sentiments after 1802, and especially between 1809 and 1816. Coleridge's turn to the right had, no doubt, multiple causes and influences, but the long, ugly spectacle of post-Revolutionary realpolitic, as well as "the grosser public acts of Napoleon" were surely potent factors in Coleridge's conversion.[16] Throughout England, 1816 brought an alarming display of civil unrest, directed, of course, against private property and the State apparatus. Coleridge reacted to this situation with his second lay sermon (1817), described by A. S. Link as a "hard-hitting analytical inquiry into the causes of the present discontent." The burden of the essay—that the effect of populist demagoguery is to elicit additional repressive measures, the stimulus to further disobedience, and so on until the whole powder keg blows up—is clearly determined by the contemporary social situation. "It is evident," Link concludes, "that Coleridge feared the possibility of a violent social revolution during the post-war period."[17]

Coleridge's decision to publish "Kubla Khan" in 1816 and to render it a substantially different statement from the one he had made in 1797–98 was certainly, to some extent, politically motivated. Others have suggested as much. According to Rudich, "Kubla Khan"'s "basic structure contrasts the political power of the State with the creative power of the Poet."[18] While I agree with Rudich that these are the operative categories (artists and statesmen: men of power, men of knowledge), and that the primary impetus behind the 1816 publication was probably contemporary political conditions, I disagree with his interpretation, one which does not observe the essential duality of the poem. Rudich does not take into account Coleridge's personal position in 1797–98, when he first composed his vision in a dream: at the height of his creativity, intimate with Wordsworth, enthusiastic about the offices and effects of poetry, and not yet disenchanted with Pantisocratic ideals. Rudich also effects a strange liaison when he pairs Coleridge's swerve from the Jacobin to the Tory school with his apotheosis of the wild, vatic poet, "the divine vessel through whose vision of nature and man, political alienation can be overcome and paradise regained."[19] If the mindless excesses and self-aggrandizement which Coleridge witnessed in the post-Revolutionary drama dismayed him, would he idealize the enthusiasm and license of the self-styled divinity, the rhapsode?

It seems more reasonable to assume that Coleridge revises and prints "Kubla Khan" in 1816 in order to *recant* his youthful extremism and to celebrate the virtues of a rational authoritarian control—aesthetic and political. "Kubla Khan," revised by the addition of the Preface with its poetic extract, contrasts the repressive, effectual, and legitimate government of the Khan with the radical (we should read that word literally) energy of a movement that is savage, self-regarding, self-indulgent, irrational, and unforeseeing. The Khan does not capitulate to these powers ("the sedition of the mob"), although he knows his empire fated to be overwhelmed by them.[20] Lines 1–11 depict the last of the anciens régimes. What will follow its extinction will be, so the poem intimates, chaos and the death of beauty—Yeats's nightmare.

The 1816 "Kubla Khan" represents Coleridge's effort to reclaim for a more sober or sadder maturity a document born of his errant youth. The poem does not just repudiate its original statement; the former Pantisocratist submits to a new control. Or, to recast this in terms of aesthetic argument, "rigid form" triumphs over "wild versatility."[21]

T. S. Eliot criticizes the imagery of "Kubla Khan": "it is not used: the poem has not been written."[22] Eliot is right; that synthesis so crucial to his (as to Coleridge's) idea of poetry does not occur in "Kubla Khan." The work, a completed fragment, makes its readers connect its separate, antithetical movements and fuse its imagery. Having studied these activities, however, we understand why this "not written" poem feels so complete. "Kubla Khan" contains all the elements necessary to a "written" or achieved poem; it lacks only the interstitial material. I suspect that serious readers of the poem have always and unconsciously supplied this material. They fill in the blanks and credit the poem with the closure which their labor produces. "Kubla Khan" is not, in its final form, a work that contrasts two poetic theories (in order to celebrate, denigrate, or integrate these constructs). The 1816 version is a work that demonstrates the fatal liabilities of the only kind of poetry Coleridge can produce. If any one work explains Coleridge's abandonment of poetry, that work is "Kubla Khan."

Strangely enough, after all the critical paces, we come full circle to Bostetter's simple and sensible conclusion. "Kubla Khan"'s imperfection represents both a personal failure on Coleridge's part and the failure or deficiency of an aesthetic ideology. Coleridge does not finish "Kubla Khan" the first time around because the aesthetic ideal he valorizes in that draft offers no assistance to the poet who loses his vision. Indeed, that particular shaping vision exacerbates the problem of suspension, cessation, or desertion. By inviting the poet's subjective appropriation of "what was originally, as it were, given to him," the romantic mode effectively arrests the artistically fertile dialectic of self and other, barring in this manner the last escape from the sole self. Coleridge does not, in the second writing (1816), complete the fragment by drawing the connections between the prefatory extract (the dangers of a voyage inward and downward) and the visionary aesthetic originally recommended. To do so would be to condemn his own poetic enterprise and to acknowledge its political implications. Instead, he makes his readers revive within *them* the amassing harmony. This avoidance of self-criticism should, as Bostetter suggests, be seen as a personal failure.

The poem, however, does for itself what Coleridge cannot do for it. It criticizes itself mercilessly, condemning its own compositional method even as it thereby unfolds. "Kubla Khan," read as a completed fragment, exposes its organicism, its spontaneous expressivity, and its escapism as a terrible tyranny. For in putting to work an ideology requiring the artist's appropriation of the actual and extrinsic into psychic space, the poem denies itself the dialectic mentioned above—where mind and Nature, vision and fact, engage in productive, self-perpetuating, self-enlarging interaction.

"Kubla Khan" is a poem that explicitly rejects what it implicitly longs for but is incapable of realizing, a scene with the poet *not* in it, to twist Robert Langbaum's phrase.[23] In this perversity, "Kubla Khan" is perhaps more of a "psychological curiosity" than we or Coleridge had imagined.[24]

CHAPTER SIX

THE COMPLETED FRAGMENT
"The Giaour"

Finding the irresolution in "The Giaour" presents no problem. Byron refers to the poem in his Advertisement as "these disjointed fragments," and the discontinuity to which he alludes is unmistakable. "The Giaour"'s form—or lack of it—has engaged critical attention from 1813, the date of its original publication, to the present, although interpretation has changed significantly over the years.

Modern scholarship focuses "The Giaour" as a kind of Rashomon tale featuring multiple narrators, each one possessed of a highly circumscribed and overdetermined understanding of a series of events.[1] A more precise and elaborate version of this view proposes that the poem's organizing fiction is that of an oral, bardic performance. The poet-bard assumes diverse and deliberately restricted roles in order to relate his material dramatically and, as it were, authentically.[2] Formally, "The Giaour" would thus seem to imitate and explore problems of narrative relativity. While this interpretive line accounts for the poem's final effect, it does not address the particular kind of irresolution which "The Giaour" displays: the withholding of an authorial, mediational continuity that would bind the several voices into a complex unity. Had Byron allowed each speaker to tell his tale in a consecutive and orderly fashion (here I refer to intra-narrative disjunctions), with the poet-bard directing the reportage, both the rhetorical effect and epistemological interests ascribed to "The Giaour" would remain substantially unchanged. Merely by juxtaposing the diverse and contradictory materials, Byron could have illustrated with equal success the radical indeterminacy of even the simplest actions, and/ or the incommensurability of action and narration.

Jerome McGann has suggested that "The Giaour"'s irresolution adds "cultural authenticity to the events of the story."[3] The obvious analogy is to Samuel Rogers's poem, "The Voyage of Columbus," a work designed to look like a transcription from an ancient and imperfect manuscript. ("The Giaour" is dedicated to Rogers.) By fragmenting "The Voyage of Columbus" and referring the resultant narrative incoherence to the physical condition of the manuscript, Rogers creates an illusion that allows him to smuggle into his modern verse the "machinery, superstitions, and imagery" from a less enlightened, more poetical age.[4] We can see that the maneuver—its object and method—duplicates the strategy of the hoax poems. Rogers's audience was not, of course, nearly so credulous as Macpherson's and Chatterton's, nor is Rogers nearly so earnest in his charade.[5]

"The Giaour" is a different case altogether. As regards motivation, Byron's poem contains little or nothing of the supernatural or superstitious—nothing that need be legitimized by the postulate of a primitive cultural source. Second, Rogers restricts his "interference" in the poem to the prose notes; he lets the fragments stand alone, and ostensibly as he found them. Byron, however, who intrudes directly into the text of "The Giaour," keeps us in mind of the modern (authorial) sensibility annotating the action. This is to say, Byron shows little concern with cultural authenticity as a formal imperative. Finally, where Rogers employs the fiction of a found, and of course, greatly defaced manuscript to explain textual ruptures, Byron declares in the Preface to "The Giaour" that he heard a complete story, and that the parts missing from his poem are alive in and (theoretically) recoverable from the balladeer's repertoire and Byron's own mind. The structural imperfection is not, then, represented as a circumstantial necessity but rather as the result of Byron's bad—which is to say, selective—memory. In short, "The Giaour"'s fragmented form fails to confer any of the advantages secured by Rogers's use of a similar technique. As the effects of the two poems differ, so must our understanding of their form.

McGann has facetiously suggested that Byron's readers assumed, "as each new and augmented edition of his 'snake of a poem' came out, that he periodically recalled additional snatches of the original lay."[6] McGann's irony underlines the disparity between the form of Rogers's poem and that of Byron's. Readers of "The Voyage of Columbus" *were* encouraged to receive such additions to the poem as Rogers might supply as subsequent discoveries or as decipherings of previously illegible passages.

McGann's joking brings up a serious, and to this study, central issue: how *did* the nineteenth century interpret the incremental expansion of "The Giaour," and how might *we* work the form?

Early reviews of the poem show that the critics did not, of course, construe the additions as Byron's happy recall of forgotten passages, nor did they regard the poem's disjointedness as a feature designed to emphasize point of view and the fallacy of empiricism and historical objectivity.[7] The critics appear to have believed Byron's statement that the Giaour's story (what they call the "Turkish original" or "catastrophe"—lines 168– 786), came to him in a complete and integrated package. In the words of one review, Byron eliminates from that "original" those "insipid ingredients which swelled the redundant narratives of our ancestors" in order to "reduce [the story] to its quintessence," by which the critic means the facts in and of themselves. Byron apparently performs this reduction by pretending to remember selected portions of the original ("Byron has professed to give us a fragment"). This distillation accomplished, the poet proceeds to add point and meaning to the tale—that is, he interprets it— in a candidly anachronistic and interested fashion. He explains the lacunae which he himself creates by juxtaposing against the original, "poetic" material a complementary but critical discourse. The early reviews tend to locate this commentary in two discrete and framing blocks (lines 1–167 and 787 to the end) rather than distributed throughout the poem.

When "The Giaour" is read as a collection of narrative fragments framed by Byron's interpretation and dramatic expansion, the significant irresolution occurs not in the gaps within the central section but in the disjunction between frame and core—that is, between modern interpretation and Turkish original, or commentary and chronicle. A contrast might be instructive here; whereas the frame or belated addition to "Kubla Khan" functions as recantation and authorial salvaging action, "The Giaour"'s surrounding passages figure as part of the original conception: intended components of a complex whole. Coleridge would seem to have hastily and desperately switched horses in midstream while Byron, to use one of his own compositional metaphors, appears to have set out knowing exactly how far his horse would take him. At the appropriate posthouse, Byron picks up his prearranged new mount and finishes the journey. (This is not to say, of course, that the destination he reached was the one he had in mind.)

Byron's contemporaries regarded the central section (168–786) as the poet's attempt to present a history as experienced and interpreted by those nearest to it chronologically and ideologically. The framing material is viewed as Byron's attempt to abstract from this history a more profound, general, and therefore belatedly useful level of meaning, both political and existential.

One of our own critics, William Marshall, has argued boldly and, to my mind correctly, that "The Giaour" *cannot* be "pieced together."[8] Although the various voices can be assembled into a coherent narrative, the gap between the Turkish original (all the voices, taken as a collective discourse) and the "translator's" material remains. The poem is not integrated by simple addition of the two discourses, even if we could combine such categorially distinct elements. In order to bridge the gap, one must ascertain the "principle of combination" or formal intention governing the series of antitheses promoted by the discontinuous architecture of this fragment poem.[9] More specifically, one must define the transitional logic obtaining between the poet's (editorially situated) query, "when shall such hero live again," and the subsequent narrative if one hopes to rationalize the poem's disorder.

Although "The Giaour" in several respects resembles a bardic oral performance, the discourse which it more closely approximates is that of an early Greek history in the manner of Herodotus. *The History of the Persian Wars* combines two types of research: Herodotus investigated the Persian Wars and he travelled in the East to collect information about present conditions and past events in those countries. The *History* is a collection of tales, each one a *logos* or repetition (one that refines and distills) of "what was said" or "what is said" about a given event. The tragic *logoi*, "almost all of which concern the fall of princes," constitute a subdivision or kind of *logos*: that is, the *kleos*.[10] The *kleos* typically consists of a historical account compiled from eyewitness reports delivered orally to the historian and necessarily relatively close to him in time. The historian then narrates the account (orally, or as with Herodotus, in writing) in such a way as to bring out the causes and conditions underlying the event, and thereby to suggest its original meaning as well as—and this is paramount—its more immediate and practical dimension. The historian elucidates the relatively recent episode so as to explain by analogy a situation or event of greater moment—one that is too multidetermined or too mediated to permit direct investigation. By his inquiry into the simpler, more directly accessible matter, the historian illuminates the complex and weighty subject and at the same time, and by this generalizing protocol, works his way around to his genuine concern, contemporary applications.

The *History* is intentionally digressive, accretive, and paratactic—a snake of a tale. Here is Herodotus's rather charming allusion to his unusual method: "Here I must express my wonder—additions being what my work always from the first affected. . . ."[11] Because Herodotus aims to establish for his subject its cultural setting, and to imagine his data by way of developing its moral and historical and (what we would call) anthropological implications, the facts "get presented, not literally, but dramatically, and sometimes almost symbolically."[12] This interest and method produce a characteristic structural jumpiness and heterogeneity. Still, the *logos* does not chase more than one hare at a time. Herodotus "set out to tell all the Stories bearing on his subject and to weave them together into some kind of unity."[13] The unity attempted (and achieved) is, of course, neither organic nor Aristotelian. Given the motley materials with which the historian works and his conscientious rejection of a predetermined controlling concept, transitions are rough and overall organization and resolution indistinct.

Before I extend and adapt this description to "The Giaour," I would like to put Byron's choice of a methodological model in perspective. It is not enough that we appreciate the utility of Herodotus's *History* to Byron; to be of critical use, the availability to Byron of the *History*—its cultural currency in Regency England—should be established.

Let me summarize Arnaldo Momigliano's account of Herodotus's position in Enlightenment and Romantic thought. "In the second part of the eighteenth century one could read scores of dissertations inspired by the principle that historians are the voice of their times and must be examined in relation to what was called the genius of their age." "The authority of Herodotus and Thucydides was steadily growing," but Herodotus, with his "wide humanity," his respect for the "imaginative" dimension of his data, his use of oral evidence, and his habit of reading his works aloud, spoke with special force to the late eighteenth- and early nineteenth-century interest in the relation between poetry and historiography, and lent support to the theory that the latter had evolved from imaginative discourses.[14] Moreover, Herodotus's sensibility and values—his narrative voice—appealed to the internationalism, curiosity, and tolerance that characterized the European intellectual community during the Enlightenment and to some extent afterwards. Herodotus, a "naïve, cosmopolitan, *historien de moeurs*," was experienced by this community as a figure not unlike Goldsmith's Citizen of the World.[15] For us, perhaps, or in this context, Byron's Don Juan is the apter comparison. Whereas Thucydides represented the first professional historiographer, Herodotus epitomized the consummate amateur. A kind of unofficial ambassador and explorer, Herodotus questioned local people, collected their accounts, described their customs and relished their oddities. Byron's activities in the Levant were, of course, far less systematic, but his interests and methods were essentially those of the father of History.

Herodotus's *History* was in one respect peculiarly timely in the early nineteenth century and peculiarly germane to Byron's interests. Herodotus's primary subject was, of course, the Persian Wars, and Byron's primary enthusiasm was the cause of Greek independence. "In his quiet way [Herodotus] had understood the Persians, and through him the Turks could be seen more objectively."[16] Momigliano refers here to the revival of interest in Herodotus in the fifteenth century, following the disintegration of the Byzantine Empire, but the observation has a clear relevance to the Turkish presence in Greece in the early nineteenth century. In "The Giaour," Byron's treatment of "the Turk" (Hassan) is surprisingly compassionate, no less so in fact than his representation of "the Venetian," that is, the Giaour. In that Herodotus practically stood for the principle of non-reductive historical relativism, the *History* might well have suggested to Byron a way to develop poetically a subject about which he could not easily be generous.

"The Giaour" opens with a meditative lament upon Greece's decline, a passage focussed by the figure of Themistocles, a famously ambiguous hero.

> No breath of air to break the wave
> That rolls below the Athenian's grave,
> That tomb which, gleaming o'er the cliff,
> First greets the homeward-veering skiff,
> High o'er the land he saved in vain—
> When shall such hero live again?

Two lines down, the poet tells us that the prospect he describes is rendered from "far Colonna's height." The reference to Colonna, the legendary secret burial spot of Themistocles (the official grave is in Turkey), reinforces the earlier allusion to Themistocles as the epitome of Greece's greatness, and perhaps an expression of her fatal weakness. The narrator's mournful and locally unanswered query—"When shall such hero live again"—and the locally unmotivated narration of the Giaour's "mournful tale" together suggest that in some sense that sad tale either is or contains an answer to Byron's general question.

This is to say that the method of Byron's poem resembles the procedure that is and was so specifically associated with Herodotus. Byron assembles in the "core" section, or the story of the Giaour, a number of eyewitness accounts that describe an event relatively close to the poet-historian in time, that is, unobscured by extensive transmission. The accounts that together make up the *historia* function indirectly to elucidate a situation far more complex, significant, and remote. Byron introduces this latter subject in his prefatory meditation on Greece and its bygone heroes, and throughout the poem, the Giaour is presented in such a way as to bring out his likeness to Themistocles, the figure whom Byron enlists to explain, as it were, Greece's fall from greatness.

Byron transcribes and distills the "Turkish original" or the story of the Giaour by way of answering his real question: what conditions initiated and explain Greece's descent from her golden age to the present brazen one? The headnote to the poem as much as announces this theme.[17] Byron reduces the *historia* to its "quintessence"—the eyewitness accounts. Then, *in propria persona*, he dramatizes, interiorizes, extends, and interprets the romance, thereby illuminating a more immediate political and moral issue: the decline of the forces of change in England and Europe generally during and, of course, after the Napoleonic Wars. This, I believe, is the ultimate question that haunts about the edges of "The Giaour."

The decision to address broad, evolutionary questions through the examination of individual character—the character of the great man—might itself represent the influence of Herodotus. The *kleos*, an oral account of the deeds and effects of a hero, is closely associated with Herodotus, for it was he who incorporated this traditionary form into written historical discourse. Plutarch's *Lives*, an exceedingly popular work in the late eighteenth and early nineteenth centuries, probably belongs to the formal tradition established by the *kleos*. Gibbon, although skeptical of "the hero" and prone to represent him as an unwitting "cog in a great system," does not suppress his nostalgia for the primitive republic, a state characterized by "heroic simplicity, freedom and individualism" and favorable to the development of the great man.[18] Byron had, of course, read Herodotus, Plutarch, and Gibbon; more important, he was from an early age enamored of the idea of heroism and, eventually, of Napoleon as an avatar of that idea. Thus the method of the *kleos* might well have seemed particularly attractive to Byron.

The broad historical inquiry which informs "The Giaour" addresses the moral and material decline of fifth-century Greece and nineteenth-century Europe as represented and potentially explained by the characters and careers of Themistocles and Napoleon, heroes whose creation of epochs of expansion seems to have called forth epochs of contraction. Byron pursues his inquiry by representing the fortunes of a fictive character who is as ambiguous in his virtues and effects as Themistocles or Napoleon. The Giaour is, of course, both destructive and creative, noble and corrupt, and Byron withholds (and disallows) a satisfying analysis of this doubleness. Because Byron's object in "The Giaour" is to study the impact of a certain kind of personality upon history, he eschews psychological analysis and "works steadily in the direction of generalizing character."[19] Byron is not concerned with the Giaour's "inward torment," nor with the "devils and angels" whose warfare he psychically entertains.[20] The reader's interest in such psychic and metaphysical questions is permitted no scope.

Byron leaves his history incomplete; he refrains from applying explicitly the "tool of inquiry" (the central romance) to the object of inquiry (the enigma of cultural greatness and decay). Byron's failure to solve the equations he sketches may represent an interest in imitating the overall method of the *History*, a work which, "though not finished throughout, is concluded."[21] This is not to say, however, that the poem's particular mode of irresolution lacks a more intrinsic or necessary rationale.

Let me provide a brief summary of the central romance, as the eyewitness accounts technique makes the narrative a bit difficult to follow. I will then present some striking analogies between the Giaour—his character and career—and Themistocles (and, by implication, Napoleon). I follow Herodotus, Thucydides, and Plutarch in my sketch.

Actually, the story is simple. Hassan, the Turk, keeps in his serai a favorite mistress, Leila, who captures the heart of the Giaour and is herself enamored of the infidel. Hassan, according to the custom of his people, punishes his faithless slave by murdering her. The Giaour avenges Leila's death by murdering Hassan. His task accomplished, he retires to a monastery where he passes the rest of his days.

The problem for the reader is to locate the "principle of combination," as one reviewer put it, that yokes the romance to the opening "corpse of

Greece" passage. Or, our job is to ascertain the "truth of character" that illuminates the figures of Themistocles and the Giaour, and explains the relevance of one representation to the other.

One effect produced by the eyewitness accounts is to endow the tragic events with an air of necessity. We may not know exactly *what* happened, but the very existence of the reports positions the action as a definite factuality, and one that resists descriptive discourse—its partiality—absolutely. The narrative voice, however, heard in the opening section and then again, indirectly, through the confessor at the end, qualifies that metaphysical determinism. Although the narrator represents Greece's debasement as well as the Giaour's as the inevitable fate of all human greatness, the reader is encouraged to meditate this fate (its moment and manner) with respect to determinate causes. The Giaour may act in the only way possible, given his character and his situation, but at no point in the poem is it suggested that the Giaour is morally blameless or that the individual must acquiesce to characterological and situational imperatives. The Giaour is unequivocally represented in the poem as the agent of his own fate, of Hassan's, and of Leila's, even as he is himself situated within a field of historical and metaphysical necessity. How do these severe contradictions answer the questions which the narrator raises in his introduction?

In selecting Themistocles as the epitome of Greece's heroic age, Byron chooses a figure as anomalous as the Giaour and in the same ways (I reverse the order of invention).[22] Themistocles, the "slave of Glory," parallels the Giaour, slave of Love. Byron's Giaour is an aristocrat by birth, sentiment, and *virtu*, but his maverick actions effectively destroy the order or ideology which is his own ground of being. He shatters Hassan's gracious feudal estate, steals Leila from her rightful owner, and allies himself with a rebel band in order to effect his own designs. In the last part of the poem, the Giaour defines the nature of his heroism by way of describing his present misery. He represents himself as a man of passionate action, one who must prefer intensity to comfort, and resistance to remorse. He neither justifies his actions or character with reference to some notion of the Good, nor does he accuse Hassan of villainy. Acknowledging the accidental nature of the roles thrust upon Hassan and himself, the Giaour identifies himself with his rival by asserting that he too would have murdered Leila had she betrayed him. The Giaour's love for Leila is clearly a love for the passion and heroic abandon she calls forth from him. The punishing quality of the Giaour's final confinement is its lack of an ideal, absolute object—no "maid [to] love," no "man [to] hate"—a condition that produces in the Giaour "the waste of feelings unemployed."

The character of the Giaour is the key to his own romance and to the larger narrative sketched in the preamble. Whereas Byron's allusion to Themistocles is generally taken as a simple contrast to the problematic heroism of the Giaour, even a cursory acquaintance with Themistocles' biographies invalidates that contrast.[23] Themistocles was not one of the "unforgotten brave." He was barely remembered two years after his exile. His career lent itself remarkably well to both positive and negative interpretation, the evidence itself surprisingly mixed. He was honored by both Persians and Spartans, lionized then vilified by his own people, the Athenians. He was both a champion of the people and a social climber, the savior of his country and the one who made it vulnerable to foreign intervention by exacerbating internal factionalism. As depicted by Herodotus, Themistocles possessed "political wisdom and clearsightedness, . . . wit and ready invention, . . . fertility in expedients, . . . strong love of intrigue." His was a "curious combination of patriotism with selfishness, . . . laxity of principle amounting to positive dishonesty."[24]

The mere facts of Themistocles' career are as two-edged as those of the Giaour's, and the poem drives the parallel home. "The Giaour" opens with the prospect of Themistocles' unmarked grave and it ends with the description of the Giaour's. The Giaour finishes his days in a community whose beliefs he tolerates but does not adopt, circumstances identical to those in which Themistocles concluded his life. As the Giaour resists assimilation by his newly adopted community, so Themistocles, in refusing to serve Darius at the decisive moment, would not confirm himself a member of the community which had received him in his disgrace. Both characters remain constant to their first love, but whether that love was for the thing itself—Leila in the case of the Giaour, Greece for Themistocles—or for the passion it aroused in them is unclear. Both men bring about the death of "courtesy and pity" and fatally upset the stability of the old order. Both eventually suffer the misery of being prepared but uncalled.

The meaning of the Giaour and of the romance in which he figures lies in their functional equivalence to the character and destiny of Themistocles. Moreover, this analogical meaning illuminates the decline of the Greek nation and, again by analogy, the decadence of Enlightenment Europe. "The Giaour" collects and interprets its material in an extremely circular way that seems finally unproductive of any insight at all. Byron's "snake of a poem" is an *ourobouros*. Perhaps the way for us to proceed toward an understanding of Byron's subject is to step outside that circle and ask why it was drawn in the first place. Byron opens the Giaour's narrative in search of a "theme on which the muse might soar." Why does the author select the themes I have isolated, and why does he pursue them in so oblique, disjunctive, and circuitous a fashion?

Byron's "Ode to Napoleon Buonaparte" dates from a period slightly later than that of "The Giaour'"s composition, yet it enacts the same conflicts and attempts the same kind of resolution as that which determines the form of "The Giaour." It therefore seems as good a way as any to escape the circular logic promoted by the structure of "The Giaour."

Napoleon is, of course, the subject of the Ode, yet in a perplexing epigraph, Byron quotes Gibbon's scornful description of the Emperor Nepos, specifically, "the Shameful abdication, [by which] he protracted his life a few years, in a very ambiguous state, between an Emperor and an Exile." As in "The Giaour," Byron interposes a mediating figure between himself and his subject: Gibbon's Nepos separates the author from the subject of his Ode, Napoleon. The method of the epigraph thus instructs us in the method of the Ode; Byron seeks to understand his tortured and complex reaction to Napoleon by finding the appropriate analogue. The Napoleon of the Ode is a "nameless thing"—as nameless, or morally and existentially ambiguous, as the Giaour, whose identity throughout the poem is strictly generic (the Giaour means "the alien"). The Napoleon of the Ode forfeits his name by accommodating himself to a diminished reality. Like Themistocles and the Giaour, the Napoleon of Byron's poem is an exile whose heroism might have survived untarnished had he disdained the lesser existence which fate decreed for him. And again, like the Giaour and Themistocles, Napoleon kept his own counsel, indifferent as to how his supporters (or enemies) might interpret his decisions.

Byron, torn by his love for the man, his scorn for the action, and his need for the hero, urgently seeks in the Ode a context within which Napoleon's apparent acquiescence to defeat might signify strength rather than weakness. Of course, if Napoleon fell first through "self-abasement" ("The Giaour," line 140), then his worldly degradation marks a real or essential corruption and is therefore just, as well as conceptually tolerable to Byron. But Napoleon's reverses and his acceptance of them could also indicate a fierce and pure genius, one that refuses to rebel against, negotiate with, or justify itself to a canting and corrupt society.

In order to determine the relative truth of these accounts, Byron tries out a series of potentially explanatory analogues; in effect, Byron seeks a context that will enable him to maintain Napoleon as an ideal. Although the Ode begins as a trenchant political analysis, Byron cannot relinquish his attachment to the idea of heroism and to Napoleon as its incarnation.

The conflict is defined through the poem as a question of names. Byron's project is to save Napoleon from the moral ambiguity—the terrible anonymity—which his actions have earned him. To this end, the author casts forth a series of names in the hope that one of them might fit Napoleon and relieve him of his epithet, "nameless thing." Lucifer, Samson, the Roman, the Spaniard, the Austrian, Tamerlane, and Cincinnatus all prove deficient in figuring as the desired analogue. Still seeking the positively explanatory context for Napoleon, Byron postulates a figure from the New World: Washington. The Ode does not, however, bring forth an evolution through which Washington might emerge as the symbol of a new context, a new category in heroes and histories. Byron simply inserts Washington into the Old World, a context that complicates and attenuates his heroism.

Returning to "The Giaour" now:

> 'Twere long to tell, and sad to trace,
> Each step from splendour to disgrace,
> Enough—no foreign foe could quell
> Thy soul, till from itself it fell.

Character, Byron tells us, is destiny, and the destiny of great men is history simplified and interpreted through long retrospect. In both "The Giaour" and the Ode, Byron attempts to explain the dubious heroism of Themistocles and Napoleon by locating each figure within the context of historical characters considered independently of their historical milieus. Byron does not look to historical conditions to elucidate the behaviors of his heroes. Although he seems to want history to explain psyche and thus vouchsafe him his heroes, Byron's notion of history—that of great men making great events—psychologizes history, rendering it useless as an explanatory system or even as an abstract logical development. Byron lacks, in other words, an antithetical method capable of producing a dialectic, precondition for the breakthrough of categories that he requires.

The Giaour's career, a series of steps from splendor to disgrace, does not finally yield the "truth of character" by means of which Byron hopes to explicate the condition of modern Greece and modern Europe. Had it done so—could it do so—Byron could have integrated the two themes (the Giaour and Themistocles, nineteenth- and fifth-century Greece) through an interpretation. Instead, the reader is left with "a broken tale" and an unnamed hero.

"Such is my name, and such my tale," concludes the Giaour. But of course, one never learns the Giaour's historical identity, only his generic designation, nor is the nature of his tale—its meaning and application—apparent.

By abstaining from particularizing the protagonist, Byron implies that the causes and meanings of world historical events are to be sought in the exploration of human character. Apparently, the only difficulty is in locating the properly, fully analogous (and therefore explanatory) *kleos* and hero. The Giaour remains "a nameless thing" because, presumably, his truth of character has not been completely illuminated. The inference is that the romance would have explained Greece's decadence and Themistocles's role in provoking, hastening, or retarding it, as well as Napoleon's character and its impact on European history, if only Byron had understood the Giaour better or had chosen a different romantic hero in the first place.

The effect of the poem—specifically, of its irresolution—is to call this inference into question. One feels that the fault lies less with Byron's powers of selection or penetration than with his method, one which interprets history as the sum of the actions and passions of great men. The reader who is alert to the aim and the rules of "The Giaour"'s formal game seeks to connect the meditation on Themistocles (that is, the glory that was Greece) with the Giaour's tale in such a way as to produce a reciprocal interpretation of the two historical epochs and agents. For the poem itself to have accomplished this task, Byron would have had to identify the conflict responsible for his procedures. The terms of this conflict are, on the one hand, Byron's desire to understand his own epoch as the cause or explanation of Napoleon's alarming and, to Byron, unacceptable behavior; and on the other, his interest in reading Europe's decline as Napoleon's effect, and Napoleon's decline as evidence of his unworthiness. Thus the method of Herodotus is adequate neither to Byron's emotional needs nor to his needs as historian and poet.

In *Don Juan*, Byron appears to accept the implications of "The Giaour"'s particular formal failure. The epic poet explicitly and repeatedly debunks the concept of absolute categories, of heroes, of truth of character, and of the subsequence of event and circumstance to character. In *Don*

Juan, Byron submits (cheerfully?) to a vision of historical and material determinism. In effect, he transcends the conflict that precipitates "The Giaour"'s form. *Don Juan*, a poem that celebrates the end of heroes and hero worship, rids Byron once and for all of his torturing impulse to define. Liberated from this stricture, Byron can name his hero confidently, comically, and insistently. "'Such is my name, and such my tale'" is a conclusion more appropriate to *Don Juan* than to "The Giaour."

. . . .

CHAPTER SEVEN

THE DELIBERATE FRAGMENT

"A Fragment," or
"When, to their airy hall"

The deliberate fragment, an instance of imitative form, makes a virtue of what it would have us believe is necessity. The work's imperfection, announced in the title or indicated typographically, figures as a formal necessity, expression of the work's governing thought. Doctrinal and formal dimensions thus claim the same impulse and the same originary moment. Under the pressure of this essentially organic projection, form is the transparency of pure meaning, and what was fragment is revealed as autonomous, complete, and coherent discourse. Of the four fragment models discriminated in this book, the deliberate fragment is, almost certainly, the most familiar to us. Shelley's "Triumph of Life," the (in)conclusion of which seems to objectify and imaginatively confirm the work's skeptical idealism, is probably the best known work of this kind.

A critique of the deliberate fragment can bring out the *uses* of form, and in so doing, may discover form and statement to enjoy a relationship, not an identity. We find that by truncating his work, the poet can project a particular genetic scenario and thereby support or emend the work's structure of ideas. While the intention that governs formal development may correspond to and/or be conditioned by doctrinal interests, the two impulses are not often identical nor do they share the same moment of origin.[1]

The deliberate fragment, insofar as it seeks to collapse form and content into a genetic and semiotic simplicity, raises questions about literary production. By moving beyond but along the lines established by the study of

several deliberate fragments, we can begin to explore the historical significance of the idea of irresolution within English Romantic letters. The
deliberate fragment poses the question: is there a sensibility, a concept, or
a conflict specific to an epoch that most readily—naturally, as it were—
promotes a discontinuous poetic? I take up this question in the Conclusion to this book.

Don Juan is probably the most effective—and certainly the most deliberate—of Romantic fragments. While one can, and Byron said he could,
endlessly invent episodes to advance the hero's peregrinations to a conclusive finale, the poem does not impel most readers to do so. One does not
really care whether Juan dies beneath the guillotine blade or in his, or
someone else's, bed.[2] The poem's sensible unfinishedness does not derive
from our being left hanging at the end but from Byron's hanging fire
throughout. The author pursues his contextuality interests, his definitions
of practical relativism (or historical determinism), and his debunking of
absolutes through the manipulation of form as well as idea. The difference, of course, between Byron's deliberate fragment and the sort I describe above (for example, "The Triumph," "A Vision of the Sea," Wordsworth's "The Danish Boy") is that Byron uses the form ironically and in
order to dismantle the myth of organic or necessary form. To examine *Don
Juan* in the context of this study would be to put the cart before the horse;
my concern in this book is to establish the norm, or the innocent practice
of a form. Byron's wry and witty burlesque of that practice is better
explored in the context of modernist poetics. Moreover, as I observed in
chapter one, our scholarship has for some time and very capably addressed
the motivation and meanings of *Don Juan*'s textual ruptures.[3] Indeed, the
deliberate fragment has been generally, although tacitly, acknowledged as
a determinate form, probably because it so clearly formulates its doctrine
and so closely associates this thematic discourse with its formal decisions.
In the interest of elucidating our practice (and to bring out some psychic
and historical issues informing Byron's methods, early and accomplished),
I consider a deeply flawed lyric from Byron's *Hours of Idleness*, 1807, "A
Fragment," or "When, to their airy hall."[4]

Jerome McGann tells us that Byron presents this volume "as a kind of
portrait of the hero as a young man."[5] That is, Byron uses the occasion of
his first public appearance to construct a persona that might serve him
throughout his poetic career. But one might guess from McGann's telling
substitution of "hero" for "artist," and from the issues raised by our reading of "The Giaour," that the project fails to produce that inevitability,

formal and conceptual, which is its *raison d'être*. The ironies and paradoxes of heroism—the overriding issue in "The Giaour" and the organizing principle of *Don Juan*—emerge very plainly in "Airy Hall." A close study of this slight and juvenile work reveals Byron's mature preoccupation with Napoleon, with romantic heroes, and with the glory that was Greece as displacements of more primitive and conflictual matters: succinctly, his commitment to the notion of heroic destiny, and his particular literary ambitions. The form of "Airy Hall"—or rather its title, "A Fragment"—exposes the contradiction engendered by these interests. Compounding the conflict, Byron's desire to conceive his experience as something to be "'gained' or 'concluded' or fulfilled" is countered by his more realistic awareness that life only feels so composed when it comes to us under the sign of fiction. These conflicting knowledges explain the ostensibly necessary, internally generated formal limits of "Airy Hall." The poem is not successful even within these limits, but its manner of failure is instructive when brought to bear on Byron's weightier projects.

Hours of Idleness is an exercise in self-invention. Through this volume, Byron hopes to produce a rounded persona as vital and credible as the living human reality. In his early twenties when he composed the volume (his perspective and experience, naturally, limited), Byron nonetheless aspires to that inclusive shapeliness one associates with memoir and not, typically, with youthful autobiography. We can see in Byron's solution to this particular formal problem the outlines of a procedure he develops throughout his writing career. Rather than look backward or inward (into memory and psyche, Wordsworth's and Coleridge's structural and material resources), Byron turns his gaze outward and to the future, there to discover his uniquely appropriate formal principles—psychic, literary, and existential. By projecting an image of a future self—a realized and individuated character—Byron might materialize systematically qualities necessarily mingled, immature, or strictly potential in the young man. For Byron to see, and to make his readers see, what he would be in the fullness of his years would be to organize a context wherein immediate conflicts might be defined and resolved. Byron's famous posturing—his projection of aspects or phases of his personality into independent characters susceptible of objective observation—clearly enacts the same approach to adult ego-formation and self-knowledge. The dimensions alone differ; Byron's postures are synchronically situated actions, whereas his projections represent temporal extensions.

In order to serve as a principle of coherence for *Hours of Idleness* and as a principle of self-construction for Byron, the projected persona must be entirely credible. The reader—and Byron—must focus this vision not as a fantasy figure nor as a hypothetical realization, but as Byron himself thirty or forty years hence: a prophetic prefiguration. This construct, designed to provide answers to questions the poet is yet too ignorant to ask, must assume a verbal form as invulnerable to disconfirmation as epitaph. At the same time, it is required to perform the services of prophecy, a more contingent, individualized discursive mode.

Byron introduces this construct—a persona—in "Airy Hall," a poem that looks very much like epitaph. The poem's subject is epitaph and it is preceded in the volume by "Epitaph on a Friend." In that poem, the speaker disparages "the sculptor's art," "Affliction's semblance," for its insincerity and artificiality. The artistic expression of sorrow is compared unfavorably to sorrow "recorded on [the] heart": marble statues are contrasted with living, weeping "statues." Although "Airy Hall" seems to proceed with this sort of self-deprecation, customary in epitaph and elegy, its stirring finale shows a significant subversion of the convention. "Lengthen'd scroll" and "praise encumber'd stone" are compared *not* to the living, sanctioning emotion, but to the historical reality which is their referential rather than expressive authority. These (funereal) arts are despised for a fundamental defect in their medium, language. This defect has nothing to do with the expressive or affective potential of language, but rather with its ontological subordination and subsequence to historical event. The critique is levelled at discourse itself, not just at literary forms valorized by their expressivity—that is, their genetic authenticity.

The poem's immediate target is honorific discourse, where the disparity between (exalted) things and (ineffectual) words is greatest.[6] A casual reading of "Airy Hall" might suggest that Byron rejects fulsome praise from a position of humility. When the narrator proposes that his epitaph consist of his "name alone," one assumes that he modestly seeks to disclaim individual merit. One might even associate this impulse with Wordsworth's dictum on epitaphs to the effect that these inscriptions be brief, vague, and general—a part of Nature rather than a figure of exception.[7] A closer reading, however, of Byron's refusal of verbal specificity—enumeration of character attributes—reveals that the levelling, generalizing impulse and devices of epitaph are made to serve highly self-aggrandizing ends. Byron's concern with brevity is motivated by his scorn for language, a pale imitation of the spectacular reality that the man himself will create existentially. Moreover, Byron does not propose that his naked name be resorbed by Nature and her ongoing, humanizing operations (Wordsworth's argument for plain denomination in epitaph), but that it figure a unique and terrible challenge. One thinks of such names as Mont Blanc or the Colosseum, names that inspire sensations of awe, isolation, and fear—names of sublimity.

Byron does not, moreover, stop at asserting the ineffability of his greatness. He suggests that he will virtually create himself. His ancestors will be, he declares, "joyful in their choice." Surely, ancestors have no choice in this matter. Byron, a member by birth in their clan, must be restored to that family, regardless of personal accomplishment. The narrator, however, indicates that his noble deeds on earth will earn him admission to an exclusive posthumous club.

What I emphasize by the above remarks is the logical contradiction installed by Byron's wish to believe in (and thus derive security from) the inevitability of his heroic destiny, and conversely, his will to experience his complete individuality and to establish his reputation by a unique and arduous achievement. He would like both to validate the odds and to beat them: to be "chosen" yet self-made. "Airy Hall" is thus pressed into service as prophecy, the depiction of a fate Byron cannot miss, but at the same time, the poem formally leans toward proleptic, encomiastic epitaph.

A second contradiction emerges when we compare the poetic statement to the verbal action. The burden of the discourse is that actions are better than words. The "being more intense" that Byron seeks to construct in "Airy Hall" and to promote through *Hours of Idleness* is the man of action, not letters.[8] In light of this distinction, why, one might ask, is Byron writing poems at all? His awareness of this paradox almost certainly explains the self-deprecating title, *Hours of Idleness*, as well as the gratuitous disclaimer of literary seriousness in the Preface to the first edition. At this point in his life, it appears that Byron would like to realize his greatness without the assistance of art—or, to fashion the more intense self from his own, historical being, conceived by his ancestors and actualized through his own initiative and performance. In "Airy Hall," Byron appears to summon his poetic powers only so as to objectify his intimations of greatness. The implied contradiction at the heart of the volume, and the poem, is that Byron must apparently experience his heroism in advance and verbally in order to produce it existentially.

Aware that he cannot, by an achieved and autonomous poem, develop an invidiously contrastive relationship between language and life, Byron calls "Airy Hall" "A Fragment." The surprising, even perverse allusion to the work's irresolution—the poem displays no lacunae, terminal imperfection, or inconclusiveness of any kind—makes a statement. It says, in effect, that this poem, like all verbal artifacts and actions, is ontologically deficient—a provisional and strictly instrumental construction. It is, the title tells us, an abstract, an outline, a bit of memorial inscription: a thing semi-real, awaiting substantiation by the *real* of history. "Airy Hall" explains its (factitious) imperfection by reference to the fact that Byron's historical actions—actions that will render his "name alone" the consummate symbol of his personality—will perfect the work. Unless we produce some such doctrinal understanding, we will not grasp the work's formal intention nor, therefore, see the work as complete within its own terms.

In that one is hard put to find this adequate inadequacy, however, "Airy Hall" cannot be said to work within its own terms. Simply, the form of the poem fails to impress itself as a reification of the governing idea. Ironically, the explanation of this failure resides in the *relationship* between form and content, and specifically in the distance between these two moments: or, in the conflicting intentions productive of the poem's argument on the one hand, and its expression on the other. Byron's formal model is, as we have seen, epitaph, but under the pressure of his need for an existential idea, his opposition of letters to life, and his repudiation of history as a behavioral determinant, the poem swerves from epitaph to prophecy. "Airy Hall," a hybrid, structurally articulates Byron's desire for existential uniqueness while it refuses the uniqueness of historical moment.

Let me contrast, very schematically, the differing aims and methods of epitaph and prophecy. Each of these discourses sums up a human being, presenting him at a point when his worldly affairs are concluded and the truth of his character stands revealed. Each speaks *sub specie aeternitatis*, and each exposes history as fate. And yet, epitaph and prophecy are very nearly mirror images of one another.

The object of epitaph is twofold—consolation and commemoration—and it achieves these ends in various ways. First, epitaph typically seeks to distract the mourner's thoughts from the irreplaceable individuality of the deceased by emphasizing the commonalty of the hereafter. The mourner is invited to ponder those universal human traits which the deceased shares with all the living and the dead. (Consider in this light Byron's exclusive afterworld, a closed meritocracy.) Hence Wordsworth's caveat, that the epitaph not analyze overmuch. The perfection of epitaph lies in "due proportion of the common or universal feeling of humanity to sensations excited by a distinct and clear conception . . . of the individual, whose death is deplored and whose memory is to be preserved."[9]

Second, epitaphs rarely call attention to the dimension of time and achievement—history—for this is where the deceased's absence is realized. Epitaph turns one's gaze to immortal things, and insofar as it suggests, if only by its form, eternal compensations, it can easily argue the vanity of earthly fame. This last is, of course, a position antithetical to the polemic of "Airy Hall."

Epitaphs—consoling fictions of the most direct and self-conscious kind —are, accordingly, organized in such a way as to give the reader a distinct and intense closural experience. Epitaph seeks to annul the interruptive fact of a death, to help the mourner forget all the things unsaid, the promise unfulfilled, or to replace this painfully disorganized conclusion with the harmony of fictive resolution.

Prophecy too, of course, is a discourse about destiny, or realized existence, but its rhetorical orientation is toward history—destiny's efficient cause. The prophetic author (or vehicle), speaks as one who knows the course of the subject's career from birth or even before birth, to death, or to the fulfillment of the prophecy, which may come long after the subject's death. Prophetic discourse, the domain of which is behavior, does not pose questions of motivation or primary meaning (psychological, metaphysical, or ethical questions). The prophetic voice sketches the living human reality which the subject must become by virtue of the actions he initiates and those that befall him. Prophecy is an entirely individualized form, applicable exclusively to one particular human being—or to one unique juncture in an expanding web of historical meanings, circumstances, traces, and tendencies. Prophecies construct a real and unique figure before the fact, while epitaphs fabricate a fictive and very generalized character after the fact. Prophecies are not consoling fictions but, by design, irritatingly enigmatic predictions. The prophetic aim is not to naturalize the nonsense of death, but to expose the nonsense of life as lived by men in the middest. Prophecy, unlike epitaph, does not deduce causality from sequence; its vision is essentially catastrophic and it focuses achieved states, not processual dynamics.

The formal intention of "Airy Hall," expressed by its placement in the volume, its implementation of familiar epitaphic devices and sentiment ("words cannot express . . ."), is that of epitaph. The very title, "A Fragment," suggests the tombstone inscription, or the condition of the partially eroded text. By representing "Airy Hall" as epitaph, Byron hopes to emphasize the causality binding his achievement to his virtues, and his virtues to his fiercely individual character—one that owes nothing to genealogy or fate and that is glorified or demeaned by its actions alone.

The poem's argument and method, however, as well as its function within *Hours of Idleness*, are best described in terms of prophecy—a self-fulfilling prophecy that would serve Byron as a kind of ideal *niveau*. The prophetic intention signifies Byron's need to confirm his historical uniqueness and to ensure, as it were, the inevitability and immortality of this character. The prophetic strain of the poem develops the meanness of authorship as compared to unmediated existential enterprise.

Prophetic discourse is typically complete and sufficient; its appearance of irresolution is the product of compression and ellipsis, as in epigram. The meaning is all there before us, it need only be unpacked. Prophecy, a cryptic rather than fragmentary form, delivers its expanded meaning in the fullness of time. At that preordained point, its perfect propriety, closure, and inclusiveness—qualities it possessed all along but imperceptibly—become manifest.

Due to the dominant and unacknowledged impulse toward prophecy, "Airy Hall" reads like a complete though condensed utterance. The achieved effect, then, contradicts the work's title. "Airy Hall" *is* a fragment, but its irresolution is not, as Byron would have it seem, the product of a perfectly self-expressive thought. The work's authentic limitation has nothing to do with imitative form, nor is it the sign of doctrinal sincerity. Quite the contrary, it arises from the incompatibility of the poem's diverse meanings.

Byron's repression of the originating conditions of his work gives rise to two ironies. First, the prophetic interest is, we recall, essentially instrumental in the poem and volume. By indulging this interest, Byron seeks to construct a personalized role model, immanent and structurally serviceable throughout his life. Yet the hallmark of prophecy (and one of its secondary attractions for Byron) is that its fulfillment is inevitable. No attempt to avert or to hasten the prophesied end can affect its eventuation in its own time. Byron's project—self-production upon a prophetic template—is a contradiction in terms.

Second, by implying the interdetermination of form and content, "Airy Hall" solicits an organicist, ahistorical mode of reception. The poem, however, develops a critique of art with reference to the ideal of real history, which is to say, it undermines its own formal premise. We perhaps find it difficult to see this contradiction because the historical truth that Byron opposes to the illusions of art is itself a highly aestheticized and historically determined artifact. Byron represents the stage of history as a fabulously responsive and equitable dimension, where actions express truth of character, where character creates itself, and where fame is the inevitable and just recognition of character. These relations (character and action, action and social reaction) have, in the poem, the appearance of natural law or absolute truth.

Ironically, the imperfection of "Airy Hall" *does* reflect its argument; that is, it betrays the poem's conceptual confusion and marks the incongruity of its formal and substantive intentions and effects. Because the form of "Airy Hall" represents an attempted correction and camouflage of content rather than its incarnation, one would have to judge the poem a failure within its own terms, those of the deliberate fragment. We hardly notice its title, and if we do, we read "fragment" as if it meant "short poem."

One does not, of course, lose very much in the failure of "Airy Hall." It is an easy concession to make; had Byron critically focussed the issues that occupy "Airy Hall," we might not have had *Childe Harold's Pilgrimage* or *Don Juan*. In those poems, Byron transvalues—because he cannot untangle—the end-stopped dialectic of "Airy Hall." In the later poems, Byron does not so much identify words as historical actions in their own right (one way of closing the poet-hero, letters-actions debate) as he attributes to historical events the same relational and provisional meaning he had formerly restricted to verbal events. The maneuver—a reductive strategy —works, where the transcendental approach of "Airy Hall" does not. Byron's mature concept of heroism is, among other things, a concept of survival—the business of making do by continual and limited acts of creative adaptation to circumstance, performed in the absence of any ideal, any principle of conclusion or perfection. With this concept, Byron embraces the historical conditions whose coercive *and* creative influence he denies in "Airy Hall." He learns to value these conditions for the range of prospects they afford, each one yielding some particular social and psychic truth. In giving up his desire to see life whole—as something that can be "'gained' or 'concluded' or fulfilled"—Byron comes to appreciate those "immediate and partial acts of apprehension" that are the human allowance and that may ultimately produce a shrewd, a working knowledge of things.[10]

Byron's transvaluation—really, an inversion—of the conflict that generates "Airy Hall" produces a philosophy of practical relativism: anything goes so long as it goes. In *Don Juan* as in "The Giaour," Byron empties history of its determinacy, its burden of absolute meanings. In his comic epic, Byron refuses to look behind effects, to convert circumstance into cause, to authorize his text. He will not be a prophet, forward- or backward-looking. We must see, though, that the discontinuities which score *Don Juan* betray the vital conflict we examined in "Airy Hall": Byron's desire to be historically effective and to be historically undetermined and unique. Or, as the categorial distinctions sketched in "Airy Hall" suggest, the textual breaks in *Don Juan* mark the incompatibility of epitaph with prophecy, form with content. The triumph of *Don Juan* is its acceptance—indeed, its thematizing—of this conflict, one that is characterized in the poem as a fact of life, to be repeatedly faced and faced down.

CHAPTER EIGHT

THE DELIBERATE FRAGMENT

The Posthumous Fragments of Margaret Nicholson

Shelley's canon contains more fragment poems than that of any other Romantic poet. Many of these were collected by Mary Shelley in her 1824 and 1839 editions and, of course, more have come to light since then. Shelley's more substantial fragments (many of the posthumous fragments are as short as two lines) are typically deliberate fragments, poems that thematize the conditions that apparently precipitated their formal ruptures. While one could profitably submit to formal inquiry Shelley's posthumously published fragments, those few pieces Shelley himself published or sought to publish are the more lucrative subjects for this particular critique, involving, as they do, questions of intention. The group of poems to which I refer includes *The Posthumous Fragments of Margaret Nicholson*, 1810; "The Daemon of the World," 1816 (two-canto extrapolation from *Queen Mab*, published in the *Alastor* volume); "Julian and Maddalo," 1819; and "A Vision of the Sea," 1820.

I address in this chapter the first and third works; since these are thematically linked, they allow for a particularly thorough exploration of structure-thought negotiations. Both *Posthumous Fragments* and "Julian and Maddalo" are in the way of the *sermo pedestris*; both feature a victim of political tyranny and of unrequited love. Both are conversations, of a sort, curiously complicated by dramatic ambiguities; both are about love, madness, and poetry—topics investigated for their insights into the imbrications of psyche and politics.

In that the deliberate fragment foregrounds thematically its formal determinants (the necessity governing its expressive mode), it offers itself as a complete and realized form. This necessity may be represented as an intrinsic imperative or it may assume the character of an extrinsic causality. This is to say that the deliberate fragment may relate its discontinuities to the condition of the author's or persona's mind (his sense of reality), or its imperfections may be derived from particular historical conditions (reality itself). With Shelley, of course, much of whose poetry studies the recipro-cally reflective fields of psyche and culture, this distinction must be used discreetly. It is precisely Shelley's subtle and dialectical understanding of the individual mind within its universe of forms (of thought) that gives his deliberate fragments such interest.

In *Posthumous Fragments* and "Julian and Maddalo," Shelley investigates individual response to an existence the rule of which is inconstancy, im-perfection, and isolation. Both works seek to ascertain the scope of indi-vidual energy in modern society; specifically, they frame questions about political efficacy, personal fulfillment, and historical determinism.

Margaret Nicholson, Shelley's pseudonymous persona, had an authen-tic and notorious historical referent. In 1786, Nicholson tried to assas-sinate George III. The effort failed, of course, and Nicholson was com-mitted to Bedlam for life. In 1810, the year Shelley wrote her poetic (auto)biography, Nicholson was still alive, and, according to Hogg, her attempt on the King's life was still "fresh in the recollection of every one."[1] The only significant historical documentation of the affair is a pamphlet entitled *Authentic Memoirs of the Life of Margaret Nicholson*, published anonymously in 1786. Shelley's volume shows him to have been conver-sant with some of the facts of Nicholson's life as recorded in this pam-phlet, but these facts are neither so specific nor surprising as to have precluded his invention of the material based on sketchy, oral information. One cannot tell to what extent Shelley imagined what he knew.[2]

Posthumous Fragments is a work in the tradition of Southey's *The Re-mains of Henry Kirke White*, 1807, and Moore's *Poetical Works of the Late Thomas Little, Esq.*, 1801. The formal intention of these works is to con-struct a literary persona out of real or fictitious literary remains. (Little was, of course, Moore's "diminished" mask.) By and large, the poetry in both these volumes is subordinated to character delineation. The editors select and present their material according to some clearly defined princi-ple, reflecting the editor's assessment of the salient and most instructive feature of the poet's life and work. Southey and Moore introduce this feature in the Prefaces to their editions. Rather than print the best (the most finished, accomplished, or ambitious) of the work left behind, the editors present those poems which most clearly exemplify what they judge to be the ruling principle, the "essentials," of the poet's life and canon. The reader is encouraged to plot the development of a single quality in the verse and a single characteristic in the man, rather than look for technical improvement or refinement of sensibility. The chief rhetorical object of these psychologically motivated works is to engage the reader's sympathy for the real or invented poet. These volumes are designed as exercises in reader-writer identification.

According to the authentic account, Nicholson's attack on the King was not a lunatic act. Fitzvictor (the pseudonymous editor of Nicholson's remains, and a code name for "Shelley") seems of the same mind, for he places the composition of the poems which he presents in the interval between Nicholson's assault on the King and her confinement for insanity. It would appear that the poetry dates from the period in which she was undergoing trial. By this fiction, the volume represents Nicholson's unofficial apology, as it were. (The real Nicholson refrained from pleading her case.) The author of Nicholson's authentic memoir—a highly unsympathetic journalist—attributes to her only one symptom of depravity: she talked to herself. This quirk aside, she is portrayed as a sober and diligent, although sullen, young woman. Shelley develops this symptom into the formal principle of his volume; each of the poems enacts or describes an experience in which the author, Nicholson, strains to hear and interpret an indistinct voice or sound. Since there are no agents represented in the volume *but* the author, the source of these voices must be, if not supernatural, the poet herself.

The poetry which Shelley writes in Nicholson's name seeks to represent critically the disjunctiveness and abortiveness that characterized her historical career. Shelley shows his heroine to have been driven to madness—literally, character disintegration—by the miscarriage of those hopes and the disconfirmation of those ideals which had served as the "essentials" of her personality. Although only two of the six poems in the volume are entitled "Fragment," the volume title designates the imperfection of what appear to be complete poems. Each bears the formal mark of its origin (an unraveling psyche) and of its theme (social deterioration), and some attempt is made to explore the interaction of these dimensions. Just as Southey presents Kirke White's fragments (those "immature buds and blossoms") by way of "discover[ing] evident proof what he would have been"[3] had he reached maturity, Shelley projects through Nicholson's fragments a vision of *her* achieved character—what she would have been had historical conditions been different. The best way to describe this character is by reference to Shelley's own categories. Had Nicholson's ordering faculties not been deranged by the particular impacts of her moment, she would have been a poet in Shelley's "restricted" (that is, literary) sense. Moreover, her social values and political interests identify her as already a poet in the general sense. The reader is meant to construe the poems *through* their discontinuities and with attention to the internal and external factors responsible for them. One is urged to read the poems with reference to each other, and the volume as a whole should "be considered as making up [her] history."[4] The form, argument, and arrangement of the poems, as well as the editor's preface, explain local instances of irresolution as reflections of Nicholson's perceived reality: a ruined world. However, when the volume is read as a poetic autobiography, each poem an episode in the persona's career, the fragments should coalesce into an integrated, continuous, and resolved work, one that achieves its (Shelley's) intention. Assembled, the fragments should represent imaginatively (which is to say, syncretically) a disintegrating mind *and* social system, developed from a position within that mind and that system. Intertextual continuity is produced largely by the recurrence of certain themes, images, and phrases; the transitions obey an associational logic and the overall effect is, not to put too fine an edge on it, melodramatic.

The recurrent elements—effectively, leitmotifs—organized as I have described, construct a kind of composite poem. The sequence as a whole describes a particular project: the production of an organized, integrated, resolved utterance. The first few poems achieve a modest success in this direction. Although the tensions that motivate the utterance are not resolved, an equilibrium is reached, and it is this that suspends the discourse in a reasonably satisfying manner. As the sequence unfolds, however, the speaker's enabling critical distance diminishes; her expression becomes increasingly disjunctive and terminally unresolved. The moment of disintegration becomes, as it were, the climax of the later poems and the source of their meaning. To cooperate with Shelley's intention, one must read off from Nicholson's fragments her ruling principle, and at the same time conjecture an order of historical actuality that consistently interrupts imaginative enterprise. The autobiographical fiction, an aid to sympathy, constructs for the reader, out of Nicholson's experience, subjective but nonetheless shared or general knowledge.

Ironically, Shelley's fiction succeeds too well. In that it ends by undermining the reader's critical purchase, it interferes with Shelley's other and primary aim: to expose from a radically antithetical position, his own, the system that produced *a* Margaret Nicholson. The success of this project requires the reader's willingness to trace Nicholson's fragmented psyche and poetry to a distinctively atomized, competitive, and cruelly irrational social dimension. Shelley's concern, however, with sympathetic or, loosely, phenomenological knowledge, leads us in just the opposite direction, toward a privatized, psychic thematization of the discursive miscarriages.

Shelley further reduces the critical option by featuring among the poems (episodes of his heroine's life) a conventional rejection scene which, for want of other biographical data, takes on a pivotal function. The inclusion, the placement, and the voice of this poem all suggest that Nicholson's character disorders and her consequently disjunctive utterance derive from a commonplace erotic disappointment. This is, of course, a suggestion entirely at odds with Shelley's political interests. That is to say, the volume does not realize its formal intention.

Oddly enough, Hogg's prosaic critique of the volume—its incongruous juxtaposition of love and revolution in the same group of poems—was astute, although for reasons other than those he cited. The skewed angle of attack, however, engendering a sort of secondary, meta-fragmentation in the volume, is extremely telling in its own right. Shelley's imagination of the fact of Margaret Nicholson reveals, by its distortions, his own historical situation. With no objective sanction, Shelley transforms a would-be political assassin into a despairing poet and a lovesick woman. Shelley's Nicholson, neither a criminal nor an ideologue, is a *poete maudite*; her madness is the sign of her sensitivity, and both evince her innate moral authority.

To valorize Nicholson's insanity by reference to her psychic refinement is, of course, to efface the mimetic function to which Shelley dedicates the discursive imperfections of the volume. Fitzvictor initially represents Nicholson's madness and its verbal insignia (fragments) as political reactions to political conditions; he ends by interpreting Nicholson's utterance as a psychic extension of these conditions, and thus completely coopted. Further, despite the polemical edge of the preface and the early poems, Shelley ultimately traces both psychic and social disorders to the unfathomable agencies of Nature.

The poems are arranged in such a way as to exhibit a clearly demarcated progression from love to madness, two states of being—specifically, of perception—revealed as polar opposites by the end of the sequence. The reader plots this evolution (a devolution) by observing the correlation of psychic states with degrees of poetic resolution; as character disintegrates, so does the poetry. Resolution signifies in this discourse a clean separation of poem from nonpoem, or representation from actuality, and we recognize this achievement in those poems that answer the questions they raise or interpret their own discourse. Such poems define by their firm margins serene, intertextual silences. As the volume proceeds, the author loses her ability to distinguish her state of mind from the extrinsic universe; the voices she projects and those of independent origin become as a monologic discourse to her. In the first two poems, for example, the authorial voice seems consciously to structure itself dialogically. That is to say, the poet knows she is poeticizing and that the world she constructs is a reflection of the real from a certain point of view. The voice that concludes the sequence, however, is deeply compromised by all that it would, and cannot, "behold and order." We hear, at the end, an unimagined expression of psychic and social chaos, the utterance of one so possessed by her culture she cannot conceive it. This is to say, Shelley represents the individual and the body politic as "connate," coextensive, and coterminous; Nicholson's career signifies and advances the progress of a corrupt social system.

Margaret Nicholson is not, of course, Shelley's persona; indeed, Fitzvictor is the inscription of this difference. By reference to him, we identify Nicholson as the sufferer who describes her own cure but cannot effect it. The narrative teaches that individuals within a given social context cannot change that context by direct action of any kind whatsoever, informed as that action must be by historically conditioned knowledge, motive, and form. One must endure one's epoch and take solace in the faith that the permanent and prolific principles of Nature, time, and the human mind will eventually reform all bad creeds and refine away error. By this logic, Nicholson can only become an effective political influence when she is transformed by Shelley into a type, universal and abstract. The idealizing thrust of the volume finds in Shelley's historical position—specifically, the *differential* between his own and Nicholson's epochal characters—the redemption of her ineffectuality. Shelley, the belated historian, represents "the essentials" of Nicholson's experience, or the psychic and sociological meaning of her history. Through Fitzvictor, Shelley tries to *represent* the paradox that the sequence shapes, and that our sympathy dismantles.

Let me briefly describe the structure of ideas developed in the volume and its sequence of forms, drawing examples from various poems.

My rapt soul dwelt upon the ties that bind
The mazy volume of commingling things
When fell and wild misrule to man stern sorrow brings.

These lines from "Fragment . . . ," the second poem in the volume, pose the question that thematically governs the entire sequence: what happens to individuals when the social sympathies are strained to the point of extinction, and how is the internal principle of harmony, a universal inheritance, affected? My language here and above echoes and incorporates phrases from Shelley's *Defence*. While one cannot in good conscience gloss one work with another written more than a decade later, it makes sense to assume that some of the themes and responses that emerge as canonically typical will be most prominent, because crudely developed, in the juvenile work.

The first poem, left untitled by Shelley but identified by subsequent editors as "War," takes up the question of social disintegration most explicitly. The speaker analyzes the institution of monarchy by formulating its effects upon the individuals who recognize its legitimacy. She organizes her critique with reference to the various classes of primary relationships that structure any social system. According to and in the language of the poem's central conceit, social infirmity, the consequence of war—tyranny's child—maims the world's body. In the poem, earth bleeds. Agriculture, represented as reflecting a healthy social organization, is displaced by the business of war, which undoes the bond between culture and Nature. This fission engenders a chain reaction, ending in the rupture of all those bonds that constitute human society. By dramatizing in a highly schematic way the relations between individuals, between individuals and their rulers, between the sexes, and between the different aspects and faculties of the human mind, the narrator represents the condition of society, state, eros, and psyche in a corrupt world.

Nicholson characterizes this state of affairs as a hell on earth, and the metaphor is not casual. The poet invokes by it a range of miseries (isolation, disunity, discord, and lovelessness), all of them states of discontinuity and fragmentation, and all of them the result of a primary alienation. The dissolution of those "ties that bind" the healthy human society generates in the poem a succession of cries and groans (orphan's sigh, widow's moan, war shrieks, dying hero's plaint). This cacophony of human misery melds into a single voice, one that levels an impassioned and, as it were, transpersonal accusation against monarchs. The narrator makes it clear, however, that this corporate utterance with its implied consolidation of interests and identities, cannot emerge in the absence of a certain consensus perception: here, a transcendent belief. By the idea, or the ideation of God, the sufferers maintain the *categories* of human virtue and happiness ("peace, innocence, and love") until such time as these abstractions might be actualized. Further, faith in a God who responds to the human voice figures in the poem as a prerequisite for social communion. Without this supreme fiction—the collective postulate of an ultimate communicative circuit—the lesser fictions that enable ordinary discourse, or fictions of consensus, decay, and so goes the social fabric. Finally, the lucidity evinced by the narrator associates her belief in a God who acts as well as listens with a politically effective expressivity. The poet's firm persuasion—a sort of therapeutic dissociation from a chaotic immediacy—enables critical thought and discourse.

Shelley's atheism would seem to cast Margaret Nicholson's belief in ironic perspective, were we to forget that Nicholson is Shelley's editorially mediated persona, not his mouthpiece. Moreover, Shelley's atheism is not really inconsistent with the poem's doctrine, for while belief is treated here as a positive and practical orientation, it is also conceived at a very abstract level. It is not faith in a Christian God—or, indeed, any particularized divinity—that focuses and invigorates the disparate invectives in the poem. What is defined by the verse is the sheer *fact* of a faith that transcends individual differences, facilitating collective, synergistic experience and expression. This position does not, of course, contradict Shelley's early or late social thought.

In the opening poem, the narrator distinguishes spiritual from phenomenal life, but she regards the dimensions as complementary and continuous. She hears God's anger and Nature's sympathy in the voices of human outrage and despair. Her vision of these correspondences and continuities establishes a ground of hope, which in turn generates indignation (lines 23–62). Whether or not kings are ultimately or even immediately responsible for the unhappy state of things is not the salient question in the poem or volume. The political issues are developed through the psychic drama, one that plots the narrator's decreasing ability to externalize her misery. "War" establishes for the reader the author-narrator's psychic norm (in the volume, her apogee); the successive revelations that make up Margaret Nicholson's inner history are to be understood with reference to this norm.

In "War," as in all the poems, the narrator's poetical expertise objectifies her mental condition. The poem, a sequence of identifications and projections, enacts on a discursive plane the narrator's cognitive distinction of self from other, and internal from external dimensions, as well as her power to surmount imaginatively those differences. The poem, treated as a record of consciousness, represents a sane—that is to say, critically controlled—response to an insane environment, and in so doing, it establishes for the volume a normative model of individual-social interaction.

Through its rhetorical device and discursive structure, "War" exemplifies the verbal ideal that is at once consequence and sign of healthy interaction between the individual and the social sphere. Questions are asked, pronouncements are made, and demands are leveled with a confidence that testifies to a vital, stable relationship between speaker (poet) and audience. Every utterance in the poem is somehow *engaged*. Words have issue; meanings are materialized in these dramatized verbal transactions.

One probably notices these expository features only because they are so curiously absent from the following poems. As the narrator's immediate griefs become more oppressive, contracting her freedom of thought, her distinction of psychic from social fact breaks down. Intellect and imagination begin to part company, and without reason's ballast, imagination wanders dangerously. The sympathy that the narrator had attributed to God and Nature is withdrawn, and the ensuing sense of isolation provokes the narrator's more extreme confusion of the real with the fantastic (see "Epithalamium"). In the third poem, Nicholson accepts the implications of her despair about historical redemption; she consents to her advancing madness, and the sign of this consent is her involuntary, which is to say, uncritical identification with all she had contemned. In viewing herself as a participant in the system, she forfeits her antithetical vantage *as well as* her power to sympathize. Again, the psychic degeneration is verbally plotted; the poem ends with an unfocused, unimpassioned imprecation—a protest made from a position of forced collaboration and with no expectation of response.

"Fragment," the fourth poem, marks the narrator's descent into hell. The psychic landscape she describes is a death-in-life. Unequal to the energies of indignation and unable to externalize her suffering, she succumbs to "blank horror." Like Beatrice Cenci, Nicholson passively reflects the evils of an evil system, so thoroughly has that system claimed her. She represents herself as an elemental force within the anarchic world she inhabits (the chaos symbolized by a hellish meteor storm); hers is a voice that, in echoing back the "frightening yell," cannot help but reinforce it.

She hears an answering strain that she characterizes as "maniac"—the voice of her double ("like he was to me"). The reader easily identifies this voice as the narrator's own projection; the author, we observe, responds as if to external speech.

The dialogue that develops this poem sketches a kind of animated pathology. The "characters" in the exchange are body (male: the "wanderer") and soul (female: she who lingers). The conceit that organizes the poem is thus a travesty of the marriage conceit that structures "Epithalamium." The fruit of this demonic union is a mad shriek, expression of a disorganized, indeterminate sense of horror.

The final poem in the volume, "Melody to a Scene of Former Times," delivers the nightmare predicted in the fifth poem, "The Spectral Horseman," and prefigured in the marriage motif of "Epithalamium" and "Fragment." The narrator's ultimate nightmare—a "dream" of "Two years of speechless bliss"—is a cruel irony. "Dream," of course, must mean delusion (and, one wonders, does "speechless" mordantly enforce this meaning?), as well as memory. The experience that prompted this dream was apparently a relationship characterized by love and trust. The nightmarish quality of the dream is, we see at once, the fact that it is *only* a dream and, moreover, a dream of something that never truly was and that can never again be dreamed. *Posthumous Fragments* crystallizes as a logical structure with this last poem. Here, Shelley identifies "the tie that binds"—the principle that maintains psychic and social integration—as erotic love. This "tie"—that of singular man to singular woman—broken, entropy finds no resistance and the whole structure of human values and achievement collapses.

The narrator's nightmare reminiscence produces one final statement, an utterance that gathers up the diverse voices heard throughout the volume: widow's moan, orphan's sigh, Benshie's shriek, and Nature's howl. The chorus does not accuse, "It moans for pleasures that are past, / It moans for days that are gone by"; it regrets the lost paradise and explains the expulsion by a human defect, the inability to sustain love. Religion and politics fall away in this last poem, culmination of the logic played out in the preceding works. "Melody" is, of course, a song, and but for the last three lines, it is a traditional plaint on the theme of constancy. By ending on this note, Shelley reduces the social and political narrative inscribed in the history of Margaret Nicholson (and broached in the first two poems), to a romantic betrayal. Nicholson's generous, fierce humanitarianism dwindles into a meditation on a private love and betrayal. What begins as a vision of universals and a trenchant critique of history's defection from that ideal concludes with a sentimental lament.

Posthumous Fragments is a reactionary work in effect if not by intention, for it expresses through its formal development not just the futility of political responsiveness but the malignant effects of such engagement on the individual. Margaret Nicholson's character as a poet, moreover, implies that the political arena holds special dangers for the artist, one who must keep his eye on higher things, his vision intact and uncontaminated by historical particulars.

In conceiving the *Posthumous Fragments*, Shelley sought, I believe, to interpret a private and inner history by way of general historical analysis. On a more practical level, he sought to express certain radical ideas he was as yet too insecure to publish under his own name. A knowledge of Shelley's later verse and prose suggests that Nicholson's romantic disappointment be read as the *consequence* of a social malaise, and that her poetic failures reflect the corruptions peculiar to her historical moment. We must remember, though, that "Melody," by virtue of its situation in the volume and its thematic relationship to the foregoing poems, figures as the *explanation* of Nicholson's poetical and psychic fragmentation. The betrayal, generalized, is a *cause*, not a symptom, of that social malaise. The poem goes so far as to hint that Nicholson's radical humanitarianism is a reflex displacement of her private anguish. In this suggestion, Shelley appears to give credence to Nicholson's official biographer, who implies that Nicholson's frequent and unacknowledged petitions to the King concerned a private affair with the two noblemen who later visited her in prison. The King's failure to notice these petitions allegedly drove Nicholson to her desperate act.

By interpreting the real Margaret Nicholson's action, and the fictive Nicholson's convictions, as reactions to a private betrayal and expressions of its psychic effects, Shelley neutralizes the radical gesture he hoped to make in this early volume. *Posthumous Fragments* dramatizes the futility of formulating antithetical ideologies; all such impulses are shown to be grounded in private life and psyche, which cannot but participate in the dominant, institutionalized ideology. The maverick either becomes the tyrant or is destroyed by him. Shelley's mature meditations on historical dialectic—the conceptual basis for his vision of spiraling historical evolution—show us the means whereby he sustains his radicalism. The dialectic requires the *continual* formulation of antithetical positions, formulations invaluable in themselves and not to be estimated by their immediate or local success, nor by their consequences for the persons who develop them. This is a severe and, of course, individually rigorous vision of historical progress. It is, however, a vision that accommodates human limitation far more generously than Shelley's earlier, more romantic idea.

Had Shelley composed *Posthumous Fragments* at a later time, he might not have represented the poetry of his fictive author as "fragments and isolated portions," but rather as "episodes to that great poem, which all poets, like the co-operating thoughts of one great mind, have built up since the beginning of the world." Rather than compare Nicholson's lamentably fragmented discourse to some notional verbal/psychic integration, Shelley would have argued the imperfection of all speech in time, since all poems, like all poets, "are in one sense the creators and in another the creations of their age" and "from this subjection the loftiest do not escape."

CHAPTER NINE

THE DELIBERATE FRAGMENT
"Julian and Maddalo"

Shelley locates Julian and Maddalo—intellectual antagonists and code names for Shelley and Byron—within a drama where the agents are both human and elemental. The opening conversation—one that establishes Julian and Maddalo as opposing perspectives on sublunary life—takes place during a ride along the Lido. Both characters remark with relish the bleakness of the landscape; the narrator (neither Julian nor Maddalo) extends their perception into a more profound and far-reaching observation. He describes life forms native to that sandy isthmus in so consistent and suggestive a fashion as to define the radical instability—literally, the rootlessness—of existence.

> I rode one evening with Count Maddalo
> Upon the bank of land which breaks the flow
> Of Adria toward Venice:—a bare strand
> Of hillocks, heaped from ever-shifting sand,
> Matted with thistles and amphibious weeds,
> Such as from earth's embrace the salt ooze breeds,
> Is this;—an uninhabitable sea-side
> Which the lone fisher, when his nets are dried,
> Abandons; and no other object breaks
> The waste, but one dwarf tree and some few stakes
> Broken and unrepaired, and the tide makes
> A narrow space of level sand thereon,—
> Where 'twas our wont to ride while day went down.[1]

All is movement—random, unsynchronized, purposeless, and externally induced.

As I noted, Julian and Maddalo are defined by their dialogue as spokesmen for antithetical philosophical positions. Julian proclaims his humanitarian—atheistical and idealistic—character, whereas Maddalo represents himself as a cynical, worldly realist whose religion is to him a kind of insurance against the mysterious agencies of fate and the real hazards and miseries of quotidian life. Their conversation eddies around several related topics. Do philosophical idealism and political meliorism lead to madness or prevent it? Can men tolerate a reality unmediated by visionary hopes; do such hopes only ultimately emphasize the meanness of existence and the ineffectuality of individual and collective will? And, even if the idealist is so resolute as to maintain his vision in the face of persistent disconfirmation, does this higher commitment remove him from the humanizing, corrective influences provided by social intercourse, the sympathy of "the kind"? Does he isolate himself in a perilously subjective and hermetic domain and thereby become his culture's other, its lunatic? These questions, put to the test in "Julian and Maddalo," are precisely the questions raised but not met by *Posthumous Fragments*. Does Margaret Nicholson go mad from "a want of that true theory . . . / Which seeks a 'soul of goodness' in things ill," or does her "theory"—her social, political, and erotic idealism—undo her?

The question is not decided in "Julian and Maddalo"; it is posed as a problem that is formally and dramatically worked, but that is not finally solved by the poem's action or argument. The nature of the poem's inconclusiveness, however, and the situational and psychic alterations the characters undergo, shape the reader's assessment of the poem's intellectual material. Neither Julian nor Maddalo wins the debate according to the conventions of such contests, but the subsequent events of their lives expose the deficiency of Julian's position more pointedly than that of Maddalo. (Or, if Julian and Maddalo make up a composite persona, the deficiency can be said to reside in the idealist rather than the realist and skeptical tendency.)

Maddalo takes Julian to an asylum so that he may observe a man who has experienced reversals so severe as to have unhinged his reason. Maddalo attributes the man's psychic disorders less to the gravity of his losses than to his inordinate vulnerability, a condition that Maddalo traces to the man's inflated expectations about political, social, and sexual matters. In exposing Julian to this pitiful wreck—an object lesson—Maddalo hopes to persuade his friend of the dangers inherent in his own generous naïveté.

Julian and Maddalo enter the madhouse, and, amid "fierce yells and howlings and lamentings keen / . . . / Moans, shrieks, and curses and blaspheming prayers," they catch "fragments of most touching melody." Maddalo's Maniac is, of course, the singer. By this dramatic device, his poetical talents ("harmonies") are suggested at the outset, and thus is the Maniac (and his literary model, Tasso) installed in the poem as a projection of tendencies latent in both protagonists.

The Maniac relates his history—not *to* Julian and Maddalo but in their presence. The friends attend "the unconnected exclamations of his agony" (Preface). It appears that this once "cultivated and amiable" gentleman is obsessed with the loss of a woman he had loved and who, he believed, had loved him. Before this affliction that broke his heart and, apparently, his mind, the man had been unusually responsive to the sorrows of other men. Like Julian (and Margaret Nicholson), he "seemed hurt / . . . / To hear but of the oppression of the strong, / Of those absurd deceits . . . / . . . which carry through / The excellent impostors of this earth / When they outface detection." The narrator allows the reader to infer the connection between the Maniac's selfless, feeling egalitarianism and his inability to sustain the particular injury—inconstancy—inflicted upon him.

The Maniac's narration—that is, its obsessive reflexivity—implies a second factor in the etiology or advance of his disease: namely, his withdrawal from society and his refusal to articulate his grief. He preserves an "incommunicable woe" for fear, he says, of imposing his distress upon others. The more plausible explanation, however, would introduce the Maniac's fear of a less than empathic response. Along these lines, we might note the significance of the Maniac's detachment both from his two visitors and from the circumstances of the moment. His discourse consists of a conversation with two imaginary partners; thus, even in his apparently object-related, dialogic speech, he remains locked within a mental universe all his own.

The Maniac's recriminations conform to the general pattern established by his discourse and demeanor. His anger, almost exclusively reflexive, underlines a solipsism so extreme as to preclude even the small relief of an extrinsic object, an enemy. By the same logic, of course, the reader is denied a critical object. The Maniac's narcissistic narration is such that the figure of the (potentially) culpable woman cannot take shape for us. Simply, we know too little of the man's beloved to blame her for his sorry state.

Julian and Maddalo leave the asylum for their own "Paradise of exiles." The phrase drives home the ironic parallel between the Maniac and his visitors. The encounter has moved and chastened the two friends. They are particularly impressed with "the wild language of [the Maniac's] grief . . . / Such as in measure were called poetry."

The emphasis in that statement—an important one—does not, I believe, fall on the qualification, "in measure," or not on the conventional meaning of that phrase. For if we read the lines as Julian's and Maddalo's denial of the essential poetical properties of the Maniac's discourse (and "measure" is certainly essential to Shelley's conception of poetry in both the restricted and general sense), then what are we to do with their comment on the height of his language (line 541), with their observation of the effect of his harmonies upon a uniquely challenging audience (lines 226–30), and with Maddalo's characterization of poets as a race of wounded and indignant men?

The text itself undoes this interpretive knot. The narrator notes that the Maniac's speech at a certain point becomes ". . . lost in grief, and then his words came each / Unmodulated, cold, expressionless; / But that from one jarred accent you might guess / It was despair made them so uniform." The unmeasure and dissonance of the Maniac's expression are located in his delivery rather than in the discourse proper. His despair flattens his speech, unmodulates it, thereby concealing the impassioned order of his vision. Julian and Maddalo, poets themselves, are able to distinguish the monotony of the delivery from the order and elevation of the discourse itself: "such as in measure *were called* poetry" (my emphasis).

The point is less trivial than it seems, for it brings out the kinship between the Maniac and his visitors, and between their verbal activities. Further, by incorporating elements of the Tasso myth into his characterization of the Maniac, Shelley reinforces the already established narrative association of poetry with madness. Margaret Nicholson's poetry—a critique—occurs in the intervals between her bouts of madness, or at least represents the most lucid of her progressively clouded visions. Insofar as Nicholson is a poet—one who orders the chaos of experience—thus far is she from being insane. The deterioration of her ordering faculty (evidenced by the increasing disjunctiveness and discord of her verse) signifies the advance of her madness. In the Maniac, poetry and madness share the same origin, the same domain, and the same growth curve. The ratio is direct.

Maddalo describes the race of poets as "wretched men / . . . cradled into poetry by wrong, / They learn in suffering what they teach in song." With this observation, a judgment on both men, the conversation between Julian and Maddalo ceases. The debate is left unresolved, its academic and shallow character revealed to the friends through their encounter with the Maniac. The enormity of his anguish embarrasses them. Julian lamely rationalizes his decision to quit Venice and to abandon the Maniac, "one whom . . . [he] would call / More willingly [his] friend." The narrator does not account for Maddalo until he reports Julian's return to Venice, twenty years later. It is then that we learn of Maddalo's flight to the mountains of Armenia. The narrative juxtapositions of statement, silence, and event create the impression that the encounter with the Maniac exposes to both men the limits of their philosophy: not only the sterility of their initial premises of debate but the arrogance of their presuming thus to settle the awful mysteries of human response. The derailment of the original dialogue, however, establishes a new course and destination for the poem. The narrative itself, as opposed to the characters, begins to pose the questions. Further, whereas the original issue had concerned self-preservation—how might the individual accommodate intellectually and behaviorally the cruel illogic of existence—the new argument develops as a social question. Through the ironies implied by the actions of Julian and Maddalo subsequent to their Venetian interlude, the poem puts as *its* question, how can the individual resist reflecting the disorder (injustice, corruption, imperfection) of existence? Or, how does one refuse to cooperate with—effectively, perpetuate and exacerbate—the evils of one's moment or its knowledges? To pose this question by way of the narrative logic of Shelley's poem is to ask, how can a man be a poet—of necessity, sufficiently detached from his historical situation to observe and organize its chaos—and yet remain a human being, sympathetically responsive to the effects of this chaos on his fellow men? This is as good as asking, how might a man make himself Christ?

The Maniac, abandoned by his lover, in turn forsakes his friends and thus betrays his social obligation; he is as compromised by the evil originally imposed upon him as is Beatrice Cenci possessed by her exploitation. Both characters fail to imagine a response that is more than and different from a reflex of their own brutalization. Neither appreciates his power to order his suffering and thereby to terminate a cycle of exploitation. Julian, by a kind of chain reaction, responds to the Maniac's flight from social commitment by imitating it. In returning to London, Julian violates his own doctrine. He grows estranged from Maddalo, from his beloved goddaughter, and from the Maniac, in the end revealing himself no friend to friendship.

As Maddalo had hoped, the experience at the asylum works both to discredit Julian's idealism and to expose the superficiality of Julian's commitment to it: The reader, who is, of course, less emotionally involved than Maddalo, is invited to judge Julian more mildly. We might infer that the visit to the asylum, while it does not prompt Julian to revise his credo, impresses upon him experientially both the frailty of "our will" and the coerciveness of ills that are innocently suffered, not "permitted" (lines 170, 171). Nonetheless, Julian's brave pronouncement,

> Much may be conquered, much may be endured,
> Of what degrades and crushes us. We know
> That we have power over ourselves to do
> And suffer

echoes hollowly and ironically by the end of the poem, for Julian's decision expresses his inability both to do (to alleviate the Maniac's misery) and to suffer (to share his sadness). The reader is not meant simply to dismiss or discredit, following Maddalo, Julian's affirmation (surely that effect could have been produced more directly) but to understand the conditions of its veracity. The "power" to do and suffer in the face of genuinely uninvited misery becomes ours only when we believe ourselves to be the agents of our destiny; and we achieve this difficult conviction only by maintaining the defenses that define individual, "essential" experience as distinct from collective life and unimplicated in social reality. In this way, one resists the categories of knowledge, feeling, and action installed by one's epoch. And yet, the insight developed in "Julian and Maddalo" is that the capacity thus to reject one's moment—the ability to imagine one's historical experience or to know oneself capable of alternative modes of being—is possible only within certain historical environments. By the narrative testimony of "Julian and Maddalo," as by the argument of Shelley's *Defence*, we learn that the effective imagination is not a universal and eternal endowment.

Upon his much-belated return to Venice, Julian seeks out Maddalo's daughter. He requests information about the Maniac, and he is informed of the man's brief happiness (the return of his lover) and his intensified despair following her hasty departure. In an uncharacteristic and unseemly fashion (compare this strained interview with that effortless rapport dramatized in lines 143–58), Julian presses to learn the circumstances of their separation. But when his godchild enlightens him, he refuses to share his knowledge with his audience. "I urged and questioned still, she told me how / All happened—but the cold world shall not know." The declaration is extremely disturbing. Julian's fear of his audience, his hostility, and his detachment are entirely new elements in the poem.

In thus arresting Julian's conversation with the reader, Shelley produces two effects. By withholding the particulars of the Maniac's case, the author characterizes the tragedy as an instance—a representative instance—of the human condition. "They met—they parted"; the bald summary encompasses the Maniac's entire history and is as a synecdoche for all human histories. The procedures and the overall form of the poem suggest that the circumstances, motives, and interpretations of our meetings and partings, our gains and our losses, are matters of indifference; the fact of our inevitable alienation from all that we love and need is the sole absolute in a world holding "little of transcendent worth." "Julian and Maddalo" circumvents the reader's impulse to accuse—to identify exploiter and victim, and thus limit the story to a personal and accidental frame of reference. As Wasserman observes, "Julian and Maddalo" depicts inconstancy as the way of all flesh.[2]

Second, in refusing to share with his readers his valued information, Julian shows himself no less skeptical of being understood and compassionated than the Maniac. This formerly frank and genial narrator retreats from his involvement with his audience, refusing (or failing) to order the narrative material in such a way as to "teach in song" what was "learned through suffering." Julian's sudden reticence is, as it were, his admission of the validity of Maddalo's original argument. His silence is an acknowledgement that in the absence of a priori sympathy and unconditional agreement, dialogue is either futile or destructively divisive. We are all imprisoned in our circle of impressions. Julian's withdrawal into his circle signifies his acquiescence to Maddalo's pessimism, his sense of irremediable anomie.

The poem closes on a note of dreadful loneliness. Maddalo is reported to be off in the mountains of Armenia. His dog is dead. His daughter, originally portrayed as a romantic sprite, has now acquired "something of Shakespeare's women." Which group? The comic heroines? Or is it Cordelia, Desdemona, Ophelia, Portia, Hermione? The gravity of the closing dialogue suggests the latter group. Julian has become guarded and importunate; the narrator implies that Julian, an emotional recluse, is unattached to life, an "unconnected man" ("urged by my affairs, / I left bright Venice"). He who once loved "all waste / And solitary places," strong in his conviction of the "boundless" soul and in the endurance of friendship (lines 14–31), has seen the boundaries of his own soul and has suffered the disintegration of a most primary friendship. Through no particular act of betrayal, a shared world of thought and feeling has dissolved.

"Julian and Maddalo" constructs a kind of fugue on the theme of irresolution and discontinuity.[3] The poem's terminal inconclusion effectively curtails the narrator's "conversation" with his reader; the original conversation between Julian and Maddalo is left unresolved, and their friendship is similarly abandoned as each pursues his affairs. The Maniac's discourse is riddled with lacunae, and, once he has unburdened himself of his displaced and abstract apologia, he relapses into wordlessness (line 268).

The impulse of *Posthumous Fragments* is a miniaturizing one; the sequence explains the big picture (war, political tyranny, social inequity, domestic tragedy) by sketching a portrait. Nicholson's "disappointment in love" is introduced toward the end of the volume as the typological source of all derangements in the superstructure. In effect, Shelley's representation is a reassuring one. By the logic of the volume, attention to the microcosm—private integrity and individual commitment—must rectify macrocosmic disorders. The formal principle of *Posthumous Fragments* is one of linear reduction and temporal regression; the earliest, and structurally most significant, episode of Nicholson's history is enacted in the final poem in the volume. *Posthumous Fragments* is what we might call a closed fragment, for its irresolution formally confirms and extends its argument. Nicholson's experience is contained and explained by the discontinuities of her discourse, and Shelley's formal decisions thereby establish a clear causal relationship between individual and collective life.

The method of "Julian and Maddalo" is expansive, its organizing principle best visualized in terms of regularly expanding concentric circles. Instead of reducing the issues to a manageable narrative and doctrinal compass in the style of *Posthumous Fragments*, Shelley complicates the original, cleanly conceptual premise with the commentary of a human and dramatic immediacy. (Additionally, Shelley complicates the political argument of the poem by the allusion to Tasso, a topic I take up below.) "Julian and Maddalo" is an open fragment; social and psychic dimensions participate in an analogical rather than causal relationship, and both existential modes are characterized by a tendency toward entropy.

"Julian and Maddalo" seeks to persuade the reader of its necessary irresolution; in attempting to imagine a full reality, the poet resigns himself to the project of writing an unfinishable poem. Moreover, since dramatic and discursive closure would undermine the poetic statement and compromise the work's ideological sincerity, so to speak, Shelley is careful to promote a generous (inconclusive, conflictual, qualified) reception.

Julian's estimate of the Maniac's lover—"Why, her heart must have been tough"—comes to seem offensively and rather stupidly facile, describing as it does Julian's own behavior. Julian's ideological lapse and his desertion of the Maniac are no less (*but no more*) reprehensible than the Lady's offense. The poem, however, refuses all such judgments by disarming its readers of their narrowly moral, or moralistic, impulses. "Julian and Maddalo" teaches us to know ourselves not in the simplicity of our beliefs but in the complex inconsistency of our feelings and actions.

Torquato Tasso—or rather, the English Romantics' Tasso—was for Shelley an available expression, so to speak, of the complex irony of human motivation and effect.[4] Shelley's Maniac is *not* Tasso; he is an allusion to Tasso—generalized in much the same manner as is Shelley's Margaret Nicholson. Both figures greatly transcend their historical models. It is what Shelley makes of the Tasso legend—how he reflects and refracts it— that bears scrutiny.

Perhaps the most striking feature of this legend in the early 1800s was its inconclusiveness and its variability. The three biographers largely responsible for Tasso's reputation in England—Manso, Serassi, and Black— offer seriously conflicting interpretations of the major events and relationships in Tasso's life.[5] Manso and Serassi—those writers Shelley is known to have read—commit certain internal inconsistencies in their efforts to explain Tasso's madness. Byron irons out these wrinkles in his "Lament of Tasso"; Shelley, conversely, not only incorporates them into the Maniac's history, he invents more.

"The causes of his imprisonment are hidden in obscurity: it is still disputed whether he was insane or not. . . . We can hardly persuade ourselves that a custody so rigorous was intended merely for the cure of a mental malady, and the works he composed during its continuance are scarcely reconcilable with madness; yet it is difficult to read his letters and believe him always sane."[6] The question posed throughout the biographies is whether Tasso feigned insanity and accepted incarceration in order to escape a more severe punishment for his love of Leonora, sister of Tasso's patron Duke. What gives Tasso's nineteenth-century biographers greatest difficulty is the fact that Tasso wrote some of his best poems during the period of his alleged insanity and after his release from Santa Anna's. Byron, who deemphasizes the insanity issue in order to develop *his* Tasso as a political victim, apparently felt that a mad poet could not deliver such a stringent political statement as a sane one. Shelley does something more subtle; he subjects his Tasso, the Maniac, to an internalized—eternal and irresistible—exploitation. For the Romantic poet, this form of slavery—to psychic demons—was, of course, the terrible, the dreamable nightmare.

Whereas Manso, Serassi, Black, and even Byron construe Tasso's madness as a feature at variance with—indeed, a contradiction of—the evidence provided by his life and works, and a diminution of his stature as a martyr to liberty and love, Shelley penetrates the deeper horror: the suspicion that Tasso's genius and his madness, both genuine, are two sides of a single coin. In this Shelley does not rehearse a legend, he invents one.

Shelley's Margaret Nicholson loses her poetical character—her psychic and verbal integrity—as her madness increases. Or, and here I draw on the psychology sketched in *The Defence*, as Nicholson's imagination—the ordering faculty—atrophies, her expressive faculty decompensates, leaving the mind's mimetic or reflective impulse preeminent. Shelley associates Nicholson's psychically "unconnected" quality—her inability to break from her mental prison house into a social mode of being—with the disjunctiveness of her discourse.

"In the infancy of society every author is necessarily a poet, because language itself is poetry; and to be a poet is to apprehend the true and the beautiful, in a word the good which exists in the relation, subsisting, first between existence and perception, and secondly between perception and expression." The language of poetry is "vitally metaphorical."[7] Shelley's concept of language defines the word (and its subsequent combinations and functions) as the incarnation of two generous, extrovert actions: the active appreciation of a relationship between self (internal being or "existence") and other (extrinsic and independent being: "perception"), and the repetition or duplication of this knowledge in a subsequent cognitive act. This act, which binds (private) perception to social being through the medium of the word, constitutes that word a metaphorical expression twice over, as it were. Clearly, language—spoken, written, or thought—is a function and product intimately bound up with individual and social consciousness and reflecting the relative soundness of both. Margaret Nicholson—the dramatic expression of a social malaise—cannot but reflect linguistically the collective character of her moment. Presumably, the more closely a writer's corporate life approaches the ideal of sociality, the more integrated and effective (i.e., integrative) his discourse.

The Maniac's poetry and his madness are, to draw upon the *Defence* again, "connate." The affective and intellectual virtue of his utterance— its effective power—originates in his isolation from social influence. A merely "amiable and cultivated" man before his sorrows, the Maniac acquires eloquence through his profound abstraction. Secluded in his tower and oblivious to the presence of his visitors and his fellow inmates, the Maniac's discourse is entirely unconstrained by rhetorical considerations —it is, one might say, entirely alienated. Simply, the Maniac produces an unaccommodated articulation of his inner world. He is "a nightingale, who sits in darkness and sings to cheer its own solitude." His auditors are "as men entranced. . . ." The man's insanity releases him from the rhetorical, communicative dimension that restricts (that is, corrupts) the utterance of all who are sane. By virtue of his madness, then, *which is his freedom*, the Maniac's language is purely expressive. Its elements "have relation to thought alone"; it need not negotiate with reality. We might recall at this point that Shelley's Maniac does not address his speech to Julian and Maddalo; they "overhear" his projections of psychic colloquy.

Julian's fantasy (lines 547–63) bears discussion in this context. His dream is to remain in Venice, where

> . . .—one may write
> Or read in gondolas by day or night,
> Having the little brazen lamp alight,
> Unseen, uninterrupted; books are there,
> Pictures, and casts from all those statues fair
> Which were twin-born with poetry. . . .

Here, in the marked resemblance of Julian's fantasy to the Maniac's reality (lines 252–56), is the prototype for the poet of the *Defence*: the nightingale who sings in the dark to cheer its own solitude, uninterrupted, unseen ("stealing his accents from the envious wind / Unseen"). Through the figure of the Maniac—an allusion both to Tasso and to his Romantic descendents—Shelley modifies the social poetics developed in the Margaret Nicholson volume. Poetry performs its social function precisely by refusing to participate in the affairs and institutional apparatus of the age. Poetry, then, is nothing if not an ideal and indirect critique of the age—a critique by virtue of its detachment from or profound noncompliance with its moment.

This is not to say that the Maniac is a surrogate for Julian, Maddalo, or Shelley, nor is he by any means a thoroughly idealized figure. He does, however, introduce certain themes that contribute to Shelley's mature understanding of the relation between individual and collective possibility, and specifically, of the poet's relation to his times. Both *Posthumous Fragments* and "Julian and Maddalo" seek to ascertain the nature of the relationship between the mimetic and expressive properties of language and to develop from this insight a posture and activity for the poet, constrained by the conditions of his moment and, no less forcefully, by the promptings of his imagination (which may or may not be a faculty independent of time and place). Both the *Posthumous Fragments* and "Julian and Maddalo" thematize madness in such a way as to explore a historically specific phenomenon: the experience of writers within a society that is hostile or indifferent to their purposes—persons isolated by their understanding and rendered unintelligible by their isolation.

Through Margaret Nicholson, Shelley delivers a series of psychic perspectives on social and political conditions. The distortion and eventual loss of discursive perspective are traced to the poet's altered sense of her audience and of her relation to it. The sequence opens with a proclamation, moves into dramatic monologue, followed by soliloquy and psychomachia. It concludes with a barely audible *cri de coeur*. The progressive disintegration and detachment of the discourse is a kind of rhetorical objective correlative for the mental condition and historical experience of the speaker. The editor's (Fitzvictor's) commentary as well as his rhetorical position establish this correspondence as the work's formal idea, its source of coherence.

To the extent that Nicholson is unable to order her experience (of alienation), she reflects it, thus reinforcing the determining conditions of her experience. Where Nicholson's art leaves off, her madness begins; each provides the other's constitutive limit. The poetic sequence, read as the representation of the poetical faculty operating within an immutable set of political, social, and psychic conditions, suggests that art emerges from historically specific dialectics between sympathy (identification or compliance with existential factiveness) and judgment (imagination of alternative categories—criticism—the ordering faculty). Once this antithesis collapses, the dialectic is, of course, compromised, and poetry reverts to its nascency: the madness of unregulated, unmodulated inspiration.

Where "Julian and Maddalo" shows a profounder understanding of this dialectic is in its demonstration that the effect of certain epochs or conditions is precisely to muddle the terms: to paralyze judgment by enlisting the individual's identification with the body politic or with its most potent, charismatic representative. "The Cenci" is, of course, Shelley's most explicit expression of this theme. There are eras in which our power to criticize is subverted and we are implicated against our will.

Let me sum up the impasse that I believe determines the structure and, specifically, the irresolution of "Julian and Maddalo." One could arrive at the same knowledge by asking what it means that Shelley recruits Tasso as a type of the Romantic poet, and what it means that he does so in 1818–19, an unhappy era for the partisans of social change.   ·

We can see, I think, that by the composite figure, Tasso-Maniac, Shelley explores the consequences of two possible responses to a repellent regime: uncompromising opposition or qualified, critical tolerance. Each option carries its own dangers, both of which finally amount to the threat of madness. Unyielding and extreme resistance to one's social dimension is, in effect, total alienation: a voice not overheard, not understood, and, eventually, forced into inward colloquy. That way lies madness. Failure to oppose a given regime in so severe a fashion, however, renders the individual prey to the blandishments and seductions of his culture. Eventually and inevitably, to remain in that society and not abjure it is to be suborned, to become *of* that society: its instrument. This is possession not by the daemon but by the tyrant. It is the predicament which Byron's Tasso most fears: "From long infection of a den like this, / Where the mind rots congenial with the abyss."

Maddalo responds to the Maniac—which is to say, to the dramatized relationship of poetry to madness—by seeking deeper exile. He rejects more vigorously and thoroughly the categories of contemporary "cultivated" existence. In the Preface to "Julian and Maddalo," the narrator describes Maddalo-Byron as "capable, if he would direct his energies to such an end, of becoming the redeemer of his degraded country." Apparently, Maddalo is confident that he can bear his self-imposed isolation and despair. What he learns from the Maniac is how far he must go to maintain his adversarial and estranged position, the condition of his sanity.

Julian returns to England. If Julian's return is, as Stuart Curran has suggested, his victory—a doctrinally, pragmatically, and ethically consistent and admirable action—then it must also be Shelley's defeat: in Blake's phrase, an act of contraction.[8]

But the return to England offers itself to a bleaker construction. In that return, we might easily read Julian's cowardice, his flight from the isolation so painfully objectified by the Maniac and already a terrible issue for the poets of the second generation. Julian seems to fear that by becoming the Maniac's friend and sympathizer, he would lose his enabling defenses, and become an exposed "nerve o'er which do creep / The else unfelt oppressions of this earth." He fears he might learn to see too clearly, feel too acutely the "irremediable woe" of existence. In short, he fears for his sanity. Julian's return is too much a reflex response to the Maniac and too qualified by Julian's earlier philosophic statement for it to signify a bold cultural confrontation.

Wasserman is exactly on target when he locates the poem's "conversation" within "the context of irrepressible under-consciousness of an imperfect and alien world."[9] I would add that above and beyond the poem's deliberate irresolution, another set of factors conditions, perhaps overdetermines its form. The textual inconclusion is, on one level, an evasion of despair, or of the difficult relation between that despair and contemporary political and social life. The "perfect" poem could not but represent the ineffectuality of the imagination in opposing the institution.

Both works, *Posthumous Fragments* and "Julian and Maddalo," have areas of blindness and insight that are both brought into being by a fragmentary, interruptive poetic method. "Julian and Maddalo," not only more assured, complex, and self-critical than *Posthumous Fragments*, is also by far the more affecting work. Julian's final silence—in effect, a withdrawal from his audience and a repudiation or despair of discourse itself—marks him as a man who has ceased to participate in his age but is nonetheless forced to remain in it and to know himself as it knows him: ineffectual and antithetical.

> . . . by the madness which interrupts it, a work of art opens a void, a moment of silence, a question without answer, provokes a breach without reconciliation where the world is forced to question itself. What is necessarily a profanation in the work of art returns to that point, and, in the time of that work swamped in madness, the world is made aware of its guilt. Henceforth, and through the mediation of madness, it is the world that becomes culpable (for the first time in the Western world) in relation to the work of art.[10]

Shelley's England is Castlereagh's England, his Europe a continent restored to its monarchs. Julian and Maddalo—Shelley and Byron—take their poetical impetus from political positions, but both poets are helpless finally to resist the reactionary mood and oppressive apparatuses of their era. *"Where there is a work of art, there is no madness"* and yet, by the logic of Foucault's spatial metaphor, where there is no madness—to inaugurate, terminate, or punctuate the work—there is no art.[11] The irresolution of "Julian and Maddalo"—"unconnected exclamations of . . . agony"—is its aesthetic imprimatur. "Julian and Maddalo" is the dark side of *Prometheus Unbound*, the disintegration which authorizes the other poem's amassing, harmonious crescendo of image, action, and idea.

And yet, from a more detached perspective, one could situate "Julian and Maddalo" *within* the tradition of *Prometheus Unbound*, a poem that "rises above the simplification entailed in [Shelley's] call to the masses ("Mask of Anarchy," 1819)."[12] "Julian and Maddalo," written just five or six months after Shelley's removal to Italy, certainly reflects the poet's experience of the repressive regime imposed in England during the 'teens, but in a more sensitive, complex, and ambivalent manner than one finds in the angry and resolute "Mask of Anarchy." The "dualism [that] underlies many of Shelley's greatest poems" is probably "Julian and Maddalo"'s most impressive feature, with respect to both formal and doctrinal development.[13] But whereas the dialectic of *Prometheus Unbound* springs from the interaction of "natural cosmos" with "individual consciousness"—the one "fluid, destructive, impassive," and the other a "fragile, delicate bloom"—the generative opposition within "Julian and Maddalo" sets *social* cosmos against individual consciousness.[14]

The "greatest poems" are those that build from this dualism the syncretic, harmonious vision for which Shelley is so justly admired. "Julian and Maddalo" delivers its two-handed truths through the vehicle of imitative form; instead of projecting a vision that contains these opposing truths, Shelley represents in a fairly direct manner the ideological bind. Perhaps it is this failure on Shelley's part to imagine what he knew that bars "Julian and Maddalo" from the company of the so-called "greatest works" of the canon. Like so much serious literature of the nineteenth century, "Julian and Maddalo" discovers the "necessity of historical change, but also and more particularly the damage done to individuals by that process," and it does so from a seemingly apolitical position.[15] "Julian and Maddalo" shows as clearly as any of Shelley's poems that his criticism of Wordsworth's program of solitude and retreat had become, by 1818, considerably more complicated, based as it was on a considerably darker understanding of the relation between the private and public sectors of modern life.[16] "Julian and Maddalo" is a bitter, self-lacerating critique of the effects of corrupt community upon individual consciousness, yet it casts a cold eye on those who retreat from that community.

This is a vision so uncompromising as to make any attempt at formal resolution an evasion and an inconsistency, evils that "Julian and Maddalo" properly avoids. (And here we distinguish formal from authorial intention, and transvalue the work's inconclusion.) "Julian and Maddalo" is a less illustrious poem than *Prometheus Unbound*. But in its formal integrity—I use that word in its ethical sense—signified by its formal imperfection, "Julian and Maddalo" is the more accessible work, the poem one turns to when the holistic grandeur of *Prometheus Unbound* weighs one down.

CHAPTER TEN

THE DEPENDENT FRAGMENT
"Hyperion" and "The Fall of Hyperion"

The history of *Hyperion* scholarship shows one marked turnabout; the majority of readers first exposed to "The Fall of Hyperion" ("first" meaning the period from 1856–1925) believed it to be the original draft from which the revision, "Hyperion," was produced.[1] Conversely, the criticism that follows Amy Lowell's 1925 biography of Keats generally represents the poems as distinct and opposite approaches to the same conceptual problem, by way of the same or similar narrative materials. Although this body of scholarship often retains the term "revision" to designate "The Fall," the poems are, in practice, treated as two first drafts, each of which seeks to explain human suffering and to apply this analysis to the business of poetry. The mythological material that objectifies the problem is, in both poems, the triumph of Olympia's gods over the Titan pantheon. "Hyperion"'s mode is typically characterized as objective, dramatic, Miltonic, and Greek, while "The Fall" is described as subjective, lyrical, Dantesque, and Romantic.

This discrepancy, or the genetic constructs it sponsors, pretty much organizes our criticism of the poems. By and large, we theorize the difference by reference to Keats's literary ambitions and experiments, his technical development, the circumstances of his life, and his state of mind at the different moments of composition.

In the main, criticism does not regard the poems as separate but equal. The premise underlying most studies of the *Hyperion*s is that if the original poem, "Hyperion," had begun to say what Keats wanted to say in the manner he wanted to say it, he would not have abandoned that poem and begun "The Fall." No matter how many virtues readers of this persuasion find in "Hyperion"—and they frequently cite instances of its superior execution, its sheer verbal power—their premise compels them to seek the structural, doctrinal, or stylistic flaw that subordinates "Hyperion" to the later poem. Apparently, the reader who honors Keats's critical judgment (that is, who registers the distinctness of the two fragments), and who respects the aesthetic values that support this judgment, must be as dissatisfied with "Hyperion" as Keats must have been. "The Fall," of course, figures by this scheme the authorized poem. Since it represents Keats's mature thought on the subject addressed in both *Hyperions*, it becomes in our criticism the work we can confidently intentionalize, or the one that best rewards critical inquiry. Once these several assumptions are made, it is a relatively simple matter to represent "The Fall" as the culmination of Keats's art and thought, and to expose "Hyperion" as a misguided and logically, properly, abortive experiment.[2]

One finds, of course, interesting and astute variations on this theme. Both critical groups—those who read the poems as a draft and revision, and those who treat them as independent and antithetical projects—designate as Keats's natural or characteristic mode the lyrical, subjective manner of *Endymion* and "The Fall." Readers who treat the fragments as distinct and opposite drafts argue that Keats seeks in "Hyperion" a release from the habitual and wearisome subjectivity of his verse. He sets himself the task of writing a long, objective poem, much as he had attempted the long, subjective poem with *Endymion*. Unable to sustain this alien style, he returns to his native mode and so composes "The Fall." Harold Bloom and Walter Jackson Bate applaud this return, whereby Keats claims his own, his deepest knowledge. Rather than repress the "myth of self" beginning to possess "Hyperion," Keats delivers himself unto that deep truth, and by that martyrdom finds his own voice and the voice of his age.[3]

On the other side, D. G. James reads Keats's abandonment of the "Hyperion" project as an admission of defeat.[4] James argues that although Keats continues to esteem "Hyperion"'s objective approach above the subjective manner of "The Fall," "Hyperion" proves to Keats his technical, perhaps even intellectual immaturity. Rather than abort the project, Keats realistically reconceives it; he selects a vehicle and a manner he can manage.[5]

Nothing is wrong with these compositional accounts; they make good sense and they have produced excellent critical knowledge. They do, however, impose upon "Hyperion" an undeserved status, that of the exercise which facilitates the primary accomplishment. Were "Hyperion" a finished work rather than a fragment, it would perhaps not suffer by this representation, that of the enabling experiment. Bate, for example, presents Keats's early sonnets, rondeaux, and *Endymion* as projects necessary to the development of Keats's art, but because these are finished works, they maintain their formal determinacy—their status as *poems*—even within Bate's evolutionary interpretive hierarchy.[6] "Hyperion," conversely, dissolves into a preliminary study, meaningful only in relation to the achieved work.

The Victorians, most of whom believed that "Hyperion" was the revised version of "The Fall," identified, as we do, the subjective as Keats's characteristic voice and method. According to their compositional account, Keats embarked upon the "Hyperion" project in the readiest, most congenial fashion; the result of that (introspective, subjective) effort is "The Fall." Because Keats learned during the course of his composition the limitations of its method and meanings, he revised his original conception. In "The Fall," he had described a vision and defined a creed, and the creed itself taught him that he must incarnate the vision in a poetic action.[7] He began to do so toward the end of "The Fall" and continued in "Hyperion." This explanation implies that Keats had to begin subjectively in order to find and to penetrate his subject; in order to put that understanding to work, however, he had to proceed in a different manner, developing what was, ". . . as it were something given to him."[8] (Woodhouse reports Keats's echo of Coleridge's prefatory comment on "Kubla Khan.") According to the Victorian account, "Hyperion" is not the culmination of Keats's art and thought (as "The Fall" is to Bloom and Bate), but the culmination of "The Fall": the showing that sub- and instantiates the telling. In writing "Hyperion," Keats advances from discussing the selfless artwork to producing it; or, in his own idiom, he makes a "thing semi-real" into an "existence."

Today, when "Hyperion"'s priority of composition is taken for granted, explicit revisionary arguments are rare, although one detects traces of revisionary interpretation in studies that advance a different structural model. It requires an awkward critical apparatus to discuss "The Fall" as a revision, which typically reduces and intensifies a given discourse, when it is so much more diffuse and uncertain and promises so much wider a scope than "Hyperion." It is simpler and seems more plausible to propose Keats's dissatisfaction with Oceanus's somewhat fatuous explanation of the vicissitudes of power ("For 'tis the eternal law / That first in beauty should be first in might"), and to identify Oceanus's voice with the author's; to remark Keats's discerning distaste for the Miltonisms of the early version; to characterize "Hyperion" as interested, selfish, or "dreaming" poetry; and to represent "The Fall" as the application of Keats's new insights, the authorized poem.

One cannot but feel, however, something mechanical and overdetermined about this line of thought, insofar as it derives from a normatively contrastive reading of neutral textual features, a reading clearly promoted by the compositional history of the two *Hyperions*.[9] Let me note that the verbal and conceptual power we so often find in "Hyperion" does not effectively qualify the interpretive necessity I observe. Indeed, this approval illustrates the inadequacy of our structural model which, by requiring "Hyperion"'s essential inferiority to "The Fall," trivializes or marginalizes our response to the affective and formal virtues of "Hyperion."

The irresolution of both poems is generally read either as a sign of Keats's failure to realize his particular objectives for the *Hyperions*, or of the limitations set by his general poetic program. Some have interpreted the incompletion of both *Hyperions* as Keats's prudent decision to quit while he was ahead, a theory no less inconsistent with practical response, and no less problematic for practical criticism than the one sketched above. In that the title of "The Fall" designates the work's narrative category—its "intended" form—readers tend to overlook the poem's actual or achieved form. They interpret "The Fall"'s projected design with reference to Keats's probable motive for curtailing the "Hyperion" venture. The nature and effects of "The Fall"'s irresolution are, if considered at all, taken up in the context of psychobiography.

"Hyperion"'s irresolution has, however, assumed remarkable importance in the criticism. By and large, this feature is construed as a symptom of the work's conceptual defect. We notice, for example, that critics tend to refer to the "fragmented" or "fragmentary" Book iii; the underlying and in some cases explicit argument is that in Book iii, Keats inadvertently stresses the weak link in his basic concept, thereby triggering the disintegration of the whole effort. In other words, the poem's particular irresolution and its particular achievement are regarded as opposing facts or features. Our criticism, lacking a visual field wherein "Hyperion" might yield a single, unified impression—that of a fragment form—tends to read the poem bifocally, hence without much form at all.

A few scholars have acknowledged that one or both poems offer a kind of closure: "In a sense, *Hyperion* is already a complete poem once Apollo has realized himself, and the poet in Keats seems to have recognized this by refusing to go on. Whatever the planned length, nothing could be added to the fragment as it is without some redundancy."[10] Harold Bloom, the author of this statement, does not investigate his impression of "Hyperion"'s perfection "once Apollo has realized himself." Had he done so, he might have traced it to his memory of the poet's transformation in "The Fall" and to his own tendency to identify Apollo with "The Fall"'s poet figure. That is, Bloom seems to derive from the later poem certain categories, insights, and expectations by means of which he (re)-structures the earlier work. Or, he reads the poems compositely but does not register this fact in his critique, one that proposes an antithetical relationship between the two *Hyperions*. Consequently, he is hard put to reconcile his observation of "Hyperion"'s perfection with his argument that Keats abandoned the poem because he was properly dissatisfied with its form or formal direction. Bloom is obliged to maintain that Keats, in the course of his work on "Hyperion," rediscovered the virtues of his habitual poetic mode, the subjective. But all Bloom can summon as textual evidence of Keats's disillusionment with "Hyperion"'s objective style is "the relative unsteadiness of what exists as Book iii."[11]

One finds another case of transferred response—this time, from "Hyperion" to "The Fall"—in Kenneth Muir's conviction that although "The Fall" is allegorical (indeed, "more allegorical than the first ["Hyperion"]"), Keats "expresse[s] [in "The Fall"] his own experience as directly as possible."[12] Surely, few would characterize a dream within a dream within a vision as a direct expression of experience. My conjecture is that Muir, in effect and unwittingly, superimposes upon "The Fall" his impression of "Hyperion"'s sensual concreteness. The unveiling of Moneta appears to Muir to be a dramatically mimetic rather than an allegorical action because he has *seen* Mnemosyne's face in "Hyperion," and because he believes that "the unveiling of Moneta is a repetition of the scene in the first 'Hyperion' in which Apollo gazes into the eyes of Mnemosyne. . . ."[13]

Compare these reactions to a Victorian view. Swinburne, who believed "The Fall" to be Keats's initial composition, describes "Hyperion" as a work "fortified and purified as it had been on a first revision, when much introductory allegory and much tentative effusion of sonorous and super-fluous verse had been rigorously clipped down or pruned away. . . ."[14] This textual account enables Swinburne to acknowledge the composite resolution which the poems together accomplish; he can account for his satisfaction with "Hyperion," and particularly with its formal adequacy to its themes, by reference to this model.

The difference between Swinburne's revisionist reading and those put forth by twentieth-century scholars, is that Swinburne, by defining "The Fall" as a draft, is not compelled to interpret its inconclusion as a sign of conceptual weakness, as modern theory must do in some way or other with "Hyperion." Instead of construing "The Fall"'s discontinuation as a rejection or forced abandonment of the poem's manner and idea, Swinburne (and presumably others who shared his understanding of the compositional chronology), accepted its status as a draft: not a culpably unrealized work but a leap headlong into the sea, a way to begin. Drafts are, by definition, imperfect. To revise a draft does not mean to recant or retract one's original formulation but to make that writing more faithful to itself or to the laws that govern it. One refines, clarifies, and intensifies by isolating the draft's ruling idea and eliminating that which is recognized as extraneous to or inconsistent with that principle. Although several of the early critics infer Keats's interest in silencing the swooning "Johnny Keats" persona of "The Fall," and attribute to Keats a certain uneasiness with the draft, they nonetheless acknowledge "The Fall" as "Hyperion"'s necessary inception. In their view, "The Fall" is not negated by "Hyperion" but completed by it; or, the two poems are essentially, conceptually continuous. Similarly, a reader who conceives the poems as draft and revision cannot but realize the extent to which his impression of the latter is informed by his exposure to the former. Morever, the fragmentary condition of the revised version would emphasize this dependency.[15]

Let me roughly discriminate the three principles of response organizing the early *Hyperion* criticism, and by these principles, let me propose a formal model: the dependent fragment. First, the narrative line of both poems seems to have been extended in either direction, in the manner of the true fragment. Second, the stylistic antitheses precipitated by the fragments were structurally interpreted rather than substantively evaluated, and the conceptual discrepancies were assimilated to a bipolar model. In this we observe a reception resembling that which the completed fragment solicits. Third, "Hyperion"'s prominent terminal irresolution was read as a formal decision, a controlled reflection of and on the poetic argument or vision. In sum, the dependent fragment takes shape under the pressure of structural expectations and activities associated with the three fragment forms treated in the preceding chapters. Further, the dependent fragment figures as the product of an episode or interval in the poet's or persona's career; the fragment thus invites the reader to rational-ize its irresolution with reference to its situation within a continuum of episodes, moments, and their respective objectifications. The formal de-terminacy of such poems depends on the reader's propensity to relate the fragment to relevant precursors or successors in the author's canon.

The scheme I propose above and the reading I will produce by it are both determined by my reading of the Victorian reception. Indeed, my revisionary construct is a mirror image of the structural model sketched in the early criticism. I have relegated that material to chapter eleven only because it seemed too detailed an account to work easily as a formal model in this context. My arrangement does not reflect my view of the relative importance of that discussion to this critique, only my sense of a rhetorical problem. For a better understanding of my procedures, then, and for substantiation of my reception conjectures, I refer the reader to page 183, below, "The Victorian Paradigm."

What is the point, one might ask, of citing the virtues of the early readings, based as they were on a factual error? We cannot pretend to be Victorians and deliberately forget what we know about the *Hyperions*, nor, of course, would one wish to exchange a truth for a falsehood. By enter-taining structural assumptions strikingly different from our own, however, we productively estrange our own most habitual reception procedures. In that these procedures have produced a contradiction between practical response and practical criticism (or, in that the critic must disparage the meaning and method of one poem in order to focus the other), a new and removed assessment might prove useful. Instead of regarding the later poem as Keats's definitive work, one might conceive it as a revision of "Hyperion," much as the Victorians conceived (and therefore construed) "Hyperion" as the revised version of "The Fall." The unaccountable expe-rience of closure which both poems facilitate in so many readers might then be explained as the result of a certain mode of reading, one that we practice unself-consciously. When we read in this manner, we bring each poem to bear on the other—*completing* each, as it were, with material drawn from its companion poem. By positing a revisionary and coopera-tive relationship between the two poems, one can relate the closure that most readers observe in "Hyperion" to the additions and subtractions of "The Fall." Conversely, the expectations aroused by "Hyperion" will be found to enhance understanding of its revision, "The Fall." Thus the reader may appreciate each of the poems, in its statement and style, as an image of Keatsian truth, even though he knows that one poem precedes the other in compositional time. By thinking in these terms, one avoids fixing Keats—the least systematic, most oxymoronic of poets—in a univocal and defended position.

I propose, then, that for both practical and theoretical reasons, we read Keats's *Hyperions* within a system of revision.[16] The practical reasons I have presented. By theoretical reasons, I mean a concern for consistency with respect to the general constructs governing our sense of Keats's oeuvre and its genesis, and our readings of particular poems. Keats is not just a poet to us, he is a poetic career, or as Bate has observed, echoing Keats's own comment on Shakespeare, a "poignantly allegorical life." Keats's ascent of the poetical ladder has become mythical; one watches him station himself where a great precursor had rested, discover the limitations of that position, step up to the next rung, and finally kick away the ladder altogether. It is difficult not to read into Keats's development a variation on the traditional poetic curriculum: systematic (re)production of the hierarchically organized literary kinds, from eclogue to epic. In Keats's case, poet-heroes and poetic styles take the place of the classical forms; Keats advances from Mathew to Hunt, from Chaucer and Spenser to Milton and Wordsworth, Dante and Shakespeare. And yet, Keats's most advanced works include elements found in his earliest, crudest pieces. Moreover, these features, far from vestigial, contribute to the greatness of Keats's masterpieces. Huntian qualities persist to the end, and Keats's last significant project is "The Cap and Bells"—a fact, whatever we choose to make of it.

Further, Keats's prose exhibits throughout a determinate and passionate attitude toward critical, creative, moral, and social acts of exclusion. This is to say that our scholarly concepts regarding Keats's poetic development should reflect our knowledge of Keats's own values and specifically, his notion of negative capability. This concept has been too frequently and too expertly discussed to require elucidation here. Suffice it to say that negative capability describes an intellectual, imaginative, and moral *largesse*, a condition prerequisite to achievement in any dimension of human enterprise. For Keats, determinacy—of idea, attitude, or relationship—is not produced by progressive rejection of possible alternatives, but by acts of incorporation whereby one alternative is brought to bear upon another in such a way as to generate a certainty partaking of both positions.

The concept of revision not only accounts for the carryover evident in Keats's poetic career, it accommodates the poet's own beliefs about the nature of intellectual growth. Moreover, the idea of revision is technically serviceable to the student of Keats's *Hyperions* since it provides a way to mediate the near dogmatism with which the poems present their respective poetic statements, and Keats's master-virtue, negative capability. The task in Keats criticism has always been to see precisely what the poem says without falsely or prematurely systematizing its meaning.

To revise—literally, see again—does not mean to reject or recant or rescind. By revising, the poet remedies the deficiencies of the original. While this correction may produce textual expansion, it typically requires elimination of original material. However, insofar as this reduction is performed in the service of conceptual and stylistic realization, it is not by nature an act of exclusion but a generative or developmental, and therefore inclusive operation.

In "The Fall," Keats uses the verb "rehearse" (line 16) to describe his narrating activity. The word is, of course, a synonym for "tell," but it is a somewhat curious verb (why not "relate," "narrate," "record," "present," or "transmit"?). "Rehearse" derives from the Old French, "rehercer"—literally, to re-harrow (root up, pulverize, stir; spoil, vex, plunder, sack, torment). The etymology, and particularly its agricultural application, suggests a remedial undoing, destabilizing, and hollowing out. One of the strongest associations to which the verb gives rise is, of course, that of the stage. The actor privately rehearses his discourse—distresses, disorganizes, undoes by repeating it—so as to render his public representation more consistent with the principles felt to determine the project at every phase of its development. Similarly, through revision (narrative rehearsal or repetition) as opposed to recantation, a writer criticizes his own, accomplished performance so as to reproduce it in finer tone, or with greater fidelity to the original impulse of the enterprise. Clearly, the initial and relatively diffuse or heterogeneous gesture is, by this process, realized, rather than displaced and discredited. To situate this dynamic in existential space is to describe a process of self-definition whereby earlier (or simultaneous but marginalized) characterological crystallizations are subsumed or sublated—that is, transcended without being surrendered.

Above, I used the phrase, "system of revision," a phrase that conjures Bloom's celebrated theory. Some time ago, Bloom demonstrated that poetic growth, like other forms of human development, does not occur through rejection of past loves and models. The student does not escape a sphere of influence by negating it and striking out in an opposite direction, since the univocal and direct refusal is no less derivative (in its mechanical perversity or simple inverseness) than a slavish imitation. Because we have incorporated the inhibiting force—hence its daunting/enabling hold on us—negation cannot exorcise it. That is, the self that negates is part of the object which it—the self—would banish.

Genuine growth occurs through the repetition of our loves and identifications in successively finer tones. Each repetition brings us closer to the question that unconsciously informs our evolution. And each revisionary achievement approximates more and more closely our own daemon. According to Bloom, the poet does not make a place for himself by direct opposition to his poetic precursors nor by denying his attraction to these models. Rather, he revises these exemplary and profoundly interiorized achievements by means of a fixed sequence of psychically determined rhetorical maneuvers. The works that Bloom's ephebe produces by this process are as much "theirs"—creatures of his precursors—as "not theirs." To understand these works, we study the psychic and rhetorical mechanisms that brought (and bring) them into being and that are inscribed in their structure—gesture, statement, silence. To appreciate the innovation of a revisionary work—the autonomy of its author—we must first appreciate the nature and extent of its dependence on its inhibiting precursor.

Bloom does not discuss the poet's need to surpass himself, a need especially urgent when the poet's earlier work seems to him derivative, or when it seems to imprison him in two achievements, his own and his precursor's.[17] He cannot, in this case, simply select another and opposite model, since he seeks not only to escape his precursor but to overcome his own imitativeness, or all the ego with which he has invested that first model (by which he models his subjectivity, or produces that alienated ego). He may adopt a substitutive procedure as a provisional move, a maneuver that, by affording him a direction in which to work, counteracts the paralysis caused by that first swerve from the old god. Thus he might substitute, say, Dante for Milton, until he can surpass both precursors by means of a more complete, effective assimilation.

The relevance of Bloom's theory—and of my synopsis—to Keats's *Hyperion* poems should be obvious by now. "The Fall" stands in the same relation to "Hyperion" as "Hyperion" stands in relation to the Intimations Ode, *The Excursion*, and *Paradise Lost*. Each poem revises an important—that is, inhibiting—precursor. This is not difficult to see in the case of the Miltonic "Hyperion," and of course Bloom has already worked out the ratios that bind "Hyperion" to Wordsworth and Milton. With "The Fall," however, where the inhibiting precursor is not Dante but Keats's own "Hyperion," the revisionary ratios are harder to see. One finds only their traces in our readings of "The Fall."

The swerve, or act of misprision that enables Keats to conceive and begin writing "The Fall," is represented in the opening eighteen lines of that poem. Here, Keats presents a curious distinction, between fanatics and savages on the one hand and poets on the other. One wonders what motivates this strangely defensive beginning; had Keats not presented the option, who would think to brand the poem that follows as "fanatical" or "savage"? These are hardly conventional terms of critical disdain, and further, according to lines 1–10, simply to record one's dreams in verse is to write poetry. The distinction is not only self-contradictory then, it seems altogether simplistic, superfluous, and inconsistent with respect to the visionary-dreamer-poet distinctions presented later in the poem.

These peculiar introductory lines serve a purpose; they grant Keats a moment of blindness toward "Hyperion" and thus enable him to begin writing "The Fall" in what he can conceive as a corrective move. That Keats has misread "Hyperion" and not Wordsworth (*pace* Bloom), is suggested by the striking verbal echoes binding this passage to the opening section of "Hyperion." The "sable charm / And dumb enchantment" into which the fanatical or savage imagination lapses, recalls "Hyperion"'s initial portrait of Saturn: rapt, "quiet as a stone," a figure in a state of suspended animation—i.e., enchanted and dumb. The Poet's "warm scribe, [his] hand" clearly recalls that powerful image from "Hyperion": Saturn's "old right hand," which "lay nerveless, listless, dead, / Unsceptred." Saturn's realmless eyes are closed, and he appears to listen to the earth for comfort; he neither dreams of heaven, nor has he visions. Rather than offer "shadows of melodious utterance" ("The Fall"), he "snatched / Utterance thus" ("Hyperion").

Now, these contrastive echoes do not make sense. Or, in that "Hyperion" is not Saturn's poem, these similitudes are not strictly logical. Yet Keats *would* have us identify Saturn with the narrator of "Hyperion." He urges us to see Saturn's tranced state as an objective correlative for "Hyperion"—that is, for the structural and moral conception of that poem, as well as its poetic manner. The reader is asked to construe "Hyperion" as fanatic or savage poetry, with respect to which "The Fall" figures an authentic, accomplished verse. Having discredited the early work, Keats can proceed to complete what is found lacking in "Hyperion" (he writes a long and polemical induction before incorporating the beginning of the original poem), and to correct what is wrong (he counterpoints each of a number of stylistic and thematic features in "Hyperion" with its conventional antithesis). I will not compare the two poems to document "The Fall"'s seeming improvement upon "Hyperion." The critics I have mentioned have already done so, carefully demonstrating "The Fall"'s advance in scope, subtlety, psychic honesty, and logical rigor (see pp. 194–95).

Finally, Keats empties out "Hyperion" with a deliberate movement of discontinuity. He replaces the "first in beauty, first in might" maxim with a vision of history conceived as a series of felicitous falls. Compared to this adaptive, evolutionary gradualism, "Hyperion"'s thesis looks decidedly crude and shallow—morally, intellectually, and as a principle of poetic organization. By rewriting this thesis in "The Fall," Keats characterizes —and damns—"Hyperion" as "dreaming poetry," poetry that needlessly vexes the world. It offers no consolation for its depiction of terrific woe— only Oceanus's facile philosophy.

Bloom's revisionary ratios imply three concomitant reading ratios. These constructive actions roughly correspond to the activities that build up the true, completed, and deliberate fragment. In order to make sense of "The Fall" as a revisionary poem, one extrapolates from the fragment an antecedent and subsequent context, the activity constitutive of the true fragment. By way of a formal beginning, and in light of the associations isolated above, one would postulate "Hyperion" as a flawed, an inadequate poem: a negative model. As an "end," we would figure the continuation of the story begun in "Hyperion": the complete installation of the Olympians, illustrated by the respective careers of Hyperion and Apollo. Because that story, as it is given in "The Fall," follows a vision of successive, inevitable triumphs, reigns, and deposings, one anticipates Apollo's eventual fall, the condition of some new regime. In other words, the reader of "The Fall" supplies a terminal closure by envisioning a succession of post-Apollonian pantheons which would temporally advance the narrative up to the vision of Eden presented in lines 19–59. This vision, balanced by its imagined recurrence following the fragment's last line, would at that point be recognized as the conventional epic beginning, *in medias res*. The chronological origin of "The Fall" thus becomes the event which precipitates "Hyperion"'s first scene: the defeat of the Titans. A continuation of "The Fall" would, given this revisionary ratio, promise a vision of Christian consolation—correction and replacement of the Pagan surmise. The modern fall into solipsism (the burden of Moneta's discourse) would, within this new and higher dispensation, figure as another *felix culpa*, precondition for another spiritual advance.

One who reads "The Fall" as if it completed "Hyperion" by positing itself as the earlier epic's contrary (the antithesis to "Hyperion"'s thesis), structurally assimilates the poems as parts of a single, internally disjunctive fragment: a work begun in one mode and completed in another. To heal the breach opened by the stylistic and structural antitheses of the two poems, one might conceive these oppositions as the result of two different impulses: an early, exuberant draft and a later, more reflective commentary and expansion. By this model, the range of antitheses engendered by the poems (enumerated on p. 194) can be worked as indifferent, strictly formal and contingent differentials rather than credited as immanent, normative, thematized, and absolute oppositions. That is, we acknowledge the composite and abstract character of all those stylistic, narrative, and conceptual antitheses. For instance, the poet figure of "The Fall" need not represent a rejection of "Hyperion"'s Apollo (and thus need not be interpreted either as an improvement upon "Hyperion"'s achievement or as a backsliding from that success). The reader might instead consider the two figures as establishing the parameters of a closed system within which a finite and organized set of images, meanings, and values (in this case, concerning the offices of poetry and the nature of the poet) can be generated. By developing contingent and relational meanings for the many oppositions set up by the two *Hyperions*, the reader shuttles back and forth, weaving the two fragments into one continuous fabric. This kind of integration establishes a single, inclusive economy of action, character, and statement by means of which we may valorize any one element without depreciating its antithesis.

The next triad of moves in Bloom's system begins with the poet's embrace of a personalized "counter-sublime," a *niveau* that displaces the precursor's sublime. The Dantesque character of "The Fall" clearly functions for Keats as an alternative sublime to Milton's, the template upon which "Hyperion" is fashioned. This is not to say that Keats permanently or freely, so to speak, adopts Dante as his new sublime. Keats merely recruits Dante as an ad hoc and antithetical substitute for Milton. The maneuver enables the young poet to imagine, thus to conquer the loss which he dreads, the rejection of the old god. Keats's selection of Dante as his surrogate sublime is not, however, a random substitution. He chooses a model that liberates him to develop his own voice, a model that puts the poet in the picture.

Askesis is Bloom's term for a movement of curtailment; the poet relinquishes his full imaginative endowment in such a way as to truncate the model poem and to confirm his distance from it. The poem which Keats truncates is, of course, not *Paradise Lost* but "Hyperion" (or if you will, *Paradise Lost* by way of "Hyperion"). Simply by ceasing to proceed with "The Fall"—that is, by withholding the expected narration of Hyperion's defeat—Keats makes the presentation of this narrative material in "Hyperion" look amateurish and diffuse. The discreet, suggestive glimpse of Hyperion which "The Fall" delivers, his defeat only intimated, looks like a symbolic concentration of what is thus made to seem tediously narrated in "Hyperion." The reader tends to forget what follows the parallel vision in "Hyperion" (Hyperion's descent to the Titan council, etc.). Thus, by curtailing or fragmenting "The Fall," Keats further reduces the already imperfect "Hyperion."

To the extent that Keats represents "The Fall"'s abrupt cessation as an aesthetic necessity imposed by the work's idea, the conventions associated with the deliberate fragment come into play. In order to see "The Fall"'s irresolution as necessary and the poem as complete, one must come to a particular understanding of the poetic statement. Below, I consider some effects of this reception imperative.

Bloom's final revisionary ratio is a phenomenon he calls *Apophrades*, or the return of the dead. The revisionary poem is deliberately "held open" to the precursor's work. The uncanny effect of this strategy is an impression of perfect authorization and reversal. It looks as if the later poet had written the precursor's work. Bloom's exotic terminology (and the seemingly arcane phenomenon it designates) aptly describes an experience common to many readers of Keats's *Hyperions*. When one rereads "Hyperion" soon after "The Fall," the earlier work looks like the actualization of that poetical ideal developed theoretically in the later poem. "Hyperion" emerges as the practical implementation of all that Keats learns in "The Fall" through his descent into subjectivity, into cultural myth, and into the Romantic idiom.

We have, indeed, a wonderful "proof" of this reception conjecture in Swinburne's "Hyperion"—a conscious revision (pastiche, reproduction) of Keats's own revisionary work. We note that Swinburne opens his poem on line 18; the ostensibly missing opening lines are now assumed to be nonexistent. In other words, Swinburne rewrites a "Hyperion" that is itself revised or rewritten by "The Fall"—in Swinburne's view, the earlier poem. Or, Swinburne reproduces in his version "Hyperion"'s revision of "The Fall"—its "deletion" of the eighteen preamble lines. Thus does

Swinburne at once *represent* that deletion and *claim* it (that is, claim "Hyperion"), as his own critical act. At the same time, the putative eighteen lines constitute a space that holds open Swinburne's "Hyperion" to both precursors: the Keats of "The Fall" and of "Hyperion" (Swinburne's "strong poem"). The strategy—a brilliantly parodic one—is for Swinburne at once a liberation *from* Keats and legitimation *by* him.

It is "Hyperion" and not "The Fall" that Bloom in fact explicates in his *Poetry and Repression*, for it is "Hyperion" that takes up a stance in relation to the tradition incarnated in Milton and Wordsworth. "Hyperion" is the poem that equals and even at times surpasses the Intimations Ode and *Paradise Lost*; it moves with a sureness and strength found nowhere else in Keats's canon, a fact readily acknowledged by most critics.

Why, then, does "Hyperion" break off before its appointed end? Or, what precisely instigates Keats's revision of "Hyperion" by way of "The Fall"? I submit that Keats fragments "Hyperion" because it figures to him so anxious an achievement. Keats's success is the sign of a loss, both of those first parents, Wordsworth and Milton, and of the self Keats had identified with those parents. Second, "Hyperion"—its expertise, self-coincidence, and power—confirms Keats as no longer a protégé. "Hyperion" names him an achieved poet, responsible for his failings and punishable for his presumptions. Further, in "Hyperion"'s discursive determinacy and achievement, Keats could have read the very form of adult experience. The poem stylistically bids farewell to the synchronicity and transitivity of childhood *durée*, replacing that happy contingency with the causal, univocal, linear *déroulement* that defines grownup temporality.

These are the fears that precipitate Keats's revision of "Hyperion." "The Fall" demonstrates on every level Keats's autonomy. We see at once by this work that Keats has escaped the influence of his great precursors and that he has surpassed himself—surpassed "Hyperion." And yet, "The Fall" maintains a posture of dependence, dependence on "Hyperion," hence on Keats's earlier loves and selves—a defensive posture.

When children first find themselves in some way approximating or transcending the models they have cherished, and thereby entering on an adulthood they are not quite ready to claim, they sometimes regress a bit, establishing a kind of pretend dependency. They invest in some object—a thumb, a blanket—the affect associated with the surpassed developmental era. They find or fashion a transitional object, symbolic of what they feel they are losing. The child, of course, "masters" the object; it is his invention and therefore, paradoxically, the very proof of the autonomy he resists. He offsets this anxious mastery, however—a repetition of the primary developmental dilemma—with an "as if" object-dependence. Because the child can take this object along with him into the difficult new world he must inhabit, he feels better equipped for the fearful transition. Hence Winnicott's name for the symbolic dependencies that facilitate sustained and genuine independence: the transitional object. The object inscribes, as it were, the abandoned gods and the surpassed, childish selves. Its very presence is the paradoxically (materially) comforting sign of these absences.

"The Fall" is full of such objects, all of them symbols of the old attachments and conflicts that Keats is loath to abandon: relics from extinct religious ceremonies, leftovers from the Edenic feast, fragments of Miltonic and Wordsworthian collations. "The Fall," a revisionary poem, is *itself* such an object. The representation of Keats's dependence (on "Hyperion" and thereby on Milton and Wordsworth, and on Keats's own identifications with his poetic fathers), "The Fall" is at the same time Keats's invention—at once the condition and enabler of his mastery, and its concrete sign.

That "The Fall" is about the process and meaning of dying into life is a critical commonplace. What, then, is more natural than that its form should emphasize its dependence on an earlier and more derivative poem as a way of defending/dissembling/enabling a detachment from the past? Dying into life, or giving up a familiar mode of being, thereby and necessarily to enter upon an uncertain but presumably more challenging and rewarding existence, is Keats's metaphor for this psychic dilemma, one which is played out in his canon on many stages. Dying, with respect both to poets and personality, means sacrificing aspects of the self that are identified with the transcended models; dying is, moreover, to invite the gods, the Tradition, the Public, to chastise one's self-assertion. Finally, when we die into life, we turn from the unlimited potential of childhood and orient ourselves toward the narrowest of definitions, the finest of tones, the extreme of sensations: death. The life gained through this terrible sacrifice is that peculiarly conflictual adult experience: the painful perplexity of bliss and its neighbor pain. Specifically, the bliss to which "The Fall"—Keats *through* "The Fall"—aspires is the production of a full literary autonomy. The pain Keats cannot unperplex is his sadness for what he thereby abandons, and his anxiety about what lies ahead: the terrors of Experience.

Although the best of our criticism of "The Fall" says as much as this in other terms, the difference is important. The terms I promote here enable us to appreciate "The Fall" without depreciating "Hyperion." Bloom's revisionary ratios, applied to reader response as well as authorial and textual rhetoric and motivation, explain "The Fall" in such a way as to accommodate, even emphasize, not just local virtues in the earlier poem but its formal adequacy to its argument. Moreover, by conceiving "The Fall" as a dependent fragment—dependent on "Hyperion"—one grasps the extent to which it "completes" "Hyperion"; or, the extent to which "Hyperion"'s felt closure is an artifact of "The Fall"'s achievement, and *vice versa*. By proposing as "The Fall"'s formal motivation its conflicted relationship with "Hyperion" and only indirectly reflecting anxieties associated with the Miltonic and Wordsworthian sublime, the critic can explain some of those covert and normative assumptions I mentioned at the outset, assumptions that organize our scholarship.

I have tried to mark out a new dimension to Keats's dramatic representation of that moving and to us perfectly Keatsian phrase, dying into life. To feel this dimension, one must conceive in the form of "The Fall"— in its particular mode of fragmentation—an analogy to the psyche's dilemma: its desire *and* compulsion to surpass its precursors and its own prior selves, and its concomitant fear of a clean success. One gains a great deal by realizing that "The Fall" does and does not surpass "Hyperion" as "Hyperion" does and does not surpass its anxiety-producing exemplars, Milton and Wordsworth. One learns to read the two unfinished epics in a manner as favorable to the imagination as it is to reality. Neither of Keats's poems breaks free entirely, because neither wishes finally to reject the precursors nor to give up its dependency.

Keats decides not to develop "The Fall" as far as "Hyperion"'s termination, although it would have been easy enough to do so; the text was already written, and the use of "Hyperion" material up to that point is one of almost direct transcription. By his refusal to extend "The Fall" beyond "Hyperion" in the chronological narrative, Keats expresses his reluctance to give up "Hyperion" with its attachments to Wordsworth and Milton, and thus to abandon that earlier phase of himself and his art. He chooses to revise his former commitment rather than repudiate it, in the belief that he thus enacts the more enduring, the authentic evolution. Keats does no more than hint at the downfall of Hyperion, the glorious god of the first poem and somehow the symbol of its precarious success. We are told that "horrors portioned to a giant nerve, / Oft made Hyperion ache"; we are shown Hyperion's fallen sovereign and are told of ominous doings on earth. But the vision of Hyperion is of a god still dominant, still brilliant, still mastering the "meek ethereal Hours." Keats refuses to develop his narrative to the point where it would assume the form of epic or tragedy with their inevitable implication of gain through loss. Keats cannot—or will not—accept a happy substitution or displacement. He wants both worlds, innocence and redemption: or in this case, "Hyperion" and "The Fall," draft and revision, Hyperion and Apollo. One might recall in this context Keats's private guess at Heaven—the repetition in finer tone of earthly existence. His surmise figures, we might say, the negation of a negation. Keats's Heaven is not this life repudiated but revised.

"Hyperion" is the last myth, a narrative mode that, in Frank Kermode's formulation, "presupposes total and adequate explanations for things as they are and were."[18] Following Kermode, myth is a fictive concord between beginning and end; in the case of "Hyperion," we see an end followed by a new beginning. The poem occurs within apocalyptic time. Its span is an interregnum, an organized duration between two orders, and like the space between tick and tock, it is a recognizable interval to us because we are familiar with other tick-tocks, other dynastic revolutions.

"The Fall" is a fiction, a narrative mode "for finding things out."[19] Unlike myth, it does not cater to our need to live by pattern rather than by fact. Keats refrains in "The Fall" from providing a tock; he will not construct a mini-apocalypse, false but consoling. He neither depicts nor even suggests Apollo's problematic but superior reign. Keats refuses to disconfirm the older, apocalyptic predictions by setting up a new verity. In place of linear sequence, Keats piles up, layer upon layer, diverse historical and ideological moments. There is no real and meaningful succession in the poem. "The Fall" takes place within the *aevum*, a kind of purgatorial time—neither the time of men nor of gods. One could also call it a time of transition or crisis. Within this mode of duration, events lose their teleological determinacy. Here, the unworthiest is rewarded, not because some singular spirit has always already redeemed him, but out of Moneta's caprice—Moneta, who stands for the order of things. Her explanation of her mercy (that is, that the poet may enjoy some unalloyed pleasure) is aggressively insufficient. The point of this rational inadequacy is that Keats *will not naturalize the peripeteia*. It remains daring, arbitrary—as opaque as Moneta's eyes. It conforms to our sense of reality.

Objects within the *durée* of "The Fall" are held in perfect stasis by the forces that pull Keats back to "Hyperion" and to all that the poem represents to him, and forward to his own autonomy. One feels as one reads a dream-like motion without movement, as if the narration were treading water. By maintaining this null space, this suspension, Keats holds off the demons of maturity—irrevocable progression.

The activity appropriate to this kind of duration is revision: a labor that knits past and future so as to create an imaginary present—false because palpable—which holds space open. One could think of revision as the practical manifestation of negative capability. "The Fall" may well be, as Bate remarks, the most existential of nineteenth-century poems.[20] It is certainly a modern poem, a poem of crisis, in that it presents time as it is lived by "men in the middest." The time of "The Fall" is disorganized; it is anchored neither to a clear beginning nor to an expected end. Or as Bloom would have it, modern poetry begins in Satan's statement (we know no time when we were not as now) and in the horror of Adam's curse: to live under the shadow of the end, ignorant as to when it will come and what it will be like.[21] "The Fall" respects our clerkly skepticism; it deals with fact—"why women have cancers"—by bringing to our attention that most basic and determining fact of our existence, the irreducible intermediateness of our experience. Even if there were a meaning to that immense, that Titanic suffering which provokes in the poem such desperate hermeneutics, and even if we could find that meaning, we could never know our discovery, for we do not see this universe or any part of it holistically, tick to tock. The condition of grownup sublunary life is, of course, desire: desire for a meaning which is always already something else, somewhere else.

"The Fall" only figures this modernity when one approaches it through "Hyperion" and as that fragment's revision-completion. If we conceive "The Fall" as "Hyperion" done right ("Hyperion" invalidated), we produce yet another metaphysics of presence, another apocalypse, another romance, finally insulting to our sense of reality and to the anguish that impells Keats's sad and searching question, why must women have cancers.

John Jones and Harold Bloom offer antithetical readings of "The Fall"'s imperfection. According to Bloom, "this supposed fragment is an entire poem."[22] "The Fall" is, of course, a genuine fragment, which Bloom *makes* into an entire poem by reading it in a revisionary manner. "There is a dearth of meaning in a strong poem," he writes, "a dearth so great that . . . the poem forces us to invent if we are to read well."[23] Bloom invents, not randomly, of course, but with reference to "Hyperion" and to the whole range of Romantic fragments and wholes. And Bloom, we know, reads very well indeed. "The Fall" is not complete in that it contains "the complete patterning of images that Romantic or belated poetry demands," but because it "impels every reader to return upon his or her own enterprise as a reader" and to read wholeness into an incomplete poem in a systematic manner.[24] "The Fall" forces the reader to reenact, along with Keats, a revisionary process, and to experience the meanings that inform that process.

Jones considers "The Fall" and "Hyperion" to be incomplete: "'The Fall"s abandonment, too, is caused by a failure of the facts of life . . . to fit the bent of his art." Keats cannot make himself "'feel the giant agony of the world,'" "cannot convince himself that getting to the top of the steps amounts to a real proving on the pulses. . . ."[25] To my mind, the giant agony is precisely what that ordeal makes immanent; and that agony is the gradual realization on the pulses that there is an absence of meaning at the heart of things, that Moneta's eyes are blank and that the trial of ascending the steps or enduring history and its ungrateful vicissitudes does not redeem us for nor remove us from all that pain. Since meaning in this life persistently eludes our reflexive intelligence, all that remains is to invent attachments, determinacies, difference—abstract, actualized relationality. "The Fall" insists that there is neither Truth nor Beauty distinct from our names for these presiding deities, names that vary with time and place. *This* is the sheer puzzle of pain, and this is why Moneta speaks ironically, for irony is not negation (which, perforce, postulates), but swerve—a turning away of meaning.

What this means for poetry—Keats's explicit question—is that no poem can really console, for it cannot materialize the word that will justify our pain. Poets do not write poems that are increasingly intelligent or apropos or beautiful. They simply revise. And if the revision is good, if the guess at Heaven is truly a vision in finer tone, the poem becomes, as it were, a transitional object, able to comfort us as we die into life, repeatedly shedding our fondest illusions and acquiring some new knowledge of terrible because pointless misery. Such poems chronicle and thereby confer upon their readers the past, the loved precursors, the outlived selves. Readers and poets depend on these poems as they once depended on the "existences" that these things semi-real represent. And yet, because poems are, precisely, *not* existences but *products* of the human, the poets in this indirect way master their dependencies and surpass their heroes. The poem, if it is very good, renders the poet the influence without the anxiety and it does the same thing for its readers.

Christopher Ricks, with great taste, insight, and affection, studies Keats as a poet of adolescence, and he characterizes adolescence as an epoch of embarrassment.[26] In the blush, Ricks reads a defensive response, expression of nostalgia for childhood's primitive, sponsored pleasure. At the same time, he recognizes the aggressive component of the sign, index of desire for adulthood, its attributes and power. Adolescence—that transitioning—is, of course, the conventional period of crisis in modern western culture. In the stress of this phase, people often resurrect the transitional objects of their childhood, or they fabricate or designate new ones. One regresses a bit in order to move forward.

It seems particularly fitting, and endearing, that Keats's most ambitious poem should take the form of a transitional object, and that it should present the properties of this object alone as capable of performing poetry's best office: to be a friend to man.

CHAPTER ELEVEN

THE DEPENDENT FRAGMENT

The Victorian Paradigm

Some of "Hyperion"'s Victorian readers attributed the poem's imperfect condition to Keats's untimely death; others surmised that the cruel reviews of *Endymion* so shook Keats's confidence that he could not proceed with "Hyperion." According to this theory, Keats published "Hyperion" as a fragment at his editors' insistence rather than from a conviction of its adequacy as a fragment poem.

Since "Hyperion" opens conventionally and firmly enough, and since its ending is so strangely abrupt, one would naturally account the work a fragment by virtue of its terminal irresolution. A reader who knew "The Fall," however, with its eighteen introductory lines (the "induction"), and its narrative extension of the scene that opens "Hyperion" (an extension that elaborates the prehistory of that first scene), would be likely to find "Hyperion"'s opening indefinite and deficient by contrast. That is, "The Fall"'s relative prefatory prolixity makes "Hyperion"'s darkness visible, at the same time providing a means of illumination. The post-1856 reader, who knew both *Hyperion*s but not their proper chronology, would have been likely to construe "Hyperion" as fragmented or truncated at both ends. Such a reader would, I suspect, associate the stark *mise en scène* that initiates "Hyperion" with the vision succeeding the opening eighteen lines of "The Fall."

> For Poesy alone can tell her dreams,
> With the fine spell of words alone can save
> Imagination from the sable charm
> And dumb enchantment. Who alive can say,

"Thou art no poet; may'st not tell thy dreams"?
Since every man whose soul is not a clod
Hath visions, and would speak, if he had loved
And been well nurtured in his mother tongue.
Whether the dream now purposed to rehearse
Be poet's or fanatic's will be known
When this warm scribe my hand is in the grave.[1]

This passage, prelude to the conventionally indicated revery ("Methought I stood . . ."), would have figured as Keats's explicit rationale for image-making. That is, Keats's motivation for writing "Hyperion" would appear to be his ambition to contribute to the great tradition, that which distinguishes the civilized from the savage. The induction clearly endorses the social value of representation above the psychic gratification of expressivity; the subject of both discourses, or both aspects of what we might consider a single discourse, is dream. In this passage, dreams are equated with "guesses at Heaven," and here the guess takes the form of a postlapsarian Eden—vision of an abandoned, a superseded paradise. A reader looking to complete or objectify "Hyperion" with reference to "The Fall" would easily associate "Hyperion"'s description of Saturn's lair—that depopulated, sunk realm—with the Christian vision of "The Fall." Both scenes, forest bowers and instances of the *hortus conclusus*, preserve within them husks of majesty: a deposed ruler ("Hyperion") and the refuse from a sacramental feast ("The Fall"). The description of both realms conjures the image of a once potent divinity: Saturn in his prime and Adam and Eve in their innocence. The objects within these bowers are shown to resist natural temporal decay.

The reader who regards "The Fall" as a first draft and "Hyperion" as the revision could interpret the guess at a Titanic heaven as an advance over the Christian, Edenic vision. The former is a vision in finer tone, as it were—less partisan (less "fanatic," to use the language of "The Fall"), or more abstract, imaginative, and archetypal than the Christian representation. Keats would seem to have used the draft to explore the significance of a dream that came most readily to him as a Christian and a reader of Milton. He conducted this exploration by painting himself into the picture, thereby penetrating its inscape, its subjective truth. Once he located this truth—the meaning of the dream—he could proceed to generate more disinterested images, such as those developed in "Hyperion." "The Fall," then, read as "Hyperion"'s initial stage, appears to enact a descent into subjectivity, prerequisite to self-transcendence. In terms of authorial psychology, "The Fall" represents a self-indulgent, narcissistic phase that developmentally precedes and is the condition for genuinely imaginative, object-related work.

Further, the reader who approaches the two fragments in the manner I have described would interpret the lengthy exchange between the poet and Moneta ("The Fall," lines 136–215) both as Keats's intellectual and emotional preparation for the writing of "Hyperion," and as his apology for abandoning "The Fall." The draft would appear to have served its purpose by enabling this difficult decision and by readying the poet to act on his resolve. This resolve—the fruit of Keats's mature understanding of his subject, earned through his labor on "The Fall"—precipitates the vision that concludes "The Fall" and opens "Hyperion." Keats, it would seem, does not discontinue "The Fall" because he dislikes its subjectivity, its *Endymion*-like diluteness and its fulsome pontification, nor because he lacks the technique to execute his idea. The obvious explanation to the Victorian reader was that Keats discovers the proper application of the wisdom he acquires through the self-reflexive method of "The Fall"; he can then begin "Hyperion," the new poem, cleanly, having already laid its conceptual and procedural groundwork. Rather than argue himself and his reader into approbation (the method of "The Fall"), he can whisper his results. "Hyperion," by this explanatory construct, emerges as the practical implementation of the insights Keats gains and the truths he propounds and sanctifies in "The Fall." Naturally, Keats suppresses "The Fall," for the great insight of that work is that poets should not vex the world with their introspective explorations. Keats would appear to have matured beyond the point of needing to publish his partial achievements in order to surpass them. He learns to trust his critical judgments; the narrative which he begins to relate toward the end of "The Fall" he now isolates in a new poem, a work that is sympathetic yet dispassionate, and as formally inevitable and stylized (hence, conducive to contemplation rather than identification) as Greek tragedy. "Hyperion" is the poem that soothes its reader without falsifying the nightmare of history.

One wants to know specifically how the Victorian reader might have utilized "the draft" (i.e. "The Fall") to satisfy his closural expectations regarding "Hyperion." Or, what did "Hyperion"'s early readers make of its sudden ending? They did not, like one modern critic, perceive "irony, despair, and death thus woven into the texture of *Hyperion* from the beginning."[2] That is, they did not expect the poem to disintegrate from its extreme internal tensions. A number of 1820 reviewers, ignorant of "The Fall"'s existence (Hunt was the only exception) seem to have shared certain expectations concerning "Hyperion"'s promised end, based on that poem alone. They anticipate Apollo's verbal response to the fact of his deification, and insofar as his new celebrity is a function of his poetical genius, the anticipated speech would figure in the poem as proof of his divine talents, legitimation of his claim to divinity. "A story which involves passion almost of necessity involves speech; and though we may well enough describe beings greater than ourselves by comparison, unfortunately we cannot make them speak by comparison."[3] The pattern thus far established in "Hyperion" had been authorial description of Titanic suffering followed by the direct discourse of the falling or fallen gods. With this precedent in mind, one would anticipate, following Apollo's painful transformation into the reigning god, a sample of his supremely poetic speech—a discourse exceeding Hyperion's in beauty and power. In fact, certain reviewers demonstrate the strength of this expectation in praising Keats for not satisfying it. They approve Keats's discerning avoidance of Milton's great error, the attempt to invent the speech of a potent god. These critics do not object to the Titan dialogue, since these gods are portrayed by Keats as fallen; such creatures would logically speak in a corrupt and therefore humanly intelligible language: ". . . the moments the Gods speak, we forget that they did not speak like ourselves. The fact is, they feel like ourselves; and the poet would have to make them feel otherwise, even if he could make them speak otherwise, which he cannot, unless he venture on an obscurity which would destroy our sympathy: and what is sympathy with a God but turning him into a man."[4]

The expectations I have discussed were, of course, modified and in some cases satisfied with the publication of "The Fall." Swinburne, who had read both poems and assumed "The Fall" to be "Hyperion"'s first draft, agrees with the 1820 reviews: "The triumph of 'Hyperion' is as nearly complete as the failure of 'Endymion.' Yet Keats never gave such proof of a manly devotion and rational sense of duty to his art as in his resolution to leave this great poem unfinished; not . . . for the pitiful reason assigned by his publishers [that is, dismay at the *Endymion* reviews] but on the solid and reasonable ground that a Miltonic study had something in its very scheme and nature too artificial . . . to be carried out at such length as was implied by his original design."[5] Swinburne has nothing but praise for the "Miltonic study" as far as it goes (and indeed, Swinburne's own "Hyperion" is far more Miltonic than Keats's). Perhaps, then, what Swinburne anticipates in a continuation of "The Fall" (in such fashion "as was implied by his original design") is the presentation of a speaking god. Were Apollo to speak, he would necessarily speak as a mortal; Keats had no alternative "unless he venture on an obscurity which would destroy our sympathy."[6] Apollo would, moreover, have to express himself in language appropriate to the master god of poetry. This commentary by Rossetti focuses the issue yet more sharply. "To deal with the gods of Olympus is no easy task—it had decidedly overtasked Keats in *Endymion*." . . . The Olympian gods would also have to be introduced: Apollo already appears in the poem, not too promisingly."[7]

Swinburne and Rossetti are sensitive to the challenge—the representation of Olympian speech—because they had observed Keats work through it in "The Fall." Specifically, they had witnessed Keats's attempt, in the "draft," to apotheosize the poet figure, a transformation to be facilitated or even effected by the "knowledge enormous" Moneta imparts to him. The poet seeks to discover his own identity and his position within Moneta's scheme of values. Her array of distinctions indirectly but adequately answers his questions, and by his initial access of knowledge, the poet is suddenly self-enlightened. He speaks, demonstrating his new elevation in a rather pompous declamation (lines 187–210), a section Keats later deleted. Perceiving the weakness of this passage, and generally the riskiness of having a character profess his own divinity, Keats diverts his hero's thoughts to the contemplation of history, other creatures, legends—which is to say, a body of knowledge appropriate to mortals. In his growing curiosity about the causes of Moneta's suffering, the narrator forgets his own anguish. His request for objective or selfless knowledge yields him the tragic vision. He is awarded the opportunity at once to observe a story unfolding and to narrate it. He becomes a man speaking as a god, rather than a god speaking as a man. He observes from an eagle's watch and delivers himself in as close an approximation to celestial language as is possible in our fallen tongue. The language undergoes an elevation in style, not a depression, such as we sense in the speech of Milton's God and Son. Keats seems suddenly to understand that the authentic poetic language is myth: neither soliloquy nor declamation, but the narration of legends woven of human history by human imagination acting within particular historical fields. In other words, the way a poet ascends to godlike expression is by resigning himself to his humanness: "grieved I hearkened." This insight is, for Keats, the desired detour around Milton's error. Proceeding from the "antechamber of his dream," the "new" poet will describe Hyperion's fall and Apollo's ascent, events that parallel the poet's experience in "The Fall" but that will now be presented "in a clear light," or in mythopoetic, impersonal terms. The enlightened narrator of "Hyperion" *is* the "old" poet of "The Fall." He will depict Hyperion's defeat (Hyperion being the equivalent of the old, immature Keats), brought on by his solipsism, and Apollo's ascendancy, earned by his curiosity about persons and situations not himself and not his own. "Hyperion"'s Apollo (the poet in finer tone) will demonstrate his deification by continuing the story begun in "The Fall." Instead of describing his sensations of divinity, however, he will relate the history of the Titanic-Olympian wars, of whose outcome he is the beneficiary. He will describe his own conception and delivery, not autobiographically, however, but by narrating the historical events and destinies that made his coming into being inevitable. "Hyperion"'s Apollo identifies himself as the temporary but full heir to an adaptive evolutionary process. He is as a moment in a Marxian or Darwinian system rather than the omnihistorical uniqueness of the Freudian subject. Having been taught by the heavenly muse (Moneta) to venture down the dark descent, into himself and into Milton's error, the narrator of "The Fall" reascends into the clear atmosphere of "Hyperion." Here he achieves the "purity, amplitude, cleanliness of the 'old poetry.'"[8] He works his way around the impasse as Milton did not. It is crucial to keep in mind the fact that Apollo's speech has already begun; it is he, the enlightened poet at the end of "The Fall," the recipient of Moneta's memory stores, who narrates "Hyperion." Thus the rest of the story, in which Hyperion's downfall would be chronicled, is unnecessary. Its result, the apotheosis of Apollo, is manifest in the very existence of the new poem.[9]

In outlining a strategy for marrying the two *Hyperion* fragments in such as way as to explain-resolve "Hyperion"'s initial and terminal situations, I observed that the two poems appear to have been construed as an original creative effort followed by a critical actualization and completion. To see this is to infer the kind of reception that we have associated with the completed fragment, a form that presents, so to speak, as the poet's belated, revisionary completion of his own fragment. To organize such a work, one figures the included disorder as a stylistic counterpoint, the reflection of an ironic, dialectical, or composite argument. We might use this reception protocol to illuminate one aspect of our own *Hyperion* criticism.

Without "The Fall," much of the material so routinely remarked by readers of "Hyperion" would either go unnoticed or would yield more, and more diverse meanings, and *vice versa*. To the Victorians, "The Fall" and "Hyperion" were distinct parts or phases of a single composition: a descent through the more familiar or accessible ideologies (the Bible, Milton, contemporary aesthetics) to a strangely new yet archaic dimension, characterized above all by its free objectivity. Whereas our criticism typically (and unself-consciously) regenerates the normative contrasts seemingly intrinsic to the compositional facts, the earlier criticism tends to focus the relational procedures and meanings of the two poems. Both critiques observe a basic opposition between the exploratory, self-reflexive, and abstract character of "The Fall," and the achieved, impersonal, and material character of "Hyperion." Both critiques register the resultant contrasts: first-person voice versus third-person narration. Or, doctrine-action, expression-mimesis, Dantesque-Miltonic, romantic-classical, spontaneous-critically remedial. The Victorians, however, seem to have grasped the strictly differential dynamics of these representations. They could see that the first-person narrative mode of "Hyperion" owes its semiotic implication and its specific charge to the third-person narration of "The Fall." This is to say, and to see, that "Hyperion"'s Miltonism is neither intrinsically significant nor superior to "The Fall"'s Purgatorial quality; it no more disconfirms "The Fall"'s Dantesque style than the Edenic feast in "The Fall" disconfirms the relics of more ancient religious ceremonies depicted in the second dream. Or, the absence of what one reader has called "end-stopped feel" in "The Fall" is intentionalized or motivated by the sensual concreteness of "Hyperion."[10] Similarly, the omniscient, invisible narrator of "Hyperion" is specifically constituted and valorized by reference to the limited narration of "The Fall." How one evaluates these differences—literally, what one makes of them—depends on one's disposition to see a trend toward improvement or deterioration from one poem to the other.

Keats's two *Hyperion* poems define a series of determinate spaces by establishing parallel fixed points. Typically, critics of the poems select from each relationship the value that helps them make a case for the superiority or inferiority of one of the two poems. Victorian readers generally believed that Keats had replaced the Christian imagery of "The Fall" with the severe grandeur of pre-Olympian motifs. Because this belief confirmed their own aesthetic values, they interpreted the revision as a proof of Keats's healthy imagination and as a logical, prudent decision on the part of any developing poet. Many scholars today believe that Keats abandoned the escapism of "Hyperion" for the psychic confrontations and philosophical seriousness of "The Fall." Because this understanding sanctions their concept of high Romanticism (which includes, of course, a concept of the modern as well), they rationalize Keats's decision in the same manner as the Victorians.

The symmetry does not undo my earlier distinction. The Victorians, who knew the *Hyperions* by a draft-revision ratio, could, theoretically, appreciate the extent to which their isolation of any one feature in "Hyperion" depended on their identification of a parallel and opposing feature in "The Fall." Modern criticism, by supposing an antagonistic relationship between the two poems, forfeits the Victorian common ground, that revisionary, interlocutive, intertextual space.[11] One effect of this loss is the trouble we have accounting for our self-evident judgments. Although the draft-revision construct naturally suggests an evaluative scheme as well, it enables the reader to focus the antitheses as distinctions or gradations within a single system. Hunt, for example, one of Keats's contemporaries whom we know to have read "The Fall," praises "Hyperion" as follows: "The author's versification is now perfected, the exuberances of his imagination restrained, and a calm power . . . takes the place of the impatient workings of the younger god within him."[12] Delightfully easy with his associations, Hunt characterizes the relationship between the two poems in terms derived from Keats's story: the impatient workings of the younger god give way to a calm power. Hunt organizes the poetic difference by way of the verb, "perfected"—which is to say, one poem completes and realizes the other rather than opposes and replaces it. The exuberance of the unrestrained imagination and the impatience of the ephebe are controlled, focussed, and therefore strengthened in "Hyperion," not negated by it. Hunt in no way condemns the boyish extravagance of the earlier poem; that would be tantamount to judging Hyperion for his differences from and necessary deference to Apollo. (Apollo, in this context, is the elder god, the analogue of the mature Keats, since he represents the later, more refined historical moment.) Hunt reads the youthful excesses— Keats's and Hyperion's—as stages in an ontogenic development, and not, therefore, negated by the consummate product but constitutive of it.

Hunt's remarks very clearly reveal how the revisionist reader integrates the *Hyperion*s, taking his cue from Keats's own representation of assimilative change and displacement within a continuum.

Finally, "Hyperion"'s irresolution, like that of the deliberate fragment, was greeted by many readers as a formal expression of the story that the poem relates. Although its truncation was understood as compositionally accidental, the resultant form was thematically intentionalized. "The *Hyperion* is a fragment—a gigantic one, like a ruin in the desert, or the bones of a mastodon. It is truly of a piece with its subject, which is the downfall of the elder gods."[13]

CHAPTER TWELVE

MEANINGS AND PURPOSES

The distinctive difference of anything is . . . the boundary, the limit of the subject; it is found at that point where the matter stops, or it is what the matter is *not*.
—G. W. HEGEL, *Selections*, ed. J. Loewenberg, trans. J. B. Baillie (New York: Scribners, 1920), p. 3. From Preface to *The Phenomenology of Mind*.

We must not falter at the prospect of revealing formlessness and imperfection in the work. . . . Rather than that *sufficiency*, that ideal consistency, we must stress that determinate insufficiency, that incompleteness which actually shapes the work. The work must be incomplete *in itself*: not extrinsically, in a fashion that could be completed to "realise" the work. It must be emphasized that this incompleteness, betokened by the confrontation of separate meanings, is the true *reason* for its composition.
—PIERRE MACHEREY, *A Theory of Literary Production*, trans. Geoffrey Wall (London: Routledge and Kegan Paul, 1978), p. 79.

Jean Duvignaud's classic study, *The Sociology of Art*, is based on the premise that form "make[s] symbolic what experience has suggested as factual. . . ."[1] This premise tends to get translated, in today's critical practice, into an investigation of cognitive paradigms. I quote Marshall Brown's lucid formulation and defense of this practice which, as I observed in chapter one, dominates the study of Romantic indeterminacy:

At every period of history a subterranean network of constraints governs the organization of human thought. Different fields develop and change in parallel not because they affect one another but because the infrastructures . . . of mental activity affect all of them. . . . The infrastructure is the precondition of thought and is by definition unconscious and unarticulated. Because it lies outside the limits of individual disciplines, it cannot really be formulated within any of them. Hence arises the necessity of comparative study. The infrastructure comes to light at the juncture of independent fields.[2]

I too am interested in the infrastructures of mental and material activity; that is, I would like to explain a particular formal invention with reference to this epochally specific symbolization of experience. But whereas Brown and McFarland investigate those junctures where various authorial systems and aesthetic disciplines converge, I focus the perimeter of a single discourse, the place where it abuts and is interrupted by a universe of facts and relationships which the work defines as outside and other and seeks opportunistically to organize. The infrastructures to which Brown refers are, I believe, ultimately explained by way of extrastructures: that social experience which prompts, within the diverse aesthetic activities of an era, certain "unconscious and unarticulated" interests.

The very success of the RFP in promoting itself as an achieved literary form has, rather perversely, obscured its own historical and thus structural specificity. Criticism has not only adopted irresolution as a twentieth-century discovery ("the undoing of metaphysical closures"), it has characterized the Romantics or their project in such a way as to conceal their priority in this matter.[3] While "the fragmentary" is, as I noted in chapter one, an established and even privileged theme, the generally syncretic impulse of Romanticist criticism effectively situates that theme in a program of "higher" or alternative perfection. In other words, "the fragmentary" is felt to dis-organize in the interest of re-organizing; it precipitates new totalities which then rationalize or replace its disorder.

The two factors responsible for the anomalous position of the RFP within our criticism are (1) the dominance (until fairly recently) of the formalist, structuralist, and deconstructive models—or, of the idealistic implementation of these methodologies—and (2) the Romantic ideology, then and now, focussed by the procedures and projections of the RFP itself.

Let me very briefly indicate how tractably the RFP submits to a structuralist poetics. If poetry is defined as an interruption of the linear, diachronic flow of language from a referent, through a code or grammar, to a listener (the communicative circuit), the fragment poem not only performs, it dramatizes the poetic function. To conceive the aesthetic as a fundamentally erotic category—the self-contained realm of gratuitous cognitive exploration, or play—is again to focus the peculiarly, even formulaically literary character of the (eternally indeterminate) fragment poem. As for reflexivity, so signal a criterion in many of our most persuasive estimations of literariness, the fragment poem so much as pronounces the strictly operational status of its topics and arguments—occasions and materials for writerly and readerly hermeneutic exercise. The fragment poet appears to refuse the semiotic and even textually constitutive authority which is his traditionary prerogative; he styles himself a feckless bricoleur, unimplicated in the tyranny of conscious intentionality. By displaying his materials only partially "sublimed" into aesthetic form (and by evincing his indifference to or disdain for doctrinal, mimetic, and communicative values), he identifies the transformational *act* (his own and the reader's), as opposed to *product*, as the essential literary fact. The fragment poem not only invites and accepts a "recuperative" (that is, appropriative) reception, its condition of being is interpretation and when that consuming/consummating transposition ceases, the poem reverts to its apparatuses. It subsides into textuality, patiently awaiting the next structural opportunism.

In short, the fragment poem, in referring all immanence to the moment of reception and in foregrounding the arbitrariness of the structures and relations that precipitate that moment, can easily look like the acme of enlightened literary production. This is to say that irresolution has become a marked quality, sign of aesthetic intentionality. By a twist of the dialectical spiral, a form that was originally offered as a most natural, spontaneous, sincere, and literary creation now looks like a most artificial, ironic, and literary construction. A strange inversion-transcendence phenomenon has turned Romanticism's ideology of writing into modernism's ideology of reading: both profoundly ahistorical orientations, profoundly indifferent to the particular interests and determinants of the artworks upon which they operate.

> Discovery commences with the awareness of anomaly, i.e., with the recognition that nature has somehow violated the paradigm-induced expectations that govern normal science. It then continues with a more or less extended exploration of the area of anomaly.[4]

The RFP was a "mistake"; the universe it entered, the canon, had, apparently, space for it but as yet no means of naming that space. Let us say that Coleridge, for whatever reasons (that "whatever" will be explored at the end of this chapter), decided to print "The Foster-Mother's Tale" and "The Dungeon" in *Lyrical Ballads*, 1798, and that Wordsworth, for his own reasons, not only went along with that decision but two years later added his own fragment poems to the volume. Perhaps these poets sensed that this "mistake" was in some ways a better (more veridical, more pleasing, more effective) representation of their own and their readers' experience than the conventional wisdom would allow them to know. The area of anomaly was explored by Coleridge and Wordsworth, then by Keats, Shelley, Byron, and the lesser Romantics. The adventure of discovery closed when "the paradigm theory had been adjusted so that the anomalous became the expected" or when the fragment poem succeeded in looking like normal science, which is to say, legitimate poetry.

The assimilation of the fragment, however (among a host of other factors), forced a shift in the original paradigm. For assimilation "demands a more than additive adjustment of theory"; the scientist must learn to see nature in a different way.[5] Structuralism and its critical progeny are the products of that difference and of many others, as well as the means by which that difference is institutionalized and perpetuated. For those who see literary nature, or culture, in this different way, the fragment poem does not occupy a position on the fringes of art and of meaning. It situates itself smack in the center: ironically in the blind spot. "Material works of art are, then, the realizations of these particular moments [in living artistic tradition]—realizations which under the influence of the further development of the artistic structure can acquire completely different meanings from those which they originally had."[6] Literary history offers no stronger case for Mukařovský's general claim than the fortunes of the RFP. These fortunes—the canonical career of the RFP—are not unrelated to the projections or mythologies of the form, and these, I will argue, are related in a precisely inverse ratio to the actual procedures whereby these poems got written.

The RFP makes a semantic gesture: the poet (or poem) can and does say what he (it) likes, how he (it) likes. That cumbrous he-it equivocation represents a more than grammatical difficulty. It focuses an organic-mechanic, presence-artifact (integrated-alienated) problematic, one that is the field of the RFP's origination and that in some fundamental way explains the form's ideas of order.

Let me develop this argument by considering briefly Rilke's reading of the torso. (Rilke's commentary figures here as an exemplary Romantic appreciation.) I quote from a critique of Rodin's sculpture: "Completeness is conveyed in all the armless statues of Rodin: nothing necessary is lacking. One stands before them as before something whole. The feeling of incompleteness does not rise from the mere aspect of a thing, but from the assumption of a narrow-minded pedantry, which says that arms are a necessary part of the body and that a body without arms cannot be perfect. . . . Rodin, knowing . . . that the entire body consists of scenes of life, of a life that may become in every detail individual and great, has the power to give to any part of this vibrating surface the independence of a whole."[7]

First, one observes that Rilke dissolves the distinction between art work and organic form (". . . that a body without arms cannot be perfect"). It takes some effort to remember that the subject here is Rodin's sculpture. Rilke's prose effectively conceals the historically specific origination of the sculpture, its character as a work rather than a creation. Second, assumptions of wholeness are not products of a "narrow-minded pedantry" but formations arising from, in this case, the observer's somatic experiences and observations, and from his assimilation of closural conventions relevant to the sculptural representation of the human body. Or, his assumptions derive from his experience with wholes suggested by the fragment in question. The feeling of incompleteness arises when he confronts an object that pronounces itself finished through some culturally meaningful sign or cue (presentation in a gallery, on a pedestal, in a volume) but that fails adequately to approximate the ideal model to which it invites comparison. Both the degree and the kind of approximation tolerable are determined by the ideal model itself (for example, torso, complete figure) and, far more importantly, by the prevailing ideology of reading. Both factors—part of the work's aura—are nonetheless extrinsic to it. They constitute what Pierre Macherey has called the work's "ghostly perfection."[8]

Third, whether or not arms and legs are a necessary part of the body is a problem for physiologists or developmental biologists; for anyone else, a body that lacks extremities is not a perfect body, nor is a sculpture that assumes this shape a "perfect" reproduction of a human body. It may be a perfect imitation—a structure that appears self-limited, autonomous, and therefore complete. But in that case, both its appearance of imperfection and the observer's assimilation of this appearance to a model of higher or "other" (that is, aesthetic) perfection, are created by those conventional or generic limits within which the torso was produced, and not by correspondence to an organic model.

To read a torso properly is, of course, to bring to it expectations of a torso genre, through which the piece becomes a perfect form rather than remaining either the representation of a damaged body or a "certain correlation of components" devoid of mimetic allusion.[9] This formal realization, not just unlike an organic or somatic autonomy, is quite nearly the opposite. Had Rilke not initially noticed the missing extremities of Rodin's sculpture, he could not have called the work a torso nor interpreted the included absence as a repudiation of (art) history. So adroitly Romantic a reader is Rilke, that he entirely represses his original perception of the work's unfinishedness, its identity as a work. This repression is not adventitious; it is induced by the devices and the contextual aura of the torso.

The RFP generates that aura or effects that repression as well. The experience that the form thereby (and, as it were, inadvertently) "made symbolic," can perhaps, by way of Rilke's blindness and insight, be conceived in terms of an organic-mechanic contradiction. For the Romantic poets, this contradiction was a political fact before it became an aesthetic opportunity. As I remarked at the outset, the English Romantic poets constitute a school or movement only nominally and in the selective retrospect of literary historians. The Romantic ideology, however—the collective response to all those conditions of writing shared but not perceived as shared by the poets—can and should be historically postulated. It is the latter, the ideology, that explains the effects of the RFP but the former, the conditions of early-nineteenth-century literary life, that explains the form's production.[10]

The single experience common to all the Romantics was that of being poets in an age that was apparently favorable to the imagination (the poetry is proof of that) but doctrinally and practically subversive of its exercise and offices. Many of the tactics and values that have come to define the Romantic mode, although multiply and complexly determined, can be appreciated as functional responses on the part of a group that felt itself threatened by the interests of the perceived dominant culture. The fragment poem—from a sympathetic perspective, an exemplary case of Romantic artlessness and purveyor of its two cardinal virtues, spontaneity and sincerity—focuses Romantic ideology more clearly than any other literary form of the period. My reading of the RFP as a corporate Romantic expression will, in effect and microcosmically, interpret the poets' adversarial posture toward and within their social institutions. My interpretation of the RFP as a determinate production should reveal its imbrication with that dominant and inimical sociality. That internal contradiction—crudely, a means-end impasse—will explain the authentic irresolution that constitutes the form.

More than a few Romanticists these days read Shelley's celebrated definition—poets are the unacknowledged legislators of the world—with the emphasis on "unacknowledged." That is, they agree to characterize early-nineteenth-century English social life as an unusually alienating, atomized environment, particularly hard on writers and artists. Their *critical manipulations*, however, tend to represent the poets as largely exempt from the *anomie* that beset other groups and classes, insofar as the strategies of the poetry are read as successfully aggressive maneuvers evincing a range of vital, "heterocosmic" interests. Mill's revealing (mis)representation of the supremely poetical mind (for him this meant the Romantics) as belonging to "those whose character and tastes render them least dependent for their happiness upon the applause, or sympathy, or concurrence of the world in general" is, for all our sociological sophistication, too often rehearsed in our practical criticism. The ubiquity and intensity within Romantic letters of the theme of poetic autonomy does not, of course, argue the poets' happy exemption from insecurity; it betrays their more severe, more defended anxiety. In the same way, those keywords of Romantic poetics—sympathy, spontaneity, sincerity—underscore a painful antagonism between poets and their public and an attempt on the poets' part to assuage that pain with a myth of familial easiness.

The RFP comes to its readers *en déshabille*. In its seeming indifference to achieved effect—a disclaimer of coercive authorial intention—the fragment invites a participatory and sympathetic (which is to say, implicated) mode of reception. The RFP is not, of course, the only Romantic product to promote this effect. Nearly all the forms, voices, and values one associates with the word Romantic characterize literary production as disinterested (spontaneous, sincere) gesture rather than material contrivance: an artless and dynamic disclosure of a human presence to a human presence. The RFP, however, projects this appearance most forcefully, and in this projection one may locate the originary intention of the form.

The above observation is bound to surprise the attentive reader of this book, who cannot but have noticed that all the foregoing critical readings and the typology that organizes them represent the RFP as an emphatically manufactured artifact, its irresolution not the result of authorial immediacy and largesse but of determinate anticipations, conflicts, retreats, and revisions. Indeed, my anatomy of the RFP amounts to a description of work protocols: particular productive acts determined at crucial points not by abstract ethical or formal imperatives but by diverse and often contradictory intentions, conditions, and decisions. The RFP should have emerged through this critique not as "dynamic disclosure" (organism, vision, or expressive overflow) but as a motivated assembly incorporating available, even prefabricated materials and units (for example, gothic-tragic; coda-preface) and manipulating these in a determinate and determined fashion over time.

The contradiction is explained by the differing situations of the two critiques. In characterizing the RFP as an artless and dynamic human disclosure, I describe a notional reception, or the form's projection of its ideal interlocutor. When I discriminate the strenuous, heterogeneous, and conflicted character of the RFP, I read off from the contradictions that constitute the work's particular irresolution its mode of production. The discrepancy—an enormous one—between these two moments or situations (production and consumption; in a formalist idiom, original and achieved intention) is not fortuitous. The RFP figures a certain reception (reductively, "holistic") so as to smooth out ex post facto a disturbingly disjunctive (mechanical) mode of production.

All the poems treated in this book install the notion of a place—the putative "poem"—where writers and readers and writings and readings happily collapse into a perfect and structurally simple moment ("How can we know the dancer from the dance?"). Following McFarland, I call such moments "modalities"; they are, more specifically, compositional scenarios or myths of origin, and I describe them below. My object in this chapter is to explain the contradiction I have precipitated by producing a series of readings which, in enacting and self-consciously articulating those moments or genetic myths, expose their factitious and interested character.

The RFP not only distinguishes text from poem, it distinguishes the poem from the actual processes of literary production, the actual conditions of literary reception, and the specifically social transactions that connect those activities. Not only does the RFP postulate a noumenal site where poetic (which, in the Romantic idiom, comes to mean "human") realization occurs, it projects this realization as a function of some perfect participation between individuals sharing the same ambitions (existential totalization and intensification) and the same skills. That is, the RFP invites the reader to participate in a poetic process which it represents as uniquely serendipitous.

Alongside, and, I propose, negating the factual or worked reality of the RFP, exists a range of compositional scenarios referable to an Aristotelian or organic closural model, to a dramatic gestural model, a visionary, and a spatial model. By "model," I mean the projection of a particular kind of integrity, completeness, and autonomy. We will see that each such scenario elaborates a denial of textual stability and determinacy, and of authorial purposiveness. The function of these genetic myths is to represent poetic composition as a gratuitous, autotelic activity arrested in a text that is as it were an interpenetrative symbol of its genesis.

The fragments that project a visionary mode of origin seem to owe their truncation to the poet's loss of his inspiration or his withdrawal from it. Shelley's "Triumph of Life" is a good example. Rather than extend his abbreviated text so as to meet conventional closural standards, the poet showcases the trace of his vision, however irregular. (A reminder: the topic here is compositional projections, not actual productions.) Indeed, the fragment's disorder, brevity, and irresolution aesthetically valorize it. They charge the poem with the absolute authority of inspiration, unadulterated by what is implicitly and, of course, pejoratively characterized as prosaic and conventional intertexture. Such poems describe a truth so severe that it redefines beauty, or a part (". . . visitations of the divinity in man") so inclusive and organized as to render it perfect. Like Rilke's archaic torso of Apollo, these fragments say to the reader, "you must change your life." You must revise all your categories in such a way as to make room for (make sense of) this new absolute. In his tacit refusal to extend "what was, as it were, given to him," the poet evinces his humility before the otherness he has brought forth; at the same time, of course, he displays his indifference to his readers' closural expectations.

A second compositional drama enacted through the visionary fragment attributes the poem's irresolution to the poet's sudden retirement. Weary of public or merely audible discourse, the poet appears to retreat into mute and perfect communion with his muse. This scenario ("Meanwhile the mind, from pleasure less, / Withdraws into its happiness") argues a more stringent disdain for reception than the projection described above, for the poet's deliberate desertion of his readers, while it arouses their curiosity, chastises it. The poet, privy to Nature's secrets, leads the reader toward the mystery, then leaves him stranded outside the temple doors. The poet's ready access to the sanctuary identifies him as a singularly privileged individual; at the same time, of course, it characterizes his readers as profane and ineffectual voyeurs.

The text of the visionary fragment "shadows forth" the transcendent experience, metonymically representing it and, under the pressure of a totalizing perception, fully constituting it. Like the Coleridgean symbol, the visionary fragment claims no object but its own realization, and it identifies that achievement with its constitutive (noumenal) elements and processes.

Analogously, but from a more material perspective, the RFP may figure its author as a perfectly unself-conscious maker whose being and action, genius and techne, object and methods, are simultaneous and indistinguishable. The more succinct and familiar description of this productive modality is, of course, "organic"; the poem's irregularities, inconclusion, and exclusively processual character approximate the condition of the organic form. (Not incidentally, these organic effects develop a critique of the artifact—the precision, regularity, reproducibility, and closure of which are dialectically depreciated.) The organic fragment, like the visionary, seems to have made itself; the poet succumbs to an inexorable and irresistible process eventuating in a poem that is, in Mill's phrase, the "natural fruit of solitude and meditation."[11]

The organic fragment, like the visionary, asserts its disinterested character. By the logic of both modalities, the poet composes spontaneously and non-teleologically. Because he contemplates no "distinct purpose formally conceived" (Preface to *Lyrical Ballads*), he has no method, strictly speaking, insofar as method presupposes a determined end. The poet's office is to lose himself that he may find the poem (that is, *its* purposes), in which he discovers a formal necessity as perfect as that of the dream or organism. The physical structure and properties of the poem authenticate its productive process (the poet's genius), just as that process authenticates the poem. Both the visionary and organic myths subordinate the text to the generative impulse that works in and through the poet whose being is everywhere reflected, but nowhere embodied or imprisoned in his text. The text itself figures as a byproduct of the poet's involuntary exercise of his genius or entertainment of his Muse.

By the organic myth, the RFP recommends itself as a viable cellular unity (a complete phase or distinct part)—the sort of natural division to which Socrates refers in the *Phaedrus*. Could the reader see whole—synchronically—he would perceive the larger organism that at once completes the fragment and constitutes its identity as a part or an "episode." That larger organism might be conceived as "that great poem, which all poets, like the co-operating thoughts of one great mind, have built up since the beginning of the world" (Shelley's *Defence*). Or, one might invoke the canon, the authorial persona, or the collection of contemporary works as the system in which the fragment operates and which defines its function and identity. The organic fragment cannot but imply that all forms, however complete and autonomous they may seem, are but partial units that participate in a vast but determinate design. *Sub specie aeternitatis*, the mutual dependence and cooperation of part and whole would become instantly manifest. The psychic uses of this representation to a group that experienced both severe internal divisions and estrangement from the body politic—topics I take up below—seem obvious.[12]

The RFP generates a third appearance, one which might seem inconsistent with the visionary and organic modalities. Rather than foreground the vital, dynamic character of the poetic work, this third modality develops the concrete presence of the text as a spatial form. Despite its obvious departure from the models discussed above, the spatial fragment shares with the others a common motivation and effect. It too designates the poet a disinterested creator, and it represents the text as an indeterminate and impenetrable phenomenon that generates time-and-place-specific interpretation but never divulges the imageless deep truth where the "poem" lives. This representation turns on a certain narrative violence; by bankrupting the operative economy of action, the poet liberates his structural units (beginning, middle, end) into a nonreferential and atemporal dimension. Poems of this kind signify as concrete and immediate presences: not an expression or narration of a (missing) thing but the thing itself. The spatial RFP is perhaps the first formal demonstration in English poetry of the now-commonplace notion that an object cannot both be and mean simultaneously and to the same observer.

Whereas the organic and visionary models represent the fragment as an experientially indivisible unity of form and content (the two dimensions fused in the moment of creation and then again during perception), the spatial mode locates this radical simplicity within the text. In all three cases, the fragment, by preventing insertion of a wedge between form and content, fends off analytic procedures and definitive explanation. At the same time, the seductive indeterminacy of the fragment solicits acts of imaginative surmise that serve to contextualize or fix the text for that reader and for the particular act of reading.[13]

It is perhaps helpful to associate the spatial fragment—its devices and interests—with an abstract expressionist mode. In both cases, the artist seeks to produce, by his discontinuous and abstractive representation of familiar forms and relationships, an anti-mimetic, polysemic, full presence. Shelley's "Ozymandias" offers a splendid topos for this fragment modality. The poem presents the desert fragments of a once-stupendous sculptural representation of a public figure. The fragments have outlasted their historical referent. The great and broken masses, as well as the legend inscribed upon the pedestal that once supported them, have entered the dimension of the nonhistorical, which is to say, the purely aesthetic—or so the poem argues. What was a stable and conventional sign has become a widely suggestive, "natural," and ultimately inscrutable presence—in the Romantic idiom, a presence not to be put by. The trunkless legs and shattered visage invite private and reflexive contemplation; paradoxically, the art work seems to have grown in power proportionately as the original referent—the first cause of the sculpture—has declined. The message of this inversion is that art becomes increasingly potent (or, practical signs become art) as temporal power, or history itself, withers away. The "colossal wreck" achieves "an immortality of reference in its very decomposition [and in the decomposition of its referent], for artists can remodel its glory to serve themselves."[14] Or, by way of a nineteenth-century appreciation of one of Pascal's *Pensées*, "*Quelle belle ruine que cette phrase isolée!*"[15]

A subtler example of this modality is Wordsworth's "A Fragment" (retitled "The Danish Boy" in 1836), originally a lyrical ballad (1800) and later classified by the author as a Poem of the Fancy. The fragment describes in an excessively static fashion a place and a person more, the two intimately integrated. "Between two sister moorland rills" there haunts "the shadow of a Danish Boy," a boy, or shadow, who sings "in a forgotten tongue" that the narrator is somehow able to decipher: "he warbles songs of war, / That seem like songs of love." The note that accompanies the poem in Wordsworth's 1827 edition provides the legend that the poem transforms into lyric and myth: "These stanzas were designed to introduce a Ballad upon the Story of a Danish Prince who had fled from Battle, and, for the sake of the valuables about him, was murdered by the Inhabitant of a Cottage in which he had taken refuge. The House fell under a curse, and the Spirit of the Youth, it was believed, haunted the Valley where the crime had been committed."[16] By eliminating the narrative that explains the boy's eternal presence (and by omitting from subsequent editions the above note), Wordsworth strips the boy's utterance of its referential value; his war songs sound like love's warblings, and who is to say which is the genuine inspiration, Eros or Mars? Further, the absence of a narrative rationale collapses form and content into a single, simple moment of intense experience. That is, the poem is "about" the transubstantiation of violent human life into continuous, eternal, and passive presence: *gens* becomes *genius loci*.[17] The form of the poem dramatizes the rendering of narrative as lyric, or catastrophic, discontinuous event as subtle and fluid sensation. The poem's subject is eternity—earthly eternity to be sure (this "shadow" boy is the companion of real ponies and wet rain)—and its form consequently reproduces temporal passage (loss) as spatial presence. The poem not only resists structural analysis of any kind, it disallows even the mild violence of paraphrase. Wordsworth's "A Fragment" is as close to inexplicable a poem as one might ever read. "Like a dead Boy," the poem is "serene," which is to say, it simply is.[18]

The salient of all three modalities—or of all the impressions promoted by the RFP—is the concern with textual reception as a means of controlling the social reception of the poet. Insofar as the RFP cannot be objectified, determined, hence depleted by any one reading (including the author's), the form prevents the reader from appropriating the poet in a vulgar way, as the provider of definable goods or services. The fragment, which keeps its own inviolate retirement, conceals both the source of the poet's/poem's power to shadow forth a magnitude, and the method by which this power is implemented. Or, to adapt Shelley's phrase, a man cannot say "I *will* compose a fragment poem." And that is to say, only some men—some special men—*can*.[19] Moreover, by casting off formality, the RFP creates an ambiance which disarms its readers of their impulse to dissect and, following Wordsworth, thereby "murder" the poem. A poet who felt fundamentally estranged from his readers could, through the publication of his fragments, create for himself a facsimile of sympathetic intercourse between trusting and trustworthy equals. As Schlegel observes: "Even a friendly conversation which cannot at any given moment be broken off voluntarily with complete arbitrariness has something illiberal about it."[20]

The effects or projections I have discriminated add up to an affective stylistics: Romantic artlessness. Although the particular uses and therefore meanings of irresolution vary from fragment to fragment and canon to canon, all the poems treated in this book disguise the worked and purposeful character of the poem and the equally, albeit differently, motivated operations of reception. A responsive watchfulness on the writer's part and a wise passiveness on the reader's side are the half-create, half-perceive of the RFP. Clearly, the chief differential between my readings and the RFP's own phenomenology is the idea of poetic labor. In chapters three through eleven, we focussed the fragment's unworked and unconditioned appearance as an effective repression of diverse constraints upon poetic composition, aspects of the work's social inscription and interests. In the following discussion, I address this appearance as a global issue, so to speak, or with reference to the aesthetic ideology we call Romanticism.

The RFP offers itself to reception under two signs: the sign of incompletion and the sign of poetry. To the extent that poetry tends to be categorially discriminated with reference to degrees of discursive organization (actual or optative), the fragment's doubleness sets up a paradox. The generation of this paradox was not an unfortunate side effect of some generic or philosophic imperative, but the RFP's formal cause.

The early reader of the RFP, confronted by that paradox, had two choices; he could revise his concept of poetry so as to accommodate or even privilege unintentionality, or he could revise his understanding of intentionality so as to include features meaningful independently and in relation to the whole work (that is, motivated features), but that occur in the absence of authorial volition or direction and that violate received aesthetic norms. In either case, the reader's idea of the poet—his character, his activity, and his effect—had to change. The end of these changes was the distinction of literary production from competing modes of production. Either route to resolution of the paradox ended in a vision of the poet as an effortless and nonpurposive creator who, in his thoroughgoing passivity, performed an invaluable and unique service for his society.

In foregrounding its want of finish, the RFP not only proclaims its failure to achieve both its formal end and the author's practical objectives, it presents these failures as a triumph. The reversal hinges on the poet's ability to persuade his readers that the fragment's irresolution signifies the rejection of a mean, mechanical success—the sort produced, for example, by "consequitive reasoning" or a vulgar means-end rationality. Applied to literary production, Keats's phrase describes a poetry that originates in the author's determination to realize an objective and that terminates with that realization. Although Keats proposes the "rat trap" as a metaphor for

epistolary design, his poetry and his remarks about poetry define an opposite virtue: doctrinal, rhetorical, and affective contingency.[21] The reader
who is familiar with Keats's reflections on negative capability will find in
the passage quoted below a submerged and bitterly defensive meditation
on poets and poetry.

> The greater part of Men make their way with the same instinctive-
> ness, the same unwandering eye from their purposes, the same animal
> eagerness as the Hawk—the Hawk wants a Mate, so does the Man—
> look at them both, they set about it and procure one in the same
> manner—They want both a nest and they both set about one in the
> same manner. . . . The noble animal Man for his amusement smokes
> his pipe—the Hawk balances about the Clouds—that is the only
> difference of their leisures. This it is that makes the Amusement of
> Life—to a speculative Mind—I go among the Fields and catch a
> glimpse of a Stoat or a fieldmouse peeping out of the withered grass
> —the creature hath a purpose, and its eyes are bright with it—I go
> amongst the buildings of a city and I see a Man hurrying along—to
> what? the Creature has a purpose and his eyes are bright with it.
> (Letter to the George Keatses, 14 Feb.–3 May 1819)

Each of the genetic myths outlined above enacts a denial; each refuses
the premise that poems are stable and determinate artifacts produced by
the purposeful, methodical, and to an extent, mechanical transformation
of content into form. Simply by failing to assume and thus to provide a
determinate form, the RFP distinguishes itself from the material, inert,
reproducible and consumable object.[22] It distinguishes its "creator" from
the artisan, and by distinguishing the proper reader of poetry from the
vulgar seeker after morals, facts, or "outrageous stimulation," the RFP not
only guards itself from both a facile and a hostile reception, it effectively
fashions its ideal audience.

By way of explaining the defensive nature of the offense carried out by
the RFP, let me sketch—very baldly, reductively, and in an admittedly
interested fashion—the professional milieu of the poets treated in this
book: their sense of audience, of metier, of each other, and of competing
productive modes and interests.[23] The overriding question here is why,
how, and with what effect does the RFP promote and valorize the appearance of disinterest and represent this condition as the *sine qua non* of
aesthetic experience.

Wordsworth designates the poet "a man speaking to men"; Keats characterizes the poet as "a sage, / A humanist, physician to all men." Wordsworth's populism and Keats's philanthropy are, of course, not so simple as these pronouncements would suggest. The proper referent for "men" is, in both cases, neither contemporary readers nor posterity. Wordsworth was notoriously contemptuous of the public and proportionately encomiastic about the "People, philosophically characterised." Keats, sharply wounded by the reviewers' alternating condescension and contempt, could not rise to Wordsworth's chilly disdain: "I have not the slightest feeling of humility toward the Public. . . . I never wrote one single line of poetry with the least Shadow of public Thought."

The Romantics address "essential" humanity, a noumenal audience, and they do so because in the 1790s, and certainly by the first few decades of the nineteenth century, a large, middle-class, unevenly educated and uncharacterized reading public had displaced or diluted what Shelley called the "select classes of poetical readers." Wordsworth's jeremiads against the taste for outrageous stimulation and Coleridge's frequent exhortations to a willing suspension of disbelief depict a prosaic and indelicate audience; more suggestively, these remarks betray the poets' fearful imagination of such a readership. Due to changes involving the critical apparatus, the disappearance of subscription publishing and literary patronage, the narrowing of literary options due to politically motivated rejections of Enlightenment intellectualism, and the economic problems exacerbated by the ill-managed war against France, the English poets were more dependent on anonymous public approval than previous generations of writers had been. More to the point, the Romantics could not but appreciate their vulnerability; theirs was the place and moment that, through Adam Smith and a whole school of economic theory, established the notion of value as a relative and conferred quality ultimately determined by a consumer's desire to possess a particular product at a given moment. An experience of subservience to market conditions is one thing; an experience seemingly legitimized by the very order of things is not just a worse but a different thing.

I will not rehearse here the origins of our own commodity culture in early-nineteenth-century England, nor will I profile a by-now-familiar figure, the alienated Romantic poet. Let me simply observe that while the socioeconomic context in which the Romantics lived and wrote was, by our standards, closer to eighteenth-century forms of organization than to the modern consumer state, the impact of various practices and values on the minds of those who were materially threatened by those innovations was greatly disproportionate to the objective insult. Simply, what could poetry, understood as an essentially traditionary and conservative discipline, offer a progressive society preoccupied with what Shelley called "transitory and particular utility"? How could poetry, perhaps the ultimate cottage industry, fire the imagination of a people entranced by the vision of Wedgewood's factories, a people not yet disenchanted into sentimentalizing the craftsman and the workshop? The Romantics could not rebuke the philistine in the manner of Yeats, Eliot, and Pound—the way of the formalist—due to historically specific associations between the idea of craft and the techniques of mechanical production, techniques associated with trade and thus with consumer-determined production. Moreover, the Romantics, situated as they were at the threshold of the machine age and occupying perforce a reactive social position, would not readily perceive the presence of labor—the human presence—in any artifact. For them, the binary alternative to reification-commodification was an aesthetic of presence, the dominant forms of which are familiar to us under the rubrics "organic," "visionary," and "prophetic."

These remarks plot, of course, the defensive (compulsory and compensatory) thrust of Romantic aesthetics. In order to survive psychically in an environment experienced as deeply inimical to their interests, the Romantics redefined the traditional actions and effects of the poet in such a way as to liberate the literary process (namely, writers) from extrinsic sources, from the textual artifact, from the audience, and most critically, from the idea of purposiveness. The new, anti-artisanal poetics amounted to an aesthetic of self-representation. If society permitted its poets no real social function, they could repudiate sociality and celebrate the inner life, at once mystifying and valorizing the essential self and its expressions. Moreover, by producing himself, as it were, rather than some objective and alienable value, the poet claimed to enjoy an existence where function and identity—public and private life—were one and the same, and he made this claim by poetically reproducing his unified sensibility. In Shelley's phrase, "one great poet is the masterpiece of nature."

Having entertained some of the motives and meanings of artlessness within the Romantic context, we may appreciate the specifically dialectical functions of the RFP's projections. Insofar as the poet displays his imperfect text with perfect aplomb, the poem's formal ineffectuality (its apparent failure to realize its intention) figures a critique of crude purposiveness and (self)interest. By this representation, the poet claims (and hopes thus to achieve) a peculiar autonomy which amounts to a peculiar power.

> Oh, fret not after knowledge—I have none,
> And yet the evening listens. He who saddens
> At thought of idleness cannot be idle,
> And he's awake who thinks himself asleep
> ("O Thou whose face hath felt the winter's wind")

Phenomenologically, the RFP's indeterminacy is a withdrawal from aggressive textual determination and a retirement into a more refined mode of creative existence. The passivity figured by the fragment's discontinuity is the sign of an imaginative wealth or energy so indisputable as to make display both superfluous and inappropriate. Moreover, a work that expresses its indifference to doctrinal, mimetic, and affective resolution also inscribes its contempt for the getting and spending economy, one that thrives, of course, on the production of readily defined needs and satisfactions, and on the standardized and normative distinction of means from ends.

The technical imperfections of the RFP signify, on one level, a contempt for craft (for the tiresome, humiliating compromises required by consumer-oriented production). More importantly, perhaps, they install in the work the figure of the poet, or the presence of an eternal, chameleon, authorial energy. The discontinuities that score the RFP—suspension of the author's shaping spirit—underline the processual, dynamic, experiential nature of the artwork, its stable appearance at any given moment an optical illusion.

One could argue, of course, that all texts resist reification, or that every reading of a text realizes a new work. Who would deny that one reader's "Essay on Criticism" is different from another's? But Pope's poem encourages us to overlook this difference in that it presents us with a more or less standard and apparently stable text. However, any one reader's (or reading's) "Christabel," insofar as he must imagine and formally integrate an extensive dramatic context before even beginning to process the given text, is *textually* unique. Unlike the finished work, the RFP foregrounds the radical relativity not just of literary response but of the literary object. Because the reader cannot but see the extent to which his engagement with the fragment actualizes the work for him, he cannot experience the work as an object awaiting his consumption. A work that is never consumed can never be exhausted. The RFP thus dignifies reader response (characterizing it as creative participation rather than passive, slavish reception) in the process of defending against its own semiotic depletion. (More prosaically, of course, it also leaves its readers forever panting, forever eager consumers.)

The English Romantics were probably the first group of writers to work the idea that readers, to varying extents, write their own scripts. To put it another way, theirs was the first poetic practice to undermine the assumption that poems and their properties pre-exist readings and their conditions. The Romantics' representational discovery of these ideas was, of course, the practical culmination of a long epistemological argument conducted by British philosophy from Bacon through Hartley. In acknowledging that causality, however, one need not reject the influence of that cruder, more immediate network of pressures sketched above. If nothing else, it affected the potency of those abstract ideas among a certain group of writers.

The Romantics were among the first few generations of poets to recognize a sharp disparity between their own professional values and those espoused by more powerful sectors within their culture. They were the first to experience the sort of market relations that still largely prevail today. When I say "market relations," I refer as much or more to the poet's sense of the market as a mercurial institution upon which he depends, as I do to the actual changes in readership and in the organization of literary enterprise.

A more general way to formulate the problem that faced the Romantic poets is as follows: how to occupy an antithetical position within a culture that offers no special immunity, allows no privileged critique to writers, and still be read. If men of letters would not and could not compete with "promoters of utility," they could reconstitute the nature (rewrite the ideology) of aesthetic work in such a way as to make its value contingent upon the writer's refusal to engage practical issues, to promote a purpose, to provide a commodity. Romantic poetry finds its salvation in the transformation of marginality into disinterest. By recommending its own freedom from worldly considerations, the poetry educates its readers to regard art as an index of society's refinement and its political well-being.

The RFP is one of many solutions to the problem outlined above: the poet's sense of exclusion from a culture he dislikes and upon whose good opinions he is forced to rely. Gerald Graff addresses this phenomenon far more fully in his *Literature Against Itself*, a book extraordinary for its insights not just into nineteenth-century aesthetic ideology but for its perception of twentieth-century intellectual dependence on that ideology. The fictional solutions that the Romantics advanced make up that representational interest and style that Jerome McGann has designated "the Romantic ideology."[24]

In assigning the RFP what might sound like contemptibly pedestrian functions, I do not minimize its intellectual boldness; neither do I identify the form as part of a program to titillate, outwit, educate, or suborn a dull and suspicious public. I merely focus the concrete origins and effects of a form which has realized its purposes so well that criticism rarely regards it as having, or having had, a purpose. As for its origins, these have been located in psychology, bibliography, textual history, and the history of ideas. The great irony of the RFP's critical history is that after Bostetter's respected but virtually unused book, *The Romantic Ventriloquists*, criticism has tended either to situate the fragment poem in some metaphysical *aevum* or to construe its production as a defiant gesture—*épater la bourgeoisie*. This view is prompted, it seems, by our interest in appropriating idealistically Romantic angst and all its expressions. The plain expedience of the RFP has not been addressed.

The only experience common to the authors of Romantic fragments was that of being poets in an age that was beginning to distinguish "men of power" from "men of knowledge," the first step in the transfer of authority from one to the other.[25] (DeQuincy's inversion is itself, we might note, rather telling.) The instinct that led Keats, in his "Fall of Hyperion," to reward the poet, "weak dreamer," rather than the man of action, or that suggested to Shelley that Prometheus confound Jupiter by recalling both the curse and the aggressiveness that impelled it, was the same instinct that recommended to Wordsworth the virtue of "wise passiveness" as a mode of cognition, and transcription of vernal "impulse" as a method of composition. Each of these instincts was a protest on behalf of a mode of being signally lacking in manifest purposiveness. Such accord among extremely diverse writers suggests that the celebration of quiescence and retirement, or what Karl Kroeber names an "Archimedean 'place to stand'," began in an experience of compelled quiescence and retirement: marginality.[26] This is not to suggest that the Romantics finally withdrew from the world of praxis, or that they did not represent this dimension in their poetry. One could say, however, that the poets were most forcefully and eloquently political in their production of designedly apolitical, or escapist forms, forms such as the RFP.

The RFP is, on one level, Romanticism's most deeply illusionary form, but to stop at that judgment is to miss the real character of the fragment, that of the disillusioned fiction. To appreciate that character, one must focus the contradiction I isolated toward the beginning of this chapter, involving the fragment's compositional scenarios—roughly, its reception protocols—and the factual reality of the work "as a provisional version of an unfulfilled intention."[27] One reason for the difficulty of this critical discrimination is that the RFP establishes a "false and confusing symmetry between authors and readers; it assumes that place, that site, which precedes and prepares for the work"—an "original" place that is hypothetically recovered through the act of reading.[28] As we have seen, the RFP, with its specifically allusive lacunae, invites a reception that, by proceeding far beyond (behind, before, between, beneath) the text, discovers "the poem," a teleological construct. This discovery effectively "finds" (constructs) poet and reader as well, and, moreover, finds them to enjoy a perfect complementarity or even identity.

My practice in this book has been to seize and elaborate that "beyond," that site of interpenetrative felicity, and to use it as a critical eminence whence to survey the work (its inscribed production) and the excursion from it. The truths of the form emerge through its usage, which is to say, through that interpretive-collaborative excursion. But criticism, if it is to remain criticism, cannot *replace* the work's fractures and conflicts with that ideal consistency it insinuates and we elaborate. Not to maintain this distinction is to be used by the form. It is the *relationship* of conflict to consistency, part to whole, text to poem, writing to reading, that counts in a critical sense.

The RFP constitutes its imperfection by reference to an abstract and ideal model that "exists alongside the work, guaranteeing both its consistency and readability."[29] Macherey finds such models alongside all fictions. He exposes them, or the structural impressions they generate, as a disguise for the real imperfections of the work, those that mark its penetration by the nonaesthetic and ideologically unaccommodated: that is, by the messiness and contradictions of history. The RFP ends or is interrupted not when visions disintegrate, shaping spirits of imagination fail, evolutionary laws fulfill themselves, or poets retire into rich interiority.

(The "distinctive difference" of the form is not, as Hegel would have it, "the boundary of the subject," but, following Macherey, is constituted by internal fissures: see epigraphs to this chapter.) As we have seen, the RFP owes its discontinuities to internal dialectics and disorder—the result of those heterogeneous and opposed interests, materials, conditions, and methods that made the poem. Simply to enumerate some of the conflicts that, in truncating, realize the poems studied in this book, is to appreciate the ideological and practical limits of that realization.

"Kubla Khan": Expressive-Mimetic, Romantic/Visionary-Classic
"Christabel": Gothic-Tragic, Wish Fulfillment-Necessity
"Nutting": Designation-Desire, Semiotic-Affective
"Airy Hall": Epitaph-Prophecy
"Hyperion" and "The Fall of Hyperion": Myth-Fiction, Repetition-
  Autonomy
"The Giaour": Kleos-History
"Julian and Maddalo": Poetry-Madness: Judgment-Sympathy

These antitheses describe the psychic and formal sites where ideological dramas get played out. Each binary opposition (re)constitutes the problematic that is the origin and the interruption of the form; succinctly, individual autonomy vs. sociality.

In other words, to read the RFP reflexively is to conceive its irresolution not as the product of a metaphysical part-whole dialectic (that is, with reference to Aristotelian, organic, and visionary ideas of order) but as the form of the diverse materials and intentions that made the work. An antithetical critique need not be a radical deconstruction; the idea is not to negate, trivialize, or undo the genetic myths outlined above, but to use them to figure a difference—ultimately, a difference between the way ideology operates in the world and in bad faith, and the way it can work in a poem and self-critically.

This is an important difference; to grasp it concretely is to understand the sensible power of the RFP. Therefore, let me clarify that difference, and by way of a trenchant observation by Marx:

It is generally by their imperfections as products that the means of production in any process assert themselves in their character as products. A blunt knife or a weak thread forcibly remind us of Mr. A., the cutler, or Mr. B., the spinner.[30]

Each of the RFP's genetic myths destabilizes and deauthorizes the text (work) in the interests of revising, in a decidedly transcendental direction, the figure of the capable poet. The reader's gaze, deflected from the physical, representational, allegorical fact of the work, is turned upon the eternally elusive, authorizing, symbolizing power of the poet—a disembodied source. The compliant reader is ushered into the presence of a whole soul brought into activity; what is thereby refused, of course, is the vision of the poet as a writer, engaged in a particular, constrained, and directed act of production. Or, Coleridge's holistic fantasy repudiates precisely those coercive and divisive appositions and oppositions, Mr. C. the poet and Mr. D. the reader. In their stead, the RFP describes a full subsumption of function by consciousness, action by being, social by psychic domain.

What we found, however, in chapters three through eleven, is that any critical account of the process whereby a reader engages that seminal, inexhaustible, authorial presence (in whose company the "poem" gets written), effectively exposes both writer and reader in their interested, purposeful, and, as it were, professional capacities. Each of the poems treated in this book aborts (*in medias res* or terminally) when its materials, procedures, and intentions disengage. To reflect, for example, upon the internal disjunctiveness of "Kubla Khan" is to focus the corrective impulse and mechanical operations of the work's prefatory material and its coda. It is, moreover, to confront one's own interest in homogenizing and completing the broken work. Gentlemen from Porlock cannot survive this kind of knowledge. Or, perhaps more accurately, such knowledge reminds us that Shelley's observation, "A man cannot say, 'I will compose poetry,'" is a negation, which by the logic of grammar and psychology, helplessly, perversely, and eternally conjures its nemesis.

To return to my point of departure, the contradiction that informs the RFP renders it, from our removed perspective, a disillusioned, as opposed to illusionary, representation. Whereas illusion—ideology as it operates in the world—is distinguished by its systematic and comprehensive presentation, such fictions are known precisely by their interrupted and conflictual statement.[31]

The RFP extends to its readers the opportunity to observe this ideological implementation and critique in an extraordinarily intimate way. Like "Lucy Gray," "La Belle Dame Sans Merci," "The Ancient Mariner," and "The Cenci," the RFP displays the gaps that separate what the poet would say from what he can say, protesting all the while the perfect conjunction of impulse and action.

We have missed the gaps and the critical opportunities they afford partly because the protests are persuasive, partly because the display is disarmingly overt, and mostly because the RFP, in distributing "authorial" or constructive responsibility between writer and reader, makes a *removed* reflexive criticism particularly difficult. The solution I have tried to demonstrate in this book involves completing the fragment in such a way as to estrange our procedures, and then, in a secondary and self-critical discourse, to describe the abyss one has just, through one's sympathy, abolished. In that abyss, where the poem *"manifests,* uncovers, what it cannot say," resides the ideological imprimatur of the RFP—its special truth.[32]

Of course, to seize this option is to submit the system that contains the RFP—a system that prescribes for art the healing of breaches and the collapsing of multeity into unity, that renders the "it is" obsequious to the "I am," and that defines sympathy as knowledge—to a radical interrogation. It is, finally, to relinquish the orthodoxy of High Romanticism.

CHAPTER THIRTEEN

APPENDIX

"The Ruined Cottage"

L'édifice intact appartenait à l'ordre de l'utile et du rationnel. Détruit, il
est restitué à celui de la poésie, puisque réintegré dans la vaste
ordonnance mystérieuse de la nature. . . .
"Les edifices modernes se taisent, mais les ruines parlent."
   —BENJAMIN CONSTANT, quoted in Roland Mortier, *La Poétique
   des Ruines en France: Ses Origines, Ses Variations de la Renaissance à
   Victor Hugo* (Geneve: Librairie Droz, 1974), pp. 200–201.

". . . fragments of the Quotidian held up to our wondering attention, of-
fered somehow as proof of their own significance."
   —MARILYNNE ROBINSON, *Housekeeping* (New York: Bantam
   Books, 1982), p. 73.

The central and titular symbol of Wordsworth's poem, "The Ruined Cottage," focuses some of the meanings that precipitate the RFP and some of
the values that the form develops. There is an ideology of action in the
poem and one of suffering; correspondingly, there is a myth of production
and a myth of reception. These several representations are organized by
the image of the ruin: the history of its formal condition and its effects
upon the two wayfarers who find themselves within its precincts. By action and passion, production and reception, I mean, respectively, all that
contributes to the making of Margaret's cottage—which is to say, its
unmaking—and all that conditions the contemplative attitudes dramatized by the two narrators in their colloquy.

   The ruin, having declined sharply in real value (as that phrase is routinely understood in a commercial context), has appreciated just as sharply in spiritual, moral, and imaginative—that is, poetical value. Whereas the thriving homestead had offered certain boons to the weary traveller (Margaret's ready smile, her offer of refreshment), the abandoned and decrepit cottage affords what the reader is clearly to regard as a more profound and permanent utility. Still a retreat from the abrasions of unconsecrated historical existence, the cottage figures in its ruined state the superior agent of renewal. Similarly, the "useless fragment of a wooden bowl" is shown to deliver a more substantial refreshment than was afforded by the original, intact, and single-function implement—the dipper. In short, the poem rings ironic changes on the worldly designations, "useful," "real," "achieved."

What is interesting in terms of the patterns developed in the Conclusion is that the real value of the cottage (and now I speak metaphysically) appreciates in proportion to its neglect. It is the entire want of anyone's practical interest in Margaret's house and grounds that so hugely increases the value of her home. This act, *a failure to act*, transforms the cottage from a directly and privately or locally utilitarian value—practical and emotional—into a symbolic, indirect, generally available and readily commutable value. Margaret is and is not the producer of this new value. The paradox is, of course, a function of the effortlessness and disinterest that define her mode of production. The less she does, the more she effects. One is reminded of Wordsworth's "Michael." The shepherd, in relinquishing his practical *and* symbolic designs for the sheepfold, produces a fragmentary structure of far greater value than the finished shelter could have realized. Who would stop to meditate an ordinary, intact sheepfold in a rural region? It is the sheepfold's imperfection that removes it from the realm of the utilitarian and introduces it into moral, spiritual, and, above all, poetic space. Margaret and Michael are, in their spiritually generative passivity, types of the Romantic poet, or, I should say, of the ideology that defines the poet as a maker of this kind.

The cottage realizes its value only in the presence of a certain kind of observer, or, if you will, under the pressure of a certain kind of perception. Without the proper greeting, the cottage is mute and blind. The poem defines and celebrates one kind of reception by dramatically opposing it to another. I elaborate the contrast below.

The primary narrator of "The Ruined Cottage" may be usefully compared to the traveller who leads the reader through "Resolution and Independence." The anxiety and spiritual torpor so clearly articulated in the later poem are, in "The Ruined Cottage," symbolically suggested through the landscape and the narrator's physical progress through it.

> 'Twas summer and the sun was mounted high.
> Along the south the uplands feebly glared
> Through a pale steam, and all the northern downs
> In clearer air ascending shewed far off
> Their surfaces with shadows dappled o'er
> Of deep embattled clouds: far as the sight
> Could reach those many shadows lay in spots
> Determined and unmoved. . . .
>
> Across a bare wide Common I had toiled
> With languid feet which by the slipp'ry ground
> Were baffled still, and when I stretched myself
> On the brown earth my limbs from very heat
> Could find no rest nor my weak arm disperse
> The insect host which gathered round my face
> And joined their murmurs to the tedious noise
> Of seeds of bursting gorse that crackled round.

Although the narrator neither names nor explains his misery, the discourse (which inscribes by that sketchy fantasy, lines 10–18, a desire for easeful death) evokes that deep despondency which the hero of "Resolution and Independence" suffers. In that poem, the narrator traces his mood to anxieties centering on his professional identity, that of the poet.

The "ruined house" is to the narrator, before he hears the Wanderer's story, "four naked walls / That stared upon each other." The enclosure represents shade, a landmark in that level expanse, and a respite for the narrator from his tedious journey. At the cottage, the narrator encounters his friend, learns of the nearby stream, slakes his thirst, and removes his hat "to catch the motion of the cooler air." By these gestures, he appropriates the spot in a certain way, one we are meant to recognize as somewhat shallow or merely sensual. In his preoccupation with his animal needs. the narrator fails to seek out finer and more enduring sources of pleasure.

The Wanderer gently rebukes him: "'I see around me here / Things which you cannot see.'" He tries to deepen the narrator's response to the place, to give him access to its springs of power now that he has drunk of its natural waters. To this end, he relates Margaret's story—a terrible tale of pointless, unavoidable, and unalleviated misery. Having heard this sad story, the narrator's perception of the cottage undergoes a striking change. He sees it now as the symbol of Margaret's misery and of the cruel indifference of Nature, God, or fate.

> O Sir! the good die first,
> And they whose hearts are dry as summer dust
> Burn to the socket.

The cottage becomes to the narrator the "memorial" mentioned by the Wanderer at the outset of his narration. It turns the narrator's gaze upon the past, replacing the concrete particularity of the cottage and grounds with their timeless moral significance. Indeed, by the end of the poem, the concrete present reality of the place is completely displaced by the concrete and present reality of the poem.

The narrator's engaged or humanized reception of the cottage—as a sign rather than a signified—leaves him weak (line 495) and feeling the "impotence of grief." He returns to the scene of meditation, and now, rather than read in the cottage the legend of Margaret's real losses and grieving, he "reviewed"

> Fondly, and traced with milder interest
> That secret spirit of humanity
> Which, 'mid the calm oblivious tendencies
> Of nature, 'mid her plants, her weeds, and flowers,
> And silent overgrowings, still survived.

Rather than focus the terrible—that is, historical—absences that the ruin inscribes, the narrator contemplates the reassuring presences, natural and supernatural, that the cottage quietly impresses upon the fond eye.

Because the narrator has achieved this position of loving detachment with respect to the ruin and the human drama it enshrines, the Wanderer can deliver his lesson, knowing that it will be well taken.

> My Friend! enough to sorrow have you given,
> The purposes of wisdom ask no more:
> No more would she have craved as due to One
> Who, in her worst distress, had ofttimes felt
> The unbounded might of prayer; and learned, with soul

Fixed on the Cross, that consolation springs,
From sources deeper far than deepest pain,
For the meek Sufferer. Why then should we read
The forms of things with an unworthy eye?
(Lines added to *The Excursion*, 1845)

'My Friend, enough to sorrow have you given,
The purposes of wisdom ask no more;
Be wise and chearful, and no longer read
The forms of things with an unworthy eye.
She sleeps in the calm earth, and peace is here.
I well remember that those very plumes,
Those weeds, and the high spear-grass on that wall,
By mist and silent rain-drops silver'd o'er,
As once I passed did to my mind convey
So still an image of tranquillity,
So calm and still, and looked so beautiful
Amid the uneasy thoughts which filled my mind,
That what we feel of sorrow and despair
From ruin and from change, and all the grief
The passing shews of being leave behind,
Appeared an idle dream that could not live
Where meditation was. I turned away
And walked along my road in happiness.'
(Butler, ed. *The Ruined Cottage & The Pedlar*, Ms. D)

The "unworthy eye" is one that reads the forms of things as directly, concretely, and privately serviceable—or, as signs of some value located elsewhere (in the past or future, for example). The worthy eye reads the forms of things as the meaning of things. Or, by way of Wallace Stevens, our own Romantic,

> For the listener, who listens in the snow,
> And, nothing himself, beholds,
> Nothing that is not there and the nothing that is.

The Wanderer turns the narrator's gaze upon the nothing that *is* there ("peace is here . . ."), and reinforces this palpable immediacy by describing the vegetable beauty of the scene—the beauty and its meaning ("an image of tranquillity") indistinguishable and thus an instance of a beauty that is truth. Having materialized and humanized the ruin's historical dimension in order to deepen the narrator's comprehension, the Wanderer then cancels that semantic dimension—rejecting the referentiality of chronicle and insisting on the pure and opaque immediacies of Nature. To the Wanderer—and by the end, to the narrator as well—the ruined cottage is *not a memorial*. It does not gesture toward an absent and authorizing reality. It is itself a full and authorizing reality and therefore the ultimate resort and restorative in a world impoverished by symbol, allegory, history: the nothings that are *not* there.[1] By the end of the poem, the "restless" narrator (line 198: "restless" is always for Wordsworth a loaded word, denoting topical enthrallments) finds a "resting-place" (line 538).

The Wanderer teaches the value of presence (here, of the physical and spiritual worlds), and he intimates the reward to be gained by those who are capable of this sort of disinterested, present-ing perception. In learning to read the cottage as a presence that is not to be put by, the narrator comes to experience a peace that passes understanding. That this twofold lesson is the object of the Wanderer's discourse is suggested by the otherwise unmotivated break in the poem, line 185. The Wanderer interrupts his narration in order to draw the narrator's attention to several immediate and ordinary natural phenomena: he notes the hour by the sun; he hears the cheerful buzz of flies and "the calm of Nature," and he properly tunes his thoughts and action to these sylvan hints. That is, he detaches himself from the history he has been relating and the historically particular meanings it includes.

In removing his attention from this dimension, and turning it upon natural (seasonal and cyclical) verities, the Wanderer detaches and reattaches the narrator as well, giving him his first lesson in distinguishing meaning from being and in giving precedence to the latter. The narrator is as yet too weak, however, wholly to relinquish the satisfactions of meaning. "In [his] own despite," the narrator thinks again of Margaret and he thinks of her as a familiar. The Wanderer's narration is responsible for that vividness, for he discoursed in such a way that "the things of which he spake / Seemed present." This power of speech that initially rouses the lethargic narrator, thereby attaching him to the story, enables his ultimate disengagement and "repose," a condition symmetrically opposed to the narrator's initial torpor and estrangement. (Compare, for example, "The insect host which gathered round my face," line 24—a plaguey irritant to the "weak" narrator—to the "multitude of flies" that "Fills all the air with happy melody," lines 190, 191.)

Margaret's experience, like her cottage, is a fragment. Her waiting, which is the primary action in her tragedy, never concludes. She does not learn whether or not her husband lives, and her lapsing into death is only, as it were, a new phase of waiting.[2] In fact, "The Ruined Cottage" is exactly what Arnold said poetry should never be: the narration of un-relieved suffering that finds no vent in action, and that leaves the reader in a paralyzing "impotence of grief." Of course, Wordsworth never published "The Ruined Cottage" as an independent poem, but within *The Excursion* it remains a distinct and unresolved segment that is not concluded in dramatic terms by the subsequent material. (The story is, of course, con-textualized and rationalized philosophically, doctrinally, and politically.) In withholding the desired conclusion—*any* conclusion—Wordsworth makes it impossible for the reader to find in the story a lesson distinct from its dramatic and discursive events, its formal unfolding. That is to say, Wordsworth discourages a moralistic response, though not, of course, a moral one. He rebukes our semiotic interest in the story, forcing us to experience both Margaret's life and the narrator's brief encounter with its residue as concrete and minute particulars, ultimately impenetrable. The poem and its narrative burdens are delivered to us in the form of the spot of time, its sheer existential insistence beyond paraphrase, beyond analy-sis, beyond historically specific and practical meaning—that is, mute and blind.

Arnold recognized that without the mercy of a determinate end, the reader remains hopelessly identified with the suffering protagonist and implicated in his guilt or sorrow. The only way to break free of such a poem is through an act of will that respects the mystery of suffering (that is, refuses the analysis that would present to consciousness an alternative). This is exactly the action taken by the narrator and the Wanderer as they deliberately, consciously extricate themselves from the vivid fact of Mar-garet's pain.

The fragmentary artifact—a life, a poem, a cottage—imposes itself as a totalizing presence capable of resisting one's inevitable attempts to *read* its irresolution: that is, to construct the "real"—as that word is routinely understood in the world which is the place of all of us—meanings of the form. When we accept this curtailment of our power, we do so because we believe the fiction that the form sponsors. The less the writer does, the greater his power to chasten and subdue, that he may then energize and raise up. And the less *we* do to interfere with this redemption, the more certain does it become.

I have argued that the RFP, in imposing itself as an autonomous and reflexive phenomenon, advances a determinate doctrine: the form structurally discovers the reciprocal antagonism between being and meaning. Meaning, or rather, referentiality, introduces the dimension of history, and history in turn brings out individual psyche as the manifestation of a collective necessity. In that nineteenth-century poetry builds its authorizing ideology on the myth of individual autonomy and of escape from history through art, it should not surprise us to find this suppression or problematizing of the whole business of reference at the center of a major Romantic form.[3]

Again, "The Ruined Cottage" shows us the technique. Jerome McGann has called our attention to the way in which history, in the form of the war and all the concomitant domestic miseries directly responsible for Margaret's tragedy, disappears from the poem.[4] We hardly notice its departure (indeed, until McGann, no one did) because Wordsworth slips in a replacement to focus and distract our thoughts: vegetable tranquillity and decay, to ring a change on a Wordsworth title. The full presence of Nature, which has no meaning but its formal unfolding and which opposes its cosmic continuity to the catastrophes of human experience, cancels out the vexing, restless thoughts otherwise excited by the story of Margaret. Restless thoughts are, for Wordsworth, as I mentioned above, topical, interested thoughts, and the condition of restlessness is for Wordsworth a species of madness, as Margaret so aptly illustrates. The vegetable life that "overgrows" not just the cottage but the primary subject of the poem is, in its aspect of pure being, the wisdom of the poem. The Wanderer's peroration (lines 508–525) clearly identifies "thoughts" with "sorrow and despair / From ruin and from change"—or, with the miseries of history, with its determinate meanings and irrevocable, unrecompensed losses. This dimension of experience is represented as "passing shews of being" and "idle dream," and is contrasted with the full and true being, the *real* of Nature's images of continuity, cycle, fulfillment, renovation: that is, images of peace.

Jaucourt, in his article, "Ruines," for *l'Encyclopédie*, 1765, volume 14, explicitly excludes from the category "the houses of peasants, bourgeois. . . . [T]hese are ruined buildings." He reserves the term "ruine" for palaces, sumptuous tombs, and public monuments (*"Ruine* ne se dit que des palais, des tombeaux somptueux ou des monumens publics. On ne diroit point *ruine* en parlant d'une maison particulière de paysans ou bourgeois; on diroit alors *bâtimens ruinés*.").[5] Wordsworth's poem opens in such a way as to promise a stringent and politically informed critique of a society that destroys its own people and refuses them even the exaltation of their tragedies. This sort of interest is raised only to be rebuked and redirected. Our attention and admiration, like those of the narrator, are clearly deflected from Margaret to Nature.

The RFP seeks to erase the appearance of labor from the poetical work: to represent that work as a text, and that text as a pretext for the immaterial poem. This is to say that the fragment tries to erase history by resisting or concealing the referential operations of language. As opposed to a narrative, allegorical discourse, the RFP offers an utterance snatched from the abyss, ". . . the imperfect eruption into visibility of the perfect and invisible—an inner light which outer light but shadow[s]. . . . a fragment broken off from silence . . . followed by the silence intended to reintegrate it."[6]

This book set out to elaborate, make explicit, and interpret such projections in terms of their genetic conditions and their real purposes: to represent the RFP not as a divinely existential moment but as a work, rich in value because deeply and very humanly interested. By now it should be apparent just how sharply this approach cuts against the grain of the RFP; it reveals the fragment's answers as negations and its questions as distractions.

Through our refusal to take its wisdoms for truths, the RFP recovers a real dignity—a human quality. This is not quite the appreciation Ruskin hoped to cultivate for Gothic imperfection, but his discussion is apropos. What humanizes the RFP, and therefore its reader, is not so much the form's mode of production (Ruskin's explanation) as its myth of production, demystified. Here is the vexed conjunction of character and destiny that one does not commonly discover in the great literary monuments— works cherished for their inevitability and resolution—but which may enable an experience no less profound. That conflict or discrepancy between what the author would say and what he can say generates a form that organizes a deception, a form that sets its legitimate concern for achieving certain limited, real objectives under the fiction of disinterested, impersonal, spontaneous, and sincere creation.

To focus the RFP as an overdetermined form, of unusual expedience to its authors, is not to subtract from its art but to bring it out. The RFP seeks to cancel its identity as a work of art. For us to respect this representation is to conspire with the form in its own undoing. Clearly, the way to revalue the RFP is by challenging its standard of value. When we submit its "modalities" to a removed critique, we restore the form to the world of praxis and poeisis. It is here, if anywhere, that full presences are realized.

. . . .

Chapter 1

1. Lucien Goldmann's comment on Pascal's *Pensées* ("paradoxical masterpieces, achieved by [their] inachievement"). Quoted in Thomas McFarland, *Romanticism and the Forms of Ruin* (New York and Princeton: Columbia and Princeton University Presses, 1981), p. 3.

2. Uri Margolin, "On Three Types of Deductive Models in Genre Theory," *ROZPRAWY* 17 (1974):5–19, 13.

3. Let me present an instructive defense of the position currently accorded the RFP: "As a formal category, strictly considered, I'm not sure that too much needs to be said about the RFP. To be sure, it is not the subject of any of the extant literature. . . . But part of the reason for this . . . is that it is very much accepted as familiar that the 'fragment' is a very important theme in Romanticism." The author of this informal commentary, David Simpson, justifies our critical silence on the subject of the RFP by invoking our practical recognition of the "fragment." By thus bracketing the word, however, he negates the formal determinacy of fragment poems at any given moment, emphasizing instead the conceptual and disembodied character of the referent. Surely the consensus use of a concept does not obviate its articulation; quite the contrary, it should supply a special motive for formal description, the caveat here being the distinction between "formal" and "formalist." What Simpson neglects is that the "fragment," a theme, is largely the product of actual poems and of the meanings that have been read off from them. As long as criticism persists in speaking of fragment poems as "the fragment," they ("it") will effectively repel analytic attempts. Or, in thematizing and unself-consciously totalizing fragment poems, we constrain ourselves to a paraphrastic critique. That there is something willful in this perverseness *and* obsequious to the projections of the works thus mystified, is a suspicion we do well to entertain.

4. McFarland, *Romanticism and the Forms of Ruin*, p. 4.

5. Marilyn Butler, *Romantics, Rebels and Reactionaries* (Oxford: Oxford University Press, 1981).

6. The best source for Romantic commentary on "the fragmentary" is the Elgin Marbles discussion and, generally, nineteenth-century appreciations of the fine arts. This is not the context of an abstract or theoretical discourse, but the marbles, along with certain paintings and sculptures, did provoke writers to reflect somewhat more generally than was their wont on the idea of the imperfect.

See, for example, the "Summary of the Opinions of Benjamin West, Esq," from "Abstract of a Report from the Select Committee of the House of Commons, on the Earl of Elgin's Sculptured Marbles, etc," *Annals of the Fine Arts* 1 (1817):241, 242:

He [Benjamin West] considers, that great improvement of our British artists, may be expected from this acquisition, as *it is in these marbles which is seen the source from which they grew, and that source is now as open as when they were carried into being,* because it came *from nature,* which is *eternal* . . .
—In comparing the Theseus and the Ilissus, with the Barberini faun, and their comparative money value, he [West] reckons the three figures to be in the very highest class of art, and the very able restoration of the mutilated parts of the latter, renders it more agreeable to view as a whole, but not more valuable, or superior in style of art, or equal to the figures of the Theseus, or the Ilissus.

Letters on Subjects connected with the Fine Arts. By B. R. Haydon, Esq. Letter 2 to the Critic on Barry's Works in the *Edinburgh Review* (August 1810):278–79 and 281:

Nothing can be more delightful than the real momentary expressions of feeling in the great artists, Rubens, Titian, Vandyke, Tintoretto, and Rembrandt; let them scrawl their brush in any way, you see by what they did, they could do more: their dashes were not those of random ignorance, but of minds in a heat, who could not stay to express more than the leading points of things, and when they were hinted were content. "What can be more unfinished," say they in excuse [of indolent indulgence of feeling as opposed to attempted excellence] "than Rubens?" The dash, we answer, that may appear careless unfinishing to the ignorant eye, to the feeling and the educated one, is known to be the result of the deepest principle; and at the proper distance will be seen by both to be the leading characteristic of the thing expressed by a touch. "He that leaves his pictures rough, like Titian," says Reynolds, "without his principles, will indeed produce *'goffe pitture,'* as Vasari calls them;" and the student that dashes, because Rubens appears to dash, without reflection, has begun at the wrong end.

Proper finishing is seizing the leading points of things with truth and correctness, that they may predominate over the subordinate parts, though the subordinate parts are not to be neglected. The reverse is the character of the French school; and of David. . . .

7. Edward Bostetter, *The Romantic Ventriloquists* (Seattle: University of Washington Press, 1963; rev. ed. 1975). Balachandra Rajan's *The Form of the Unfinished: English Poetics from Spenser to Pound* (Princeton, 1985) appeared too late for me to profit by its methodological innovations and critical insight. With Rajan's ambitious, wide-ranging study, Bostetter's intensive work, and McFarland's philosophical investigations we now have what looks like the framework for a richly historical study of the Romantic fragment.

8. As Michael Riffaterre has so effectively argued, questions of genre and the literary period cannot be dissociated. Riffaterre, "The Stylistic Approach to Literary History," *NLH* 1 (Autumn 1970):39–56. My remarks throughout this chapter are informed by this issue of *NLH*, an issue devoted to problems of literary reception, genre, and form in relation to our notions of literary history. My inves-

tigations of works and responses produced in the early nineteenth-century in England will, I hope, add to our understanding of that interval: its ideas of order and its determinate disorders. I will not, however, initially characterize that era or its ideologies in order to deduce its forms.

9. Pierre Macherey, *A Theory of Literary Production*, trans. Geoffrey Wall (London: Routledge and Kegan Paul, 1978). My understanding of the lapses, lacunae, disjunctions, and irresolution so emphatically represented by the RFP is largely indebted to Macherey's work.

10. For an excellent critique of this tendency, see Paul Hamilton, *Coleridge's Poetics* (Stanford: Stanford University Press, 1983), pp. 18 and 7–26.

11. Hans Jauss, "Literary History as a Challenge to Literary Theory," *NLH* 1 (Autumn 1970):13, 14.

12. My omission of Blake requires a more substantial defense, in light of the *Zoas* and, more importantly, with respect to the overall relation of engraving (and coloring) to text in his oeuvre.

I approach this question by way of some recent commentary by students of "the fragmentary" in Romantic and modern art, a commentary that draws upon the concept of the "non finito" in Renaissance aesthetics for its explanatory model. See Eric Rothstein, "'Ideal Presence' and the 'Non Finito' in Eighteenth-Century Aesthetics," *Eighteenth-Century Studies* 9 (1976):307–32; and David Rosand, "Composition/Decomposition/Recomposition: Notes on the Fragmentary and Artistic Process," in *Fragments: Incompletion and Discontinuity*, ed. L. Kritzman and J. Plottel (New York: New York Literary Forum, 1981), pp. 17–30. Irresolution in Renaissance sculpture and painting is typically read as the sign of a conception so mighty that it outstrips the artist's powers of execution; or, it so fills him with sublime ambition that he becomes impatient of mere detail or "finish"; or again, it insists on an unconventional and unaccommodated representation. Michelangelo's sculptural fragments, "Slaves"—mighty, muscular figures straining to detach themselves from their stony medium—could stand as a topos for this conceptual model.

This model, consistent with certain received notions about Romantic art, consorts neither with the conditions of literary enterprise in early nineteenth-century England, nor with the feel of most RFPs. These are subjects I address at some length in the conclusion to this book. For now, let me note that the fragment poem, like so many Romantic inventions, was etiologically a defense against the poets' experience of marginality; its underlying purpose was to turn that ignominy to advantage. Insofar as marginality means, in real terms, enforced passivity or impotence, the logical sublimation of this experience was the valorization of a voluntary passivity, suggesting a retirement into unlimited *potentias* and disdain for manifest and effective action. There is an easy indifference—even diffidence— an apparently effortless grace about the RFP that is meant to suggest the artist's disdain for exertion rather than his exhaustion in the face of surpassing ambition. Valery's pronouncement—"a work is not so much finished as abandoned"—more accurately describes the RFP's projection than does Ruskin's "no great man ever stops working till he has reached his point of failure." The very notion of work is inappropriate to the RFP—by its own account, an easy gesture. By omitting from his composition (conventional) signs of artifice, the poet communicates not so much his contempt for finish per se (although this attitude *is* involved) as for the labor thereby expressed and the servility thus implied. The poet's feigned indifference to reception amounts to a claim of autonomy, and the withholding of closure is of tremendous expedience in this strategy.

Blake's political and intellectual context—that of the Enlightenment, with its belief in the efficacy of art and the practical uses of vision—deeply informs his fragments, and his whole canon. The Renaissance "non finito" is, for Blake, an apt phenomenology ("The road of excess leads to the palace of wisdom." "You never know what is enough unless you know what is more than enough."). All Blake's poems (except, perhaps, the *Songs of Innocence and of Experience*) suggest urgent exploration—a strenuous and Promethean essay that cannot conclude, it can only cease, for its vision so far exceeds historically available materials and representational techniques. Irresolution, for Blake, is a political tactic, whereby the poet resists incarceration in any one state. Irresolution is not indeterminacy or ambiguity, but rather an approximation to the eternally metamorphic and self-objectifying form of fire, a determinate configuration at any given moment. To talk about Blake's fragment poems is to talk about Blake in the most comprehensive way, and it is, moreover, to talk about the aesthetic and political interests of the Enlightenment. Hence my omission of Blake from this inquiry.

13. Robert Ogilvie, *Latin and Greek: A History of the Influence of the Classics in English Life from 1600 to 1918* (London: Routledge and Kegan Paul, 1964), pp. 37–39. See also M. L. Clarke, *Greek Studies in England 1700–1830* (Cambridge: Cambridge University Press, 1945).

14. *Collections from the Greek Anthology by Rev. Robert Bland, J. H. Merivale, and Others* (London: Longman, Rees, and John Murray, 1833): "The merit to which the poems in the *Greek Anthology* have a claim, consists generally in the justness of a single thought conveyed in harmonious language. Very little can be done in the space of a few couplets, and it only remains for the writer to do that little with grace . . . the lover of poetry will sometimes find a grateful pause from grandeur and elevation, in the milder excellence of suavity and softness . . ." (p. xv). "The Fragments of Philemon that have come down to us bespeak a mind tranquil and unruffled . . ." (p. liii). ". . . [T]hey [the epigrams] found an admirer in Dr. Johnson, who filled up the intervals of pain . . . in translating several of them into Latin. . . . They were considered in general as pleasing and light pastimes to the poet and his readers, and no unfair demands were made upon such modest professions" (p. lx). "Of the many poetical compositions ascribed to [Archilochus], we possess, with the exception of a single Epigram . . . only a few scattered fragments; some elegiac—but mostly lyrical. . . . The memorial of his life, so far as is necessary to the explanation of the few fragments of his works which remain to us, may be reduced to the compass of the following facts" (p. 2). From George Burges, *The Greek Anthology as Selected for the Use of Westminster, Eton, and Other Public Schools, Literally Translated into English Prose* (London: Henry Bohn, 1852): "As regards the intrinsic value of such fugitive pieces, Bland has correctly observed that—'from the histories and orations and nobler poems which have come down to us, we know how to appreciate the bold and masterly characters of the heroes and states-

men of Greece and Italy; but for private events and domestic occurrences, we must look to fugitive pieces; for there we meet with records beneath the dignity of history, and catch a glimpse of the characters and customs of an otherwise little-known age . . .'" (p. v).

15. Norman Maclean, "From Action to Image: Theories of the Lyric in the 18th Century," in *Critics and Criticism*, ed. R. S. Crane (Chicago: University of Chicago Press, 1952), pp. 422–51.

16. My quotations from *The Works of the Poets of Great Britain and Ireland; with Prefaces Biographical and Critical*, ed. Samuel Johnson, 8 vol. (London: Andrew Miller, 1800), 1:252, 250.

17. Perhaps the simplest and best evidence for the privileged relationship between the Romantics and their fragments is the negative data supplied by seventeenth- and eighteenth-century publications. The poetic fragments printed throughout the years, say, 1600–1770, simply do not comprise an appreciable proportion of the literary output over any given interval. Moreover, the fragments that do emerge are rarely (if at all) regarded as major works in their own time, nor are they distinguished by successive generations of readers and critics. I present some highlights of this publishing history in chapter two.

18. It might be noted that some of the volume titles popular in the Romantic period—*Fugitive Pieces, Foliage, Sibylline Leaves*—suggest an interest in emphasizing the partiality of compositional practice, hence of the resultant artifact. In effect, these titles (as well as such generic designations as "Bouquet" and "Garland") encourage the reader to consider the included poems with reference to one another and as making up one whole. Seemingly finished entries are, in this manner, rendered incomplete and/or discontinuous. Here is an excerpt from Coleridge's Preface to *Sibylline Leaves*, 1817:

> The following collection has been entitled *Sibylline Leaves*, in allusion to the fragmentary and widely scattered state in which they have been long suffered to remain. It contains the whole of the author's poetical compositions, from 1793 to the present date, with the exception of a few works not yet finished, and those published in the first edition of his juvenile poems. . . . They may be divided into three classes. . . . The whole is now presented to the reader collectively, with considerable additions and alterations, and as perfect as the author's judgment and powers could render them.

19. Francis Jeffrey, review of "The Giaour" *Edinburgh Review* 21, July 1813, in Donald Reiman, *The Romantics Reviewed: Contemporary Reviews of British Romantic Writers* (New York: Garland Publishing Co., 1972), part B, 2:842:

> This, we think, is very beautiful—or, at all events, full of spirit, character, and originality;—nor can we think that we have any reason to envy the Turkish auditors of the entire tale, while we have its fragments thus served up by a *restaurateur* of such taste as Lord Byron. Since the increasing levity of the present age, indeed, has rendered it impatient of the long stories that used to delight our ancestors, the taste for fragments, we suspect, has become very general; and the greater part of polite readers would now no more think of

sitting down to a whole Epic, than to a whole ox:—And truly, when we consider how few long poems there are, out of which we should not wish very long passages to have been omitted, we will confess, that it is a taste which we are rather inclined to patronize—notwithstanding the obscurity it may occasionally produce, and the havoc it must necessarily make, among the proportions, developments, and *callidae juncturae* of the critics. The truth is, we suspect, that after we once know what it contains, no long poem is ever read, but in fragments;—and that the connecting passages, which are always skipped after the first reading, are often so tedious as to deter us from thinking of a second;—and in very many cases so awkwardly and imperfectly brought out, that it is infinitely less laborious to *guess at* the author's principle of combination, than to follow out his full explanation of it.

Jeffrey registers the extent and the nature of "The Giaour'"s irresolution and, as we learn later in his review, this quality becomes for him the preeminent textual feature. In expressing—albeit facetiously—his own and his contemporaries' preference for fragments over wholes, Jeffrey articulates the formal determinacy of the fragment within the particular and dominant literary ideologies of the day. Further, he applies the reception protocol associated with "proper" fragments to complete works as well. A passage such as the one quoted above to some extent confirms the kind of response I postulate and investigate throughout this book.

20. Macherey, *A Theory of Literary Production*, p. 70.

21. Peter Bürger, *Theory of the Avant-Garde*, trans. Michael Shaw, Foreword by Jochen Schulte-Sasse (Minneapolis: University of Minnesota Press, 1984), pp. xx, xxxix, 91.

22. Jauss, "Literary History," p. 10.

23. The Romantic reader whom I postulate here is, of course, as much of a construct as my Romantic poet—both notional figures that reflect my own historical situation as forcefully as they seek to reflect the conditions of early nineteenth-century English intellectual life. The "informed reader . . . is neither an abstraction nor an actual being but a hybrid—me." Stanley Fish, "Literature in the Reader: Affective Stylistics," *NLH* 2 (Autumn 1970):145. Like Fish today, I resist this necessity.

Chapter 2

1. Preface to "Hellas," in *Shelley's Poetry and Prose*, ed. Donald Reiman and Sharon Powers (New York: W. W. Norton and Co., 1977), p. 409.

2. Georg Lukács, *Soul and Form*, trans. A. Bostock (London: Merlin, 1974), p. 13.

3. *Shelley's Literary and Philosophical Criticism*, ed. John Shawcross (London: Henry Frowde, 1909), p. xxxviii.

4. *The Complete Works of Percy Bysshe Shelley*, Julian edition, ed. Roger Ingpen and Walter Peck (New York: Charles Scribner's Sons, 1924–30), 9:345; and

7:223 ff. "A Discourse on the Manners of the Ancients Relative to the Subject of Love."

5. Ibid., 7:154, from "Three Fragments on Beauty."

6. Ibid., 7:223.

7. The ruin or fragment "miniatures in order to manifest" the whole: See E. S. Shaffer, *"Kubla Khan" and The Fall of Jerusalem: The Mythological School in Biblical Criticism and Secular Literature 1770–1880* (Cambridge: Cambridge University Press, 1975), pp. 142, 334 (note 20). In this, the fragment approximates the Coleridgean (i.e., synecdochic) symbol; it partakes of that which it represents.

8. Ingpen and Peck, eds., *Complete Works*, 7:228.

9. Reiman, ed., *Shelley's Poetry and Prose*, "A Defence of Poetry," p. 504.

10. Ingpen and Peck, eds., *Complete Works*, "On Life," 6:193–94. Reiman, ed., *Shelley's Poetry and Prose*, p. 475.

11. Ingpen and Peck, eds., *Complete Works*, 7:223.

12. George Lessing, *Dramatic Works*, ed. Ernest Bell (London: Bell and Sons, 1895–1902), p. xviii.

13. Ingpen and Peck, eds., *Complete Works*, Letter to Thomas Love Peacock, Nov. 9, 1818, 9:345.

14. The editions of Thomas Chatterton's Rowley poems, and the essays defending or denying their authenticity upon which this discussion is based, are as follows: A Collection of cuttings, manuscripts and plates relating to Chatterton, including an autograph letter of his sister Mary, the correspondence between George Dyer, Robert Southey . . . , 2 vols., 1769–1818; Thomas Chatterton, *Poems, supposed to have been written at Bristol, by Thomas Rowley, and others, in the fifteenth century; . . . to which are added, a Preface, an Introductory Account . . . and a Glossary*, ed. Thomas Tyrwhitt (London: T. Payne and Son, 1777); Thomas Chatterton, *Poems, supposed to have been written at Bristol, by Thomas Rowley, and others, in the fifteenth century . . . to which is added an appendix, . . . tending to prove, that they were written, . . . by Thomas Chatterton*, 3rd ed., ed. Thomas Tyrwhitt (London: T. Payne & Son, 1778); Horace Walpole, *A Letter to the editor of the Miscellanies of Thomas Chatterton* (Strawberry Hill: Printed by T. Kirgate, 1779); Jacob Bryant, *Observations upon the Poems of Thomas Rowley* (London: T. Payne & Son, T. Cadell, and P. Elmsly, 1781); Thomas Chatterton, *Poems, supposed to have been written at Bristol, in the fifteenth century, by Thomas Rowley . . . with a commentary, in which the antiquity is considered, and defended. By Jeremiah Milles* (London: T. Payne & Son, 1782); A Collection of extracts from periodicals and newspapers on Chatterton and his work, 2 vols., 1782–1950; Thomas James Mathias, *An essay on the evidence, external and internal, relating to the poems Attributed to Thomas Rowley* (London: T. Becket, 1783); Thomas Chatterton, *The Works of Thomas Chatterton containing his life by G. Gregory, D.D.*, ed. Robert Southey and Joseph Cottle, 3 vols. (London: Longman and Rees, 1803); John Sherwen, *Introduction to an examination . . . Respecting the antiquity and authenticity of certain Publications* (Bath: Longman, Hurst, Rees and Orme, London, 1809); Thomas Chatterton, *Chatterton's Ella, and other pieces, interpreted; or, Selection from the Rowley Poems in modern reading by James Glassford, esq.* (Edinburgh: Printed for private circulation,

1837); Thomas Chatterton, *The Poetical Works of Thomas Chatterton . . .*, ed. C. B. Willcox, 2 vols. (Cambridge: Grant, 1842); Thomas Chatterton, *The Poetical works of Thomas Chatterton; with an essay on the Rowley poems by Walter W. Skeat and a memoir by Edward Bell* (London: Bell and Daldy, 1871).

Editions of James Macpherson's Ossian Fragments and published remarks on their authenticity: James Macpherson, *The works of Ossian, the son of Fingal. In two volumes. Translated from the Gaelic Language by James Macpherson, with dissertation by Hugh Blair*, 3rd ed. (London: T. Becket and P. A. Dehondt, 1765); John Clark, *An answer to Mr Shaw's Inquiry into the authenticity of the poems ascribed to Ossian* (Edinburgh: Printed for T. Longman, and T. Cadell, London; and C. Elliot, Edinburgh, 1781); James Boswell, *Boswell's Life of Johnson*, 3rd ed. (London: C. Dilly, 1799; reprint ed. London: Oxford University Press, 1969); James Macpherson, *The Poems of Ossian, in the original Gaelic, with a literal translation into Latin, by the late Robert Macfarlan, A.M. together with a dissertation on the authenticity of the poems by Sir John Sinclair, bart., and a translation from the Italian of the Abbé Cesarotti's dissertation on the controversy respecting the authenticity of Ossian* (London: G. and W. Nicol, 1807); Patrick Graham, *Essay on the authenticity of the poems of Ossian; in which the objections of Malcolm Laing are particularly considered and refuted . . . to which is added an essay on the mythology of Ossian's poems, by W. Richardson* (Edinburgh: J. Ballantyne & Co., 1807); Edward Davies, *The claims of Ossian examined and appreciated: an essay on the Scottish and Irish poems published under that name; in which the question of their genuineness and historical credit is freely discussed* (Swansea: Printed for the author, 1825); Thomas Bailey Saunders, *The life and letters of James Macpherson, containing a particular account of his famous quarrel with Dr. Johnson, and a sketch of the origin and influence of the Ossianic poems* (London: S. Sonnenschein & Co., 1894; reprint ed. New York: Haskell House, 1968).

15. Barbara Herrnstein Smith, *On The Margins of Discourse: The Relation of Literature to Language* (Chicago: University of Chicago Press, 1978), pp. 47, 52.

16. Thomas Gray responds in a manner unusual for his times. While he confesses his skepticism concerning Macpherson's editorial account, he declares himself delighted with the poetry. J. B. Saunders, *The Life and Letters of James Macpherson* (1894; reprint, New York: Haskell House, 1968), pp. 86, 87.

17. Chatterton's career, like his canon, was a matter of fragments. "Chatterton is like Keats and Coleridge, a poet of many starts and few finishes." Donald Taylor, *Chatterton's Art: Experiments in Imagined History* (Princeton: Princeton University Press, 1978), p. 7. Not only did Chatterton write four fragmented "attempts at epic" and a fragment of a sermon, he declared that *all* his poems had been transcribed from bits of vellum. The fiction undoes the closural determinacy of every work, each one potentially completed or continued on the missing pieces of manuscript.

As for Macpherson's oeuvre, here is a belated comment on its discontinuity: ". . . it [the controversy] began in a gentle form with the publication of a few random fragments. . . . But when he collected a large number of these waifs and strays of Highland poetry, and under the notion that he was dealing with fragments of a regular epic assigned to them all a like antiquity, and gave them a unity which perhaps they did not possess; when he rendered them in an orderly form, and in a free and polished paraphrase, and presented the six books of *Fingal* and the eight of *Temora* as translations of epic poems composed by Ossian in the third century, and handed down from mouth to mouth for fifty generations, suspicion ripened into an open attack on the translator's honesty." Saunders, *Life and Letters of James Macpherson*, p. 9.

18. Instead of dispelling the confusion, the debates perpetuated it. Southey noted this irony in 1803: ". . . a faithful description of the manuscripts on vellum is more useful in determining the authenticity [of the Rowley poems] than long essays pro and con." Southey and Cottle, Preface, in *The Works of Thomas Chatterton*. Browning too remarks the scholarly amateurism of the debates in *Foreign Quarterly Review* 29 (1842):465–83. Both Southey and Browning fail to distinguish the manifest argument of the essays from their meaning: the confirmation of certain literary assumptions. See Robert Folkenflik, "Macpherson, Chatterton, Blake, and the Great Age of Literary Forgery," *The Centennial Review* 18 (1974): 378–91.

19. Saunders, *Life and Letters of James Macpherson*, p. 172.

20. Milles, *Another Edition*, see p. 24: "The superiority of Rowley's poetry [to other fifteenth-century verse] is therefore no conclusive argument against the authenticity of it. If learning was little cultivated in that age, we must not infer that it did not at all exist; and that no man, at that time, could have a taste for classical learning and antient poetry. . . ." See also pp. 3 and 4.

21. Ibid., p. 26. "The style of Chatterton never rises to the dignity of Rowley; nor does Rowley descend to the mediocrity of Chatterton."

22. Much of the so-called "external evidence," pro and con, is in the nature of character witness.

23. Bryant, p. 29 (see also p. 154).

24. Milles, *Another Edition*, p. 18. And, below, Edmond Malone, *Cursory Observations on the Poems Attributed to Thomas Rowley*, 1782, intro. James Kuist, The Augustan Reprint Society, pub. no. 123 (Los Angeles: William Andrews Clark Memorial Library, University of California, 1966), p. 11. "Many of the stones which this ingenious boy employed in his building, it must be acknowledged, are so old as those at Stone-henge; but the beautiful fabrick he has raised is tied together by modern cement, and is covered with a stucco of no older date than that of Mess. Wyat and Adams." pp. 11, 12. While Malone admits the authenticity of Chatterton's poetical elements, and the impressiveness of Chatterton's practical achievement, he cannot conceptualize a more than mechanical assimilation of materials from the literary past.

In passing, we might observe that Keats's chameleon poet ideal takes on a more specifically Romantic meaning when set against this background of assumptions and proscriptions. Similarly, the idea of authorial caprice acquires a more pointed meaning when it is understood as a repudiation of contextual determination or of a mode of reception that subordinates the imagination to the accidents of its historical environment.

25. ". . . for the present question is not, whether the author was called Rowley or Chatterton; but, whether the poetry itself was composed by a learned priest in

the fifteenth century, or by an illiterate charity-boy of the present age." Milles, *Another Edition*, p. 3.

26. Saunders, *Life and Letters of James Macpherson*, p. 203. The quotation belongs to David Hume.

27. Linda Kelly, *The Marvellous Boy* (London: Weidenfeld and Nicolson, 1971), p. 80.

28. Sir Walter Scott's anonymous review of the Southey and Cottle edition of Chatterton's works in *The Edinburgh Review* 4 (1804). Coleridge's "Monody on the Death of Thomas Chatterton," and his admiration for the boy and his poetry. See Norman Fruman, *Coleridge, The Damaged Archangel* (New York: George Braziller, 1971); also, Donald Smalley, ed., *Browning's Essay on Chatterton* (Cambridge: Harvard University Press, 1948). Browning's essay published in *Foreign Quarterly Review*, July 1842.

29. Taylor, *Experiments in Imagined History*, p. 4.

30. Ingpen and Peck, eds., *Complete Works*, Letters, 9:346–47. Letter to Peacock, 9 Nov. 1818.

31. Here are some Romantic voices from our own age: "As Coleridge put it, we know a man for a poet by the fact that he makes us poets. We know that he is expressing his emotions by the fact that he is enabling us to express ours." R. G. Collingwood, *The Principles of Art*, p. 118, quoted in Taylor, *Experiments in Imagined History*, p. 19. "The perceiver of Chatterton's art need only be willing and knowledgeable to move from sensuous accompaniment to the more central mental world where the work lives." Ibid., p. 19.

32. Wordsworth attacks Chatterton on the same grounds as those he lays out in his Macpherson critique. He calls Chatterton's Saxon Poems ". . . essentially unnatural," and his critique seems largely motivated by the reviewers' inability to distinguish between "a real ancient medal and a counterfeit of modern manufacture." Wordsworth's furious attack on both Macpherson and Chatterton (an attack at odds with his idealized representation of Chatterton in "Resolution and Independence") might well be informed by his resentment at the critical response to his *Lyrical Ballads*. He refers in the Essay, Supplementary to the Preface, to the "unremitting hostility with which [the *Lyrical Ballad* poems] have each and all been opposed." Percy's *Reliques*, less of a *literary* sensation than Chatterton's and Macpherson's works, presented less of a threat to Wordsworth. He praises Percy's volume highly, although he knew of course that Percy "new modelled, and in many instances . . . composed" the "authentic" ancient ballads.

33. Gregory, *The Works of Thomas Chatterton*, cxviii.

34. John Davies, *Nosce Teipsum. This Oracle expounded in two Elegies. 1. Of Humane knowledge. 2. Of the Soule of Man, and the immortalitie therof. Hymnes of Astraea in Acrostike Verse. Orchestra, or A Poeme of Dauncing. In a Dialogue betweene Penelope, and one of her Wooers. Not finished* (London: R. Hawkins, 1622), p. [157] (or sig. L₂ʳ); John Davies, *The Poetical Works of Sir John Davies* (London: T. Davies, 1773), p. [137].

35. Abraham Cowley, *The Works of Mr. Abraham Cowley; consisting of Those which were formerly Printed: and Those which he Design'd for the Press; Now Published out of*

the Authors Original Copies (London: Herringman, 1668), p. [iii–iv] (or sig. A₁ᵛ-A₁ʳ).

36. Abraham Cowley, *A Poem on the Late Civil War. By Mr. Abraham Cowley* (London: [Langly Curtis], 1679), pp. [iii–iv]. Changes in quote: line 3, Abraham Cowley's for AC's; line 7, following for Copy add; line 8, unquestionably for questionably; line 13, add all, Write for write; and line 15, always for Always, Inspir'd for Inspired, comma added after piece.

This text also appears in: [John Dryden], *Examen poeticum: being the Third part of Miscellany poems*, 2d ed. (London: Tonson, 1706), pp. [385–86]; [John Dryden], *Miscellany Poems. Part III*, 4th ed. (London: Tonson, 1716), pp. 227–28; [John Dryden], *Miscellany Poems. Part III*, 5th ed. (London: Tonson, 1727), pages unknown.

Curtis's preface was slightly modified in the 1716 edition. In particular, line 8 questionably was changed to unquestionably. Cf. Allan Pritchard, ed., *Abraham Cowley: The Civil War* (Toronto: University of Toronto Press, 1873), pp. 6–7. It should also be noted that this passage appears first in the 1679 edition under the title "From the Publisher to the Reader."

37. Samuel Johnson, ed., *The Works of the Poetry of Great Britain and Ireland; with Prefaces Biographical and Critical* (London: Andrew Miller, 1800), 4:26–27.

38. Ibid., pp. 35–36.

39. Christopher Marlowe, *Hero and Leander; By Christopher Marloo* (London: E. Blunt, 1598), sigs. A₃ʳᵛ. Changes in quote: line 1, we for wee; line 2, duty for dutie, wee to we (2); line 6, been for beene; line 7, memorie for memory, minde for mind; line 9, shall for shal; line 19, liking. . . . At this time seeing that; line 1, duty for the one add, yourself for your selfe, and for the other to; line 2, allowance. . . .

40. Charles Churchill, *Poems*, 2 vols. (London: J. Churchill and W. Flexney, 1763–65); the final 8 pages at the end of vol. 2.

41. Joseph Cottle, *Poems* (Bristol: J. Cottle and G. G. and J. Robinson, 1795), p. xvi.

42. Ibid., p. i.

43. William Mason, "Memoirs of the Life and Writings of Mr. Gray," in William Mason, ed., *The Poems of Mr. Gray, to which are prefixed memoirs of his life and writings, by W. Mason* (York: Printed by A. Ward; sold by J. Dodsley, London, and J. Todd, York, 1775), pp. 1–416. Gray's poems constitute a separately numbered section of 111 pages located after the "Memoirs." Mason, "Memoirs," pp. 236–37; Mason, ed., *Poems*, pp. 78–81.

44. Edmund Waller. *Poetical Works of Edmund Waller*, ed. Robert Bell (London: J. W. Parker, 1854), is not at the University of Pennsylvania. Instead, I used: Edmund Waller, *The Second Part of Mr. Waller's Poems; Containing His Alteration of the Maids Tragedy, and whatever of his is yet unprinted* (London: T. Bennet, 1690), sig. a₂ᵛ-a₄ʳ.

45. Mason, "Memoirs," pp. 233–35. Change in quote: line 5, highly for high.

46. John Mitford, ed., *The Works of Thomas Gray*, 2 vols. (London: J. Mawman, 1816), 1:p. [7](1st count), or sig. A₃ʳ. "The following couplet, which was in-

tended to have been introduced in the poem on the Alliance of Education and Government, is much too beautiful to be lost." Or, Caroline Southey prints several fragments "apropriated" from the "sketches and beginnings in his [Robert Southey's] note-books and among his papers," *Robin Hood: A Fragment, with other Fragments and Poems by Robert Southey and Caroline Bowles* (Edinburgh and London: Blackwood, 1847) p. xvi. Or, J. Weston, ed. *The Remains of Robert Bloomfield* (London: Baldwin, Cradock, and Joy, 1824):

> The poetical merits of Robert Bloomfield have been long established; and the public favor which attended his previous writings can leave no doubt as to the reception of the following Fragments. They are the gleanings of that rich harvest which in days gone by, afforded to many a luxurious treat. . . . They must be welcome to his former admirers, who will immediately recognize in them the same sweetness, simplicity, and feeling, which distinguished his earlier productions.

Also, see Mary Shelley's Preface to Shelley's *Posthumous Poems*,1824 and 1839. "Many of the Miscellaneous Poems, written on the spur of the occasion, and *never retouched*, I found among his manuscript books, and have carefully copied. . . . I do not know whether the critics will reprehend the insertion of some of the most imperfect among these; but I frankly own, that I have been more actuated by the fear lest any monument of his genius should escape me. . . . Every line and word he wrote is instinct with peculiar beauty" p. viii.

Mary Shelley's delicacy strikes what we may call an eighteenth-century note, or seems to reflect a fragment sensibility not much different from those we have examined. Still, there *is* a difference between the kinds of fragments Shelley presents, and those "treasures" we find in early eighteenth-century editions. Many of the fragments in *Posthumous Poems* consist of no more than two lines; the longer pieces come to one or two stanzas. These fragments lack the narrative organization one tends to find in earlier fragments; moreover, Mary Shelley, while motivated by textual interests, also discriminates in the fragments she presents a "peculiar beauty," a sort of irreducible poetical character.

47. John Herman Merivale, *Poems, Original and Translated*, 2 vols. (London: W. Pickering, 1838), 2:342.

48. Ibid., 1–2.

49. Alexander Boswell, *Clan Alpin's Vow: A Fragment* (Edinburgh: G. Ranson, 1811), p. 37.

50. Albany Fonblanque (?), *The Examiner*, 13 June 1824, in Donald Reiman, *The Romantics Reviewed: Contemporary Reviews of British Romantic Writers* (New York: Garland, 1972), part C, 1:454.

Chapter 3

1. *The Poetical Works of William Wordsworth*, ed. Ernest de Selincourt and Helen Darbishire (Oxford: Clarendon Press, 1940–49), 2:504. References to Wordsworth's poetry from this edition.

2. Wordsworth, "Written in Germany; intended as part of a poem on my own life, but struck out as not being wanted there," in *Poetical Works*, 2:504. Because I am investigating ways in which "Nutting" might have been and could be read, and not its actual composition, I do not address the so-called "overflow" lines, unknown to Wordsworth's contemporaries. My interest is in that hypothetical discourse from which the text appears to have been excerpted—or, which we are invited to extrapolate. The formal point of departure is, of course, the fact that the poetic beginning is not a true beginning and that its ending is, by its own report, so to speak, only a provisional arrest.

3. David Perkins, *Wordsworth and the Poetry of Sincerity* (Cambridge: Harvard University Press, 1964), p. 204.

4. Geoffrey Hartman, *Wordsworth's Poetry, 1787–1814* (New Haven: Yale University Press, 1964, 1971), pp. 73–74.

5. Ibid., p. 74.

6. David Simpson, *Wordsworth and the Figurings of the Real* (London: Macmillan, 1982), p. 28. Also, see Simpson, *Irony and Authority in Romantic Poetry* (Totowa, N.J.: Rowman and Littlefield, 1979), pp. 74–75. On naming: "Its 'meaning' has been established, but that act is also a ravishing." On p. 76, Simpson discusses "act[s] of epistemological aggression" in the context of Wordsworth's narratives of designation.

7. Simpson, *Irony and Authority*, p. 59.

8. Arnold Hauser, *A Social History of Art* (New York: Vintage Books, 1958), 3:183.

9. Perkins, *Wordsworth and the Poetry of Sincerity*, p. 128.

Chapter 4

1. Ernest H. Coleridge, ed., *"Christabel": A Facsimile of the Manuscript* (London: Frowde, 1907), pp. 17, 18. References to Coleridge's poetry from *Coleridge: Poetical Works*, ed. E. H. Coleridge (Oxford: Oxford University Press, 1969).

2. John O. Hayden, ed., *Romantic Bards and British Reviewers: A Selected Edition of the Contemporary Reviews of the Works of Wordsworth, Coleridge, Byron, Keats, and Shelley* (Lincoln: University of Nebraska Press, 1971), p. 140. From the *Critical Review*, 5th ser., 3 (May 1816).

3. John Wain, ed., *Contemporary Reviews of Romantic Poetry* (London: Harrap, 1953; rpt. 1969), p. 108.

4. Charles Lamb (?), *The Times*, 20 May 1816, in Reiman, *Romantics Reviewed*, part A, 2:891: "For our own part, indeed, we know not whether the fragmental beauty that it now possesses can be advantageously exchanged for the wholeness of a finished narrative. In its present form it lays irresistible hold of the imagination. It interests . . . more by what it leaves untold, than even by what it tells." See James Gillman's speculative "conclusion" to "Christabel" in *The Life of Samuel Taylor Coleridge* (London: William Pickering, 1838). According to E. H. Coleridge, the poet declared, "if I should finish 'Christabel,' I shall certainly extend it and give new characters, and a greater number of incidents" (*Christabel: A Facsimile*, p. 50).

5. Hayden, *Romantic Bards*, p. 142.

6. *Parodies of the Works of English and American Authors*, collected and annotated by Walter Hamilton (London: Reeves and Turner, 1888), 5: 127–37.

7. Hazlitt is credited with observing "something disgusting at the bottom of his subject," something of the "charnel-house" (Hayden, *Romantic Bards*, p. 146). See Elisabeth Schneider, "The Unknown Reviewer of 'Christabel': Jeffrey, Hazlitt, Tom Moore," *PMLA* 70 (June 1955):417–54.

8. Thomas Love Peacock, "Essay on Fashionable Literature," in *Thomas Love Peacock: Memoirs of Shelley and Other Essays and Reviews*, ed. Howard Mills (London: Rupert Hart-Davis, 1970), p. 106.

9. *The Times*, 20 May 1816, in Reiman, *Romantics Reviewed*, part A, 2:891.

10. Hayden, *Romantic Bards*, p. 143. And E. H. Coleridge, *Christabel: A Facsimile*, p. 15. See Mills, ed., *Peacock*, p. 107: "In 'Christabel,' the poet writes as one 'who sees the action and does not guess at its cause.'" The remark occurs in the context of a discussion of Geraldine's inability to cross the threshold into Langland Hall without Christabel's assistance. According to Peacock, the poet says "belike through weariness" in the character of an uninformed spectator.

11. Reiman, *Romantics Reviewed*, part A, 2:505–8, from the *European Magazine* Nov. 1816 Review by George Felton Mathew.

12. Reiman, *Romantics Reviewed*, part A, vol. 2:890, 891. And Lewis M. Schwartz, "A New Review of Coleridge's 'Christabel,'" *Studies in Romanticism* 9 (1970):114–24. Unsigned review from *The London Times*, May 20, 1816 (review commonly attributed to Charles Lamb).

13. Reiman, *Romantics Reviewed*, part A, 2:506, 507.

14. Samuel Taylor Coleridge, *Biographia Literaria*, ed. George Watson (London: J. M. Dent, 1971), chapter 14, pp. 168, 169. Coleridge explicitly cites "the 'Christabel'" as one of the poems written "with this view" in mind. Also, Edwin Thumboo, "'Christabel,' Poem or Fragment," *The Literary Criterion* 11 (Winter 1973):13–19. ". . . the need to evoke the sense of the *real* through the poetry" puts "Christabel" in the context of Coleridge's characteristic concern with the creation of a particular kind of poetry—his interest in "'the two cardinal points of poetry, the power of exciting the sympathy of the reader by a faithful adherence to the truth of nature, and the power of giving the interest of novelty by the modifying colours of the imagination'" (p. 18).

15. Reiman, *Romantics Reviewed*, part A, 2:506. And, see Reiman, part A, 2:868 and 870. *Scourge and Satirist*, July 1816. "Yet that we may not be accused by Mr. Coleridge of doing wilful injustice to his merits, we shall insert his own apology for writing as he lists. 'A little child, a limber elf. . . .'" The reviewer concludes his comments on "Christabel" and leads into a discussion of "The Pains of Sleep" by citing Coleridge's "ascription of his negligence to rage and pain" and "a morbid sensibility of mind. . . ."

16. To Edward Bostetter, Geraldine is "an incarnation of sadism" and "the product of an 'excess' of divine love." *The Romantic Ventriloquists: Wordsworth, Coleridge, Keats, Shelley, Byron* (Seattle: University of Washington Press, 1963), pp. 125, 126. James Gillman imagines Geraldine to be Christabel's lover in dis-

guise (*The Life of Samuel Taylor Coleridge*, p. 302). Douglas Angus represents her as an "ageless witch figure symbolizing a repressed guilt-laden incestuous attachment for the mother," while Derwent Coleridge sees her as "no witch or goblin but a spirit executing her appointed task with the best good will." Douglas Angus, "Themes of Love and Guilt in Coleridge's Three Major Poems," *Journal of English and Germanic Philology* 59 (1960):663. To Arthur Nethercot, Geraldine is both a vampire and a creature sent to expiate her sins by doing good offices for Christabel. *The Road to Tryermaine: A Study of the History, Background, and Purposes of Coleridge's 'Christabel'* (Chicago: University of Chicago Press, 1939). Also see Michael D. Patrick, *Christabel: A Brief Critical History and Reconsideration*, Salzburg Studies in English Literature, *Romantic Reassessment* (University of Salzburg, 1973).

17. Norman Fruman, *Coleridge, The Damaged Archangel* (NY: George Braziller, 1971), p. 355. "If we find motive and causation. . . ."

18. Robert Siegel, "The Serpent and the Dove: 'Christabel' and the Problem of Evil," in *Imagination and the Spirit: Essays in Literature and the Christian Faith*, ed. Charles Huttar (Grand Rapids: Eerdman's, 1971), pp. 159–87; see especially pp. 167–169.

19. Thumboo, "'Christabel,' Poem or Fragment," p. 17.

20. Robert Kiely, *The Romantic Novel in England* (Cambridge: Harvard University Press, 1972).

21. Vladimir Propp, *Morphology of the Folktale*, trans. L. Scott (Bloomington: University of Indiana Press, 1958).

22. Kiely, *The Romantic Novel*, p. 7.

23. Preface to "Christabel." A few modern critics seem to grasp this. According to Humphrey House in *Coleridge* (London: Hart-Davis, 1953), Coleridge was trying to "explore [in 'Christabel'] more deeply the serious psychological areas which such stories [that is, gothic] just touch in their own trivial way" (130). See Nethercot, *The Road to Tryermaine*, pp. 200, 201. Or, consider Bostetter's association of "Christabel" and "The Dark Ladie." Bostetter suggests in passing that the latter was intended to form the first part of "Christabel." In "The Dark Ladie," the heroine is inexplicably scorned by her friends and received in a very qualified fashion by her fiancé. She resents his offer to marry her secretly, on the grounds that he had openly pledged his troth. One assumes that in her righteous indignation, she will reject him and languish away. Bostetter's association of the two poems suggests that he senses a similarly tragic fate for Christabel, but the terms of his analysis prevent him from acknowledging this reaction. To analogize "Christabel" to "The Dark Ladie," Christabel's knight will return, but finding her corrupted by Geraldine and cast out by her father, will alter the terms of his marriage proposal. Christabel, in anger and self-loathing, will break the engagement. Eventually, Geraldine will be unmasked and both Leoline and the knight will realize their guilt. The curve is that of tragedy, not romance.

24. Kiely, *The Romantic Novel*, p. 8.

25. House, *Coleridge*, p. 122.

26. Kathleen Coburn, ed., *The Notebooks of Samuel Taylor Coleridge* (Princeton:

Princeton University Press, 1973), vol. 3: notes 3720, 18:33 (from notebook 30).

27. E. F. Watling, trans., *The Theban Plays* (New York: Penguin, 1947), Introduction, p. 14.

28. Barbara Herrnstein Smith, *On the Margins of Discourse: The Relation of Literature to Language* (Chicago: University of Chicago Press, 1978), p. 74.

29. Barbara E. Rooke, "An Annotated Copy of Coleridge's 'Christabel,'" *Studia Germanica* 15 (1974): 179–92 (see pp. 187–89; 187 [22.R11. 1-5]; 188,189 [28.R15. 9–14] and PW 204–09; 191 [37.R, 35.7–10]).

30. Daniel Lerner, ed., *Parts and Wholes: The Hayden Colloquium on Scientific Method and Concept* (New York: Macmillan, 1963), p. 1.

31. Shaffer, *"Kubla Khan" and The Fall of Jerusalem*, p. 94.

32. Geoffrey Hartman, *Wordsworth's Poetry, 1787–1814* (New Haven: Yale University Press, 1964, 1971), p. 11.

33. As a possibly illuminating contrast, consider Wordsworth's reluctance to acknowledge the acts of selection—willful and inevitable—productive of his immediate poetic materials (see discussion of "Nutting"). On the other hand, Wordsworth openly, even dramatically, displays his interpretive activities. Coleridge's inhibitions are just the reverse; in "Christabel," he foregrounds his production of "primary" poetic materials. It is the reflective, secondary, editorial dimension of the compositional act that disturbs him, and prompts his particular modes of fragmentation.

34. David Simpson, *Irony and Authority in Romantic Poetry* (N. J.: Rowman and Littlefield), 1979, p. 143. Excerpt from Coleridge's *The Friend*, 1:518, ed. Barbara Rooke.

35. Michael Cooke, *Acts of Inclusion: Studies Bearing on an Elementary Theory of Romanticism* (New Haven: Yale University Press, 1979), p. 221.

Chapter 5

1. See A. C. Goodson, "Kubla's Construct," *Studies in Romanticism* 18 (Fall 1979):405–25. References to Coleridge's poetry from *Coleridge: Poetical Works*, ed. E. H. Coleridge (Oxford: Oxford University Press, 1969).

2. Hayden, *Romantic Bards and British Reviewers* (Lincoln: University of Nebraska Press, 1971), p. 149, from *Literary Panorama*, 2d ser., 4 (July 1816).

3. Shaffer, *"Kubla Khan" and The Fall of Jerusalem*, p. 95. Shaffer reads "Kubla Khan" as a "symbolic summary of [Coleridge's intended epic's] entire action and significance." "It was indeed a fragment of a vast intention; and yet a whole poem" uniting "essential epic brevity with universal scope" (p. 142). More specifically, Shaffer describes the form of "Kubla Khan" as follows: "a fusion between a traditional ballad form, with its sense of essential rhythms and consonances, and the irregular, 'sublime' ode forms, which raised the minstrel into a rhapsode" (p. 94).

In that Shaffer remarks the "piecemeal, traditional, inconsistent character of the [Biblical] text, and its construction out of mobile 'elements'" and associates this description with Coleridge's formal ambitions for "Kubla Khan," her structural concept of the poem can be understood as congruent with mine. For the completed fragment is "a collection of independent and often conflicting fragments" (p. 78) "put together by an editor"—or, by a poet acting in the capacity of an editor.

4. Woodring, *Politics in English Romantic Poetry* (Cambridge: Harvard University Press, 1970), pp. 29, 30. Also see Carl Woodring, "Coleridge and the Khan," *Essays in Criticism* 9 (October 1959):361–68.

5. Norman Fruman, *Coleridge: The Damaged Archangel* (New York: Braziller, 1971), p. 543, n. 34.

6. Arguments for a partisan reading, or one which interprets "Kubla Khan" as a presentation of a determinate resolution, are found in John L. Lowes, *The Road to Xanadu* (Boston: Houghton Mifflin, 1927); Geoffrey Yarlott, *Coleridge and The Abyssinian Maid* (London: Methuen, 1967); John Shelton, "The Autograph Ms. of 'Kubla Khan' and an Interpretation," *Review of English Literature* 7 (1966):32–42; Kathleen Coburn, "Coleridge Redivivus," in *The Major English Romantic Poets*, ed. C. D. Thorpe (Carbondale, Ill.: Southern Illinois University Press, 1957); Paul Magnuson, *Coleridge's Nightmare Poetry* (Charlottesville: University of Virginia Press, 1974); Elisabeth Schneider, *Coleridge, Opium, and "Kubla Khan"* (Chicago: University of Chicago Press, 1953).

Among those who regard "Kubla Khan" as the playing out of an unresolved aesthetic conflict are George Watson, "The Meaning of 'Kubla Khan,'" *Review of English Literature* 2 (1961):21–29; Alan Purves, "Formal Structure of "Kubla Khan," *Studies in Romanticism* 1 (1961–62):187–91; E. H. Coleridge, *Complete Poetical Works* (Oxford: Clarendon, 1912); Richard Fogle, "The Romantic Unity of 'Kubla Khan,'" in *The Permanent Pleasure: Essays on Classics of Romanticism*, ed. R. Fogle (Athens: University of Georgia Press, 1974), pp. 43–52.

7. Woodring, "Coleridge and the Khan," p. 364.

8. These structural assumptions give rise to certain methodological problems for the critic. The partisans must deduce Coleridge's sympathies from his descriptive manner as evidenced in his treatment of the two poetic alternatives. Since both descriptions are vivid, attractive, and morally either neutral or ambiguous, these readers must support their inference with interpretation of Coleridge's character and his characteristic forms, as well as with source studies and gleanings from his other writings. In adopting this approach, one inevitably uses "Kubla Khan" to reinforce whatever theory already governs one's understanding of Coleridge's life and art.

The compromisers construe the poem's irresolution as a sign of intellectual or emotional failure; Coleridge does not conclude because he cannot confront the implications of the logic developed in the poem. While this can be a legitimate and useful premise, the readers who advance it conceive the formal limitation of "Kubla Khan" as a hindrance to analysis in that it represents a miscarriage of original intention. The assumption underlying this approach as well as the partisan method is that analysis must aim to elicit and display "that sufficiency, that ideal consistency" (Pierre Macherey, *A Theory of Literary Production*, trans. Geoffrey Wall (London: Routledge and Kegan Paul, 1978), p. 79) imperfectly realized in the poem but nonetheless active as its organizing principle. Because that sufficiency and unity is, in "Kubla Khan," an (unrealized) ideal, criticism directs its efforts toward depicting that model in reference to which the poem is incomplete: what "Kubla Khan" should or would have been had not X, Y, or Z interfered with its execution. The poem certainly invites this response, but once we have accepted the invitation, we should go on to investigate the impulse in which it originated and the meaning it carries. We should, moreover, transfer that X, Y, or Z to its proper position in the equation—not in the sum but in the given factors or the problematic of the work.

9. John Beer, quoted in John Cornwell, *Coleridge, Poet and Revolutionary 1772–1804* (London: Allen Lane, 1973), pp. 183–84.

10. Michael Cooke, *Acts of Inclusion* (New Haven: Yale University Press, 1979), p. 220. Also, p. 221: "mind and matter [poised] between a wild versatility and a rigid unresponsive form."

11. Consider Coleridge's conversation poem as a formal attempt to realize this aesthetic and metaphysical ideal. Like the dome in air, the conversation poem presents its formal condition, or decisions, as a literal translation or transposition of its material—its doctrinal and/or dramatic content. The moment and process of composition are identified with the moment and process of primary or existential event. Or, figure and referent, word and thing are collapsed into each other. The conversation poem ends at a transformed beginning, thus emphasizing its formal and conceptual inevitability and thus, its impenetrability.

12. Norman Rudich, "Coleridge's 'Kubla Khan': His Anti-Political Vision," in Rudich, ed., *Weapons of Criticism: Marxism in America and the Literary Tradition* (Palo Alto: Ramparts Press, 1976), pp. 236, 237.

13. Cf. Shaffer, *"Kubla Khan" and The Fall of Jerusalem*, p. 185: Coleridge's "syncretist universalism[:] all the images exist in each other's contexts [and thus they] ultimately meet themselves in the extended context of each other's image" and, p. 153: "The seer—and particularly the poet, whose affair it is to make known to the world his commerce with the divine—is liable to death for his presumption."

14. J. R. de J. Jackson, *Coleridge: The Critical Heritage* (London: Routledge and Kegan Paul, 1970), p. 223. *British Review*, 1816: "We shall . . . consider the rescue of such a muse as that of Mr. Coleridge from suffocation by submersion as some gain to the cause of true poetry."

15. Woodring, *Politics*, p. 31.

16. Woodring, *Politics*, p. 28.

17. A. S. Link, "STC and the Economic and Political Crisis in Great Britain, 1816–20," *Journal of the History of Ideas* 9 (Jan.–Oct. 1948):323–38 (see p. 327).

18. Rudich, "Coleridge's 'Kubla Khan,'" p. 216.

19. Ibid., p. 217.

20. Ibid., p. 234.

21. Cooke, *Acts of Inclusion*, p. 221.

22. T. S. Eliot, "The Use of Poetry and the Use of Criticism," in *Selected Prose of T.S. Eliot*, ed. Frank Kermode (New York: Farrar Strauss Giroux, 1975), p. 90.

23. Robert Langbaum, *The Poetry of Experience: The Dramatic Monologue in Modern Literary Tradition* (London: Chatto and Windus, 1957).

24. Preface to "Kubla Khan," 1816.

Chapter 6

1. References to Byron's poetry from *Lord Byron: The Complete Poetical Works*, ed. Jerome J. McGann (Oxford: Clarendon Press, 1981). William Marshall, "The Accretive Structure of Byron's 'The Giaour,'" *Modern Language Notes* 76 (1961):502–9; Karl Kroeber, *Romantic Narrative Art* (Madison: University of Wisconsin Press, 1960); Robert Gleckner, *Byron and the Ruins of Paradise* (Baltimore: Johns Hopkins University Press, 1967); M. K. Joseph, *Byron the Poet* (London: Gollancz, 1964).

2. Jerome McGann, *Fiery Dust: Byron's Poetic Development* (Chicago: University of Chicago Press, 1968), pp. 141–64.

3. Ibid., p. 142.

4. Ibid.

5. Henry Mackenzie, in his *Man of Feeling*, 1771, ed. Brian Vickers (London: Oxford University Press, 1967), employs the fiction of textual fragmentation for rhetorical purposes. Mackenzie describes his acquisition of a "bundle of little episodes, put together without art, and of no importance on the whole, with something of nature, and little else in them." He cautions, in a note to the opening chapter, "the Reader will remember, that the Editor is accountable only for scattered chapters, and fragments of chapters; the curate [who had used the manuscript as gun wadding] must answer for the rest" (pp. 5, 7). Curiously, however, Mackenzie's novel or apologue betrays no narrative marks of its physical life as gun wadding—no fragmentation, that is. Mackenzie's fiction of discovery resembles Scott's account, prefatory to *Waverly*. In both cases, the device of the found manuscript qualifies the status of the doctrine developed by the fictions; the genetic account has no formal impact, nor, once we have registered the historical status of the discourse as a whole, no real rhetorical force.

6. McGann, *Fiery Dust*, p. 143.

7. The following reconstruction of the early readings of "The Giaour" is based on Donald Reiman, *The Romantics Reviewed: Contemporary Reviews of British Romantic Writers* (New York: Garland Publishing Co., 1972), part B, 2:842–47; part B, 5:2001–12.

8. William Marshall, "The Accretive Structure," p. 502. "The point which [E. H.] Coleridge did not perceive and I hope to illustrate here is that all the 'fragments' in the poem, representing the result of accretion with occasional verbal alteration and no more than trivial deletion, do not constitute a whole that can be pieced together."

9. Reiman, *Romantics Reviewed*, part B, 2:842.

10. My comments on the *kleos* are informed by David Grene, University of Chicago, Woodward Court Lecture.

11. *The History of Herodotus*, trans. George Rawlinson, ed. E. H. Blakeney (London: Dent, 1910), 1:298.

12. J. A. K. Thomson, *The Art of the Logos* (London: Allen and Unwin, 1935), p. 146. Or, Grene: "while the aim of the *kleos* is historical—to establish exact and accurate fact—its form is imaginative and poetic."

13. Thomson, *Art of the Logos*, p. 175.

14. Arnaldo Momigliano, *Studies in Historiography* (London: Weidenfeld and Nicholson, 1966), pp. 77–79, 82.

15. Ibid., p. 77.

16. Ibid., p. 138.

17. Advertisement. "The tale which these disjointed fragments present, is founded upon circumstances now less common in the East than formerly; either because the ladies are more circumspect than in the 'olden time'; or because the Christians have better fortune or less enterprise. The story, when entire, contained the adventures of a female slave, who was thrown, in the Mussulman manner, into the sea for infidelity, and avenged by a young Venetian, her lover, at the time the Seven Islands were possessed by the Republic of Venice, and soon after the Arnauts were beaten back from the Morea, which they had ravaged for some time subsequent to the Russian invasion. The desertion of the Mainotes, on being refused the plunder of Misitra, led to the abandonment of that enterprise, and to the desolation of the Morea, during which the cruelty exercised on all sides was unparalleled even in the annals of the faithful."

18. Marilyn Butler, *Romantics, Rebels and Reactionaries: English Literature and its Background, 1760–1830* (New York: Oxford University Press, 1981), p. 25.

19. Thomson, *Art of the Logos*, p. 189.

20. McGann, *Fiery Dust*, p. 158.

21. Blakeney and Rawlinson, ed. and trans., *History of Herodotus*, p. xv.

22. According to Herodotus, Thucydides, and Plutarch, Themistocles' defects were mean ones—greed, cunning, political and social ambition. Still, his commitment to the unification of Athens and Sparta and to the implementation of a strongly aggressive policy toward Persia was unequivocal. Where he differed from other military statesmen was in his sense of the practical importance of enlisting popular support. After his triumph at Salamis, the result of his shrewd strategems, Themistocles was indicted for treason and banished by his aristocrat rivals, Miltiades and Aristides. Exiled to Persia, Themistocles offered his services to Darius. He received office and served loyally until his death. When asked, however, to help plot against the Greeks, Themistocles (according to Plutarch) committed suicide rather than betray his nation. Thucydides and Herodotus offer a less glamorous account: that is, Themistocles died of a fever. Although a monument to Themistocles was raised in Asia Minor, it is said that his bones were, at his desire, brought home and secretly buried in Attica. Historians regard Themistocles' death as marking the end of the Persian War era. The period was followed by 150 years of internecine struggles. Then came the Peloponnesian Wars and the end of the Athenian empire. See G. Botsford and C. Robinson, *Hellenic History* (New York: Macmillan, 1950), p. 119.

23. Gleckner, *Byron and the Ruins of Paradise*, p. 102.

24. Blakeney and Rawlinson, ed. and trans., *History of Herodotus*, p. xix.

Chapter 7

1. References to Byron's poetry are from *Lord Byron: The Complete Poetical Works*, ed. Jerome J. McGann (Oxford: Clarendon Press, 1981). It might be useful to recall in this context Seymour Chatman's observation, "It is popular to argue monistically, that form and content are one, a position ultimately Plato's, but which gained great support in the Romantic period. . . . A recent . . . version is that of French structuralism" (*New Literary History* 1 (Autumn 1970):217–28). One general, ideological purpose of the RFP, and one I discuss at some length in the conclusion, is precisely the identification of form with content, whereby the discourse effectively fends off the sort of analysis that might expose the overdeterminations of both those dimensions. Of all the fragment kinds treated in this book, the deliberate fragment projects this illusion most powerfully.

2. Thomas Medwin, *Conversations with Lord Byron*, ed. E. J. Lovell (Princeton: Princeton University Press, 1966), pp. 164–65.

3. Jerome McGann, *Don Juan in Context* (Chicago: University of Chicago Press, 1976).

4. See Kurt Heinzelman, "Byron's Poetry of Politics: The Economic Basis of the 'Poetical Character,'" *Texas Studies in Literature and Language* 23 (Fall 1981): 361–88. In his study of Byron's conflict-ridden establishment of an authorial self and name, Heinzelman interprets some of the contradictions that structure the argument of this essay. Heinzelman relates the conflicts evident in Byron's undistinguished early poetry to an economic situation both peculiar to Byron and symbolic of a more inclusive social experience.

5. McGann, *Fiery Dust: Byron's Poetic Development* (Chicago: University of Chicago Press, 1968), p. 23.

6. Cf. *Childe Harold's Pilgrimage* 1:3. Here too Byron's target is literary encomium, and here he lays bare the motivated illusions of symmetry between act and phrase. "Nor florid prose, nor honied lies of rhyme / Can blazon evil deeds, or consecrate a crime." The immediate issue here is a moral one, but the observation seems essentially in line with this discussion of "Airy Hall."

7. W. J. B. Owen and Jane Smyser, eds., *The Prose Works of William Wordsworth* (Oxford: Clarendon Press, 1974), 2:59.

8. See Byron's preface to cantos 1 and 2, *Childe Harold's Pilgrimage*, 1813: "It had been easy to varnish over his faults, to make him do more and express less. . . ."

9. Owen and Smyser, eds., *Prose Works*, p. 57.

10. McGann, *Fiery Dust*, p. 39.

Chapter 8

1. References to Shelley's poetry are from *Shelley: The Complete Poetical Works*, ed. Thomas Hutchinson (Oxford: Oxford University Press, 1934). Thomas J. Hogg, *The Life of Percy Bysshe Shelley* (London: Moxon, 1858), 1:264.

2. According to Hogg, *Posthumous Fragments* was composed in earnest, as a serious polemic and as Shelley's own statement. Margaret Nicholson was not, in other words, in the picture at all. Hogg advised Shelley not to publish the poems in the manner he had intended. He criticizes their many "irregularities and incongruities," chief among which is the idea "that revolutionary ruffians were the most fit recipients of the gentlest passions." What makes the volume, in Hogg's view, "the concentrated essence of nonsense" is precisely the "incongruity" of love and violent political interests in the same narrative. Hogg reminds Shelley that "correctness . . . constituted the essence of short [compositions]," and further remarks the imprudence of the venture. Hogg records that Shelley saw the wisdom of his representation and decided to publish the poems as a parody, revising so as to make this intention clear. The two friends then cast about for a possible author or persona, and once they had hit upon Margaret Nicholson, Shelley again revised so as to make the poems consistent with the facts of Nicholson's case.

The name "Fitzvictor," the editor of the volume, provided the cognoscenti's clue to the real authorship of the volume, Victor being Shelley's pseudonym in the Victor and Cazire poems written in collaboration with Elizabeth Shelley. Shelley sent the first copies of *Posthumous Fragments* to "trusty and sagacious friends at a distance, whose gravity would not permit them to suspect a hoax." Sure enough, "they read and admired . . . charmed with the wild notes of liberty," and so did all who read the work in Oxford. The volume was enormously popular, much to Hogg's amazement. "What a strange delusion to admire our stuff—the concentrated essence of nonsense." Hogg declares that the "object and purpose [of the] burlesque [was] to ridicule the strange mixture of sentimentality with the murderous fury of revolutionists, that was so prevalent in the compositions of the day." Shelley, he says (in reference to "War"), hoped to "astonish a weak mind [and] captivate the admirers of philosophical poetry." Hogg wonders at the "acceptance, as a serious poem, of a work so evidently designed for a burlesque" (pp. 261–68).

The one modern critic to consider the volume (only, however, as a problem in textual history) assumes the serious, politically motivated character of Shelley's parody. Bruce Dickins, "The U.L.C. Copy of *Posthumous Fragments of Margaret Nicholson*," *Transactions of the Cambridge Bibliographical Society* 3 (1963):423–27. The occasional clumsiness of the poems seems to be more the result of Shelley's impulsiveness and artistic inexperience than an indication of parodic intent. The reception of the volume, Shelley's known libertarian sympathies, his atheism, and his concern with feminist issues, all suggest that Hogg was not so persuasive a mentor as he says nor so accurate a biographer. Moreover, one wonders why Shelley would write such a work as the *Posthumous Fragments* in the first place if he was prepared to mock and discredit its doctrine—its *raison d'être*—later, and for such reasons as Hogg advanced. And, if Shelley hoped for an ironic reading, why did he send the volume to "persons he thought likely to sympathize with the antimonarchical sentiments expressed" (Dickins, p. 425)? I believe we can feel confident of the earnestness of Shelley's venture.

3. Robert Southey, ed., *The Remains of Henry Kirke White* (London: Longmans and Rees, 1825), pp. xlix, lii.

4. Southey, ed., *Remains of Henry Kirke White*, p. xlix.

Chapter 9

1. References to Shelley's poetry and prose from Donald Reiman, Sharon Powers, eds., *Shelley's Poetry and Prose* (New York: W. W. Norton and Co., 1977).

2. Earl Wasserman, *Shelley: A Critical Reading* (Baltimore: Johns Hopkins University Press, 1971).

3. For a representative range of interpretations of the poem's formal ruptures, see the following: James E. Hill, "Dramatic Structure in Shelley's 'Julian and Maddalo,'" *ELH* 35 (1968):84–93; Raymond D. Havens, "'Julian and Maddalo,'" *Studies in Philology* 27 (1930):648–53; G. M. Matthew, "'Julian and Maddalo' The Draft and the Meaning," *Studia Neophilologica* 35 (1963):57–84; Stuart Curran, *Shelley's Annus Mirabilis: The Maturing of an Epic Vision* (San Marino, Calif.: Huntington Library, 1975), pp. 137–42; Carlos Baker, *Shelley's Major Poetry: The Fabric of a Vision* (Princeton: Princeton University Press, 1948), pp. 119–53.

4. C. P. Brand, *Italy and the English Romantics: The Italianate Fashion in Early 19th-Century England* (Cambridge: Cambridge University Press, 1957); C. P. Brand, *Torquato Tasso, A Study of the Poet and of his Contribution to English Literature* (Cambridge: Cambridge University Press, 1965).

5. William Boulting, *Tasso and his Times* (London: Methuen, 1907), and *Godfrey of Bulloigne; or, The Recovery of Jerusalem*, trans. Edward Fairfax, with "The Lives of Tasso and Fairfax," by the editor, Charles Knight, 7th ed., rpt. from original folio of 1600 (London: G. Cox, 1853). See Knight, "Life of Tasso," pp. 7–38.

6. Wilde, *Conjectures and Researches*, 1:6, 7.

7. This and the following unidentified quotations are from Shelley's *Defence of Poetry*.

8. Curran, *Shelley's Annus Mirabilis*, p. 141. See Wasserman, *Shelley: A Critical Reading*, pp. 80, 81.

9. Wasserman, *Shelley: A Critical Reading*, p. 66.

10. Michel Foucault, *Madness and Civilization: A History of Insanity in the Age of Reason*, trans. Richard Howard (New York: Random House, 1965; Vintage, 1973), p. 288.

11. Ibid., pp. 288–89.

12. Marilyn Butler, *Romantics, Rebels and Reactionaries: English Literature and its Background, 1760–1830* (New York: Oxford University Press, 1981), p. 148.

13. Ibid., p. 148.

14. Ibid.

15. Ibid.

16. Ibid., pp. 140, 141.

Chapter 10

1. References to Keats's poetry from *The Poems of John Keats*, ed. Miriam Allott (London, New York: Longman, Norton, 1970).

"Hyperion" was published in Keats's *Lamia* volume in 1820. The first mention made of "The Fall" is in Monckton Milnes's (Lord Houghton's) *Life, Letters, and Literary Remains of John Keats* (London: Edward Moxon, 1848), l:244. "The Fall" was not printed, however, until 1856–57, when Houghton entered it in vol. 3 of *Biographical and Historical Miscellanies of the Philobiblion Society.*

Houghton first expresses confusion about the compositional sequence, but by the second edition of the *Life and Letters*, he appears, as Sidney Colvin says, to have "drifted definitely into a wrong conclusion on the point . . . printing the piece ['The Fall," which Houghton refers to as the Vision] in his appendix as 'Another Version'. . . ." Here, Houghton writes, "'on reconsideration, I have no doubt that it was the first draft.' Accordingly it ["The Fall"] is given as an 'earlier version' in Mr. W. M. Rossetti's edition of 1872 . . . and so on, positively but quite wrongly, in the several editions by Messrs. Buxton Forman, Speed, and W. T. Arnold." Sidney Colvin, *Keats,* in *English Men of Letters* series, vol. 24, ed. John Morley (1889; rpt. New York: AMS Press, 1968), p. 231. The only dissenters to this view were "Mr. W. B. Scott and Mr. R. Garnett," and later, Rossetti (Colvin, *Keats,* p. 23).

2. Harold Bloom, *The Visionary Company: A Reading of English Romantic Poetry* (New York: Doubleday, 1961), p. 447.

3. Bloom, *Visionary Company*; Bloom, *Poetry and Repression: Revisionism from Blake to Stevens* (New Haven: Yale University Press, 1976); Walter Jackson Bate, *The Stylistic Development of Keats* (New York: Humanities Press, 1958); and Bate, *John Keats* (New York: Oxford University Press, 1966).

4. D. G. James, "The Two *Hyperions*" in *Keats: A Collection of Critical Essays,* ed. W. J. Bate (Englewood Cliffs, NJ: Prentice Hall, 1964), pp. 161–71.

5. James, "The Two *Hyperions*," p. 164. Also, see Bernard Blackstone, *The Consecrated Urn: An Interpretation of Keats in Terms of Growth and Form* (London: Longmans, Green, 1959), p. 240.

6. Bate, *John Keats,* pp. 147, 410.

7. Colvin, *Keats,* p. 153; M. B. Forman and John Masefield, *The Poetical Works and Other Writings of John Keats* (New York: Charles Scribner's Sons, 1938), quotes Monckton Milnes's (i.e., Houghton's) note to "Another Version of Keats's 'Hyperion,'" 3:259. Also, William Michael Rossetti, *Life of John Keats* (London: Scott, 1887), p. 189.

8. Quoted in J. Murry, *The Mystery of Keats* (London: Nevill, 1949), p. 198.

9. Bate, for example, assembles some impressive statistics to demonstrate "Hyperion"'s Miltonic character and to illustrate the stylistic advances represented by "The Fall" (see *Stylistic Development*). Bate's data, however, fail to explain the presence of a phrase like "Me thoughtless" in "The Fall," or the fact that Keats asked Woodhouse to mark out for him the Miltonic passages in that manuscript. One cannot, it seems, argue that Keats simply slipped now and then, and yet maintain that the single, most compelling motivation for the later poem was a Miltonic repudiation.

10. Bloom, *Visionary Company,* p. 417.

11. Ibid.

12. Kenneth Muir, ed., *John Keats: A Reassessment* (Liverpool: Liverpool University Press, 1958), p. 115.

13. Ibid., p. 114.

14. Rossetti, *Life*, p. 186.

15. See Keats's rejected Preface to *Endymion*: "So this Poem must rather be considered as an endeavour than a thing accomplish'd: a poor prologue to what, if I live, I humbly hope to do. . . . I should have kept it back for a year or two, knowing it to be so faulty:—but . . . I would rather redeem myself with a new poem." Keats's representation of *Endymion* as a prologue to the poems he plans to write and thus essentially continuous with and part of the amassing project, suggests the same structural logic I have proposed as governing the *Hyperions*' intertextuality. Moreover, Keats's use of the verb "redeem" resonates suggestively against the Christological imagery of "The Fall." The poet of that poem—Keats's mature persona—redeems the flawed success of "Hyperion" and of its central symbol, Hyperion-Keats.

16. Harold Bloom, *The Anxiety of Influence: A Theory of Poetry* (New York: Oxford University Press, 1973). In using this phrase, I draw upon Bloom's concept of the revisionary ratio, but I restrict my reference to one phenomenon his theory suggests but does not address: the poet's need to surpass himself in order to consolidate and to *work* his transcendence of the precursor's influence. Moreover, Bloom is careful to maintain the abstract, analogical character of his argument; he treats text and psyche as two tropological and mutually illuminating structures. Bloom is careful to obstruct the reader's tendency to apply the Freudian groundplot reductively. I have been less concerned to eliminate the biographical dimension, since my interest is with the work as actually or possibly read and written, not as it 'reads itself' or 'writes itself.' My interest is, to put it another way, cruder and more historically oriented than Bloom's—not how "The Fall" situates itself within the tradition, but how the reader situates "The Fall" in a fragment tradition and in relation to "Hyperion."

Let me refer the reader, at this point, to Peter Larkin's "Wordsworth's 'After-Sojourn,'" *Studies in Romanticism* 20 (1981):409–36. Larkin's analysis of Wordsworth's negotiations with his diverse *personae* brings up some of the issues developed in this chapter. "This fragile rotation of roles succeeds in not compromising temporality only by being itself compromised by a radical and self-willed inequality of utterance. 'Early' and 'late' are not redeemed from being virtual equivalents of success and failure, but are moved closer to a problematic interdependence" (p. 410).

17. Bloom's description of the state he calls Kenosis (undoing, regression, isolation) opens itself to the logic I have outlined here, deriving from the poet's anxiety *vis à vis* his own oeuvre. Bloom's failure to consider this phenomenon might explain the ambiguity surrounding his representation of revision—the enabling-defensive sequence—as a perpetual activity. As I understand his theory, one would expect to find a single revisionary poem, or a series of transformations of this poem in a given poet's canon. The same tropes should not be deployed time after time, since conflicts *are* resolved, and anxieties are, if not annihilated, displaced and transformed. Once the stance is achieved, or the space cleared, those works that follow should have an easier time of situating themselves within the tradition—or at least a different manner of self-assertion, for the incorporation of their

own works into the tradition must change the literary universe for them as for other poets. I think Bloom's emphasis on the repetitive character of the revisionary process is justified, but the motivation for it should be located in the space of self-confrontation, or narcissistic anxiety.

18. Frank Kermode, *The Sense of An Ending* (New York: Oxford University Press, 1967), p. 39. See Tzvetan Todorov, "The Two Principles of Narrative," *Diacritics* 1 (Fall, 1971):40, for distinction between mythological and gnoseological narrative organization.

19. Kermode, *Sense of An Ending*, p. 39.

20. Bate, *John Keats*, p. 591.

21. Bloom, *Poetry and Repression*.

22. Ibid., p. 123.

23. Ibid., p. 140.

24. Ibid., pp. 123, 140.

25. John Jones, *John Keats's Dream of Truth* (London: Chatto and Windus, 1969), p. 102.

26. Christopher Ricks, *Keats and Embarrassment* (Oxford: Clarendon Press, 1974).

Chapter 11

1. All references to Keats's poetry from *The Poems of John Keats*, ed. Miriam Allott (London: Longman, 1970).

2. Blackstone, *The Consecrated Urn: An Interpretation of Keats in Terms of Growth and Form* (London: Longmans, Green, 1959), p. 228.

3. Lewis M. Schwartz, *Keats Reviewed by His Contemporaries: A Collection of Notices for the Years 1816–21* (Metuchen N. J.: Scarecrow Press, 1973), pp. 224, 226, 227; see also p. 281.

4. Schwartz, *Keats Reviewed*, p. 226.

5. William Michael Rossetti, *Life of John Keats* (London: Scott, 1887), p. 185.

6. George Lafourcade, *Swinburne's Hyperion and Other Poems* (London: Faber and Guyer, 1927), p. 100. Also, it is likely that Swinburne omits the central figure of Hyperion from his poem in order to avoid the difficulties of divine speech altogether.

7. Rossetti, *Life of John Keats*, p. 187.

8. Bate, *John Keats*, p.335.

9. "Benjamin Bailey remembered that 'Keats said this description of Apollo [a passage from *The Excursion* upon the Greek Mythology] should have ended at the "golden lute" and have left imagination to complete the picture, how he "filled the illumined groves." ' " John Middleton Murry, *Keats* (New York: The Noonday Press, 1955), p. 322.

10. John Jones, *John Keats's Dream of Truth* (London: Chatto and Windus, 1969), p. 74.

11. Thus we find statements like Blackstone's where he describes "the character of the first 'Hyperion' as abstract, adamantine, massive, and of the second, as

personal, psychological, exploratory, and tentative" (Blackstone, *Consecrated Urn*, p. 242). Blackstone is fully aware that "the second poem," "The Fall," is the later work, yet he honestly records his unprejudiced or naïve response to the poems. He admits that the later work has qualities one would expect to find in the earlier, and *vice versa*. His valuable description of his own reading shows him treating "The Fall" as the preliminary foray, in which the general plot, outline, allegorical system and central problem are mapped out, that they might be developed and applied in the "abstract, adamantine, and massive 'Hyperion.'" Yet Blackstone is forced to declare that Keats "abandons conventional epic ('Hyperion') for a psychological one" (p. 262). Here, we see that Blackstone's historical position and his habit of regarding "The Fall" as the more advanced and ambitious poem compel him to interpret what is simply a difference as an improvement, thus to contradict his own spontaneous sense of the works as they first appeared to him, synchronically as it were.

12. Schwartz, *Keats Reviewed*, p. 227.
13. Ibid., p. 224.

Chapter 12

1. Jean Duvignaud, *The Sociology of Art*, trans. Timothy Wilson (New York: Harper and Row, 1972), p. 44.
2. Marshall Brown, "Mozart and After: The Revolution in Musical Consciousness," *Critical Inquiry* 7 (Summer 1981):701.
3. Peter Bürger, *Theory of the Avant-Garde*, trans. Michael Shaw, foreword by Jochen Schulte-Sasse (Minneapolis: University of Minnesota Press, 1984), pp. xx, 34, 91. This approach has always seemed peculiarly suited to investigations of Romantic openness. The first part of the nineteenth century saw an unprecedented disintegration of social, political, and economic systems, and this situation no doubt promoted an unusual sensitivity to psychic disjunctiveness and conflict. This sensitivity surely conduced to the "discovery" of the fragment as a mimetically appropriate form: the symbolic articulation of historical experience.

The influence of one Enlightenment intellectual fashion—analytic reductionism —might also be conjectured as a contributing cause of the fragment's popularity. The fragment can readily figure as an inductive particular or experiential datum innocent of ideological overdetermination. Consider in this light Byron's famous response to Saint Peter (*Childe Harold's Pilgrimage* canto 4, stanza 157): "Thou seest not all; but piecemeal thou must break, / To separate contemplation, the great whole. . . ." The fragment here is represented both as an epistemological ideal and an irreducible sensory element.

Third, the blossoming of a mature historical consciousness, involving recognition of the relativity of event as well as interpretation, must have suggested the fragment's potential as a propositional form, a means of conceptualizing experience without inadvertently advancing a naïve absolutism or positivism. The fragment's eternally provisional status would render it theoretically invulnerable to disconfirmation. Inasmuch as Romantic historical thought is haunted by a sense of crisis—the suspicion that a full and achieved reality is always already somewhere, sometime, else—the fragment would again figure as an existentially reflective form.

Finally, the higher criticism, with its paleographic enthusiasm, its concept of the Bible as a compilation of fragments by many hands (Alexander Geddes, see Elinor Shaffer, *"Kubla Khan" and "The Fall of Jerusalem"* [Cambridge: Cambridge University Press, 1981], p. 78) and its general interest in conceiving all the great world systems as partial expressions of a unitary and holistic meaning which exists only noumenally, had to enhance the intellectual and spiritual authority of the fragment.

4. Thomas Kuhn, *The Structure of Scientific Revolutions*, International Encyclopaedia of Unified Science, 2nd edition (Chicago: University of Chicago Press, 1970), pp. 52–53. Also see Paul Feyerabend, *Against Method: Outline of an Anarchistic Theory of Knowledge* (London: NLB, 1975). I paraphrase and reduce Feyerabend's argument: Discoveries are made by illogical, counterinductive constructs (that is, observations overdetermined by some unarticulable concept) which do not make sense (cannot be organized or rationalized) until enough have accumulated.

5. Kuhn, *Scientific Revolutions*, p. 53.

6. Jan Mukařovský, *A Prague School Reader in Esthetics, Literary Structure, and Style*, trans. P. Garvin (Washington, D.C.: Georgetown University Press, 1964); *Structure, Sign, and Function*, trans. J. Burbank and P. Steiner (New Haven: Yale University Press, 1977). In the latter volume, see "Standard Language and Poetic Language," pp. 17–30, and "The Concept of the Whole in the Theory of Art," p. 78.

If the poetic fragment had not initially and dramatically occurred within a literary system that celebrates authorial impulse, explosion of form, and instances of semiotic and rhetorical indeterminacy—and if readers had not been prepared to regard reading maneuvers as dimensions of textual design—the RFP might not have emerged as an instance of anticlosure. Its irresolution might have remained an unmarked feature, irrelevant to a literary reception.

Irresolution as a historically specific closural form is an aspect of the more fundamental study of poetic closure, a study initiated, and most expertly and elegantly pursued by Barbara Herrnstein Smith, *Poetic Closure: A Study of How Poems End* (Chicago: University of Chicago Press, 1968). Smith discusses closure, anticlosure, and (by inference), nonclosure as products of the presence, peculiar disposition, or absence of certain formal elements. She allows reception its contribution to closure, but her focus is on the work's positive features—the absolute and, it seems, ahistorical (even physiological) limits on textual construction. Through her anatomy of closural styles, however, Smith invites us to pay more attention to reception history. A work that seems unresolved to one generation of readers may offer a maverick resolution (and be an instance of anticlosure) to another generation. The nineteenth century not only produced fragment poems, it produced an atmosphere, and an audience, capable of transforming inherited and subsequent poetic fragments into literary forms. We are that audience.

7. Rilke, *Auguste Rodin*, quoted in Albert Elsen, *Rodin* (New York: Museum of Modern Art, 1963), p. 180.

8. Pierre Macherey, *A Theory of Literary Production*, trans. Geoffrey Wall (London: Routledge and Kegan Paul, 1978), pp. 42, 77–84, 98–101.

9. Mukařovský, "The Concept of the Whole in the Theory of Art," p. 75.

10. Jerome McGann has recently discriminated "the Romantic ideology" and explored the procedures by which it is effectuated. I refer the reader to this outstanding and inclusive critique, and specifically to its sympathetic but removed explanations of Romanticism's most disinterested gestures and effects. *The Romantic Ideology: A Critical Investigation* (Chicago: University of Chicago Press, 1983).

11. Leigh Hunt, *Foliage: Or Poems Original and Translated* (London: Ollier, 1818), p. 19. ". . . for it is not industry, but a defeat of the ends of it, and a mere want of ideas, to work and trouble themselves so much as most of our countrymen do."

"But he said to me: 'My grace is sufficient for you, for my power is made perfect in weakness.' Therefore I will boast all the more gladly about my weakness, so that Christ's power may rest on me" (St. Paul, 2 Corinthians 12: 19). The female, the organic, the child, and the aristocrat all owe their ideological authority to an appearance of passivity so thoroughgoing, so confident, and so predicated on inner wealth and self-coincidence as to make assertive, aggressive behaviors look like confessions of vulgar inadequacy. The Romantics appropriated and adapted to their purposes several mythologies already inscribed within the cultural consciousness of the age; that is, rather than invent an ideologically serviceable self-representation, they activated certain established associations conducive to the enhancement of their prestige. The associations that most interested the Romantics were those that aligned worldly ineffectuality with spiritual power—a power so absolute as to make exertion or display unnecessary.

The most obvious source of this politically serviceable formula was, of course, the Passion. The central Christian narrative—and the host of saints' and martyrs' lives it engendered—brings together the unlikely combination of terrible suffering and terrific power. Christ is, of course, God *before* his ordeal; through his trial, he evinces his divinity. The gain in spiritual power is proportional to the decline in temporal authority (which, of course, is recovered almost immediately).

This definitive Christian logic, applied to situations involving individuals less certain of their election, undergoes a change of sequence, such that the capacity and willingness to suffer greatly *confer* divinity. "Suffering enormous hath made a god of me." Romantic suffering often takes the form of simple passivity: "Consider the lillies of the field; they sow not neither do they reap." The proverb might easily serve as the text for Wordsworth's "Resolution and Independence" or even for Shelley's "Ode to the West Wind." According to Romantically mediated Christian doctrine, those who yield themselves most fully to a higher power, relinquishing particular human ambition and aggressiveness, may realize a force far in excess of conventional embodiments of power. The Romantic appropriation of Christian iconography and ideology is, of course, a commonplace. The practical political uses of the christological model, however, have been less thoroughly investigated.

The same holds true for the Romantic idealization of the child, another ideologically potent image inherited from the Christian tradition and politicized during the Enlightenment. Wordsworth's famous celebration of the child, "Mighty Prophet! Seer blest!" develops the important association of innocence—lack of ego—with power. The child's insight is in direct proportion to his intellectual and affective passivity or quiescence. Truths "rest upon" him because he gives no thought to the labor of seeking after them. We might recall in this context Coleridge's phrase, "little child, limber elf . . . who always finds and never seeks." The less the child *does*, the more he *is* and receives.

The reticence or passivity of women, traditionally interpreted or experienced as a sign of depth and interiority, intimates the possession of a power too great and subtle for display. The political, social, and economic marginality of women is, in this mythology, associated with internal power capable of generating force invisibly and thus realizing its will indirectly. The seductive retirement associated with the feminine, coupled with the suggestion of dark, chthonic, generative efficacy, made this image a natural for Romantic adaptation.

Last, the Romantics appropriated certain associations attaching to aristocratic modes—or myths—of being. That is, the aristocrat is traditionally defined by his exemption from Adam's curse: the need to labor for one's living. The income of the nobleman comes to him freely from a Nature which thereby acknowledges and consecrates his inalienable virtue. Of course, the aristocrat's passivity and disdain for the obvious exercise of his powers is accompanied by worldly power and privilege, the spiritual and secular positions' equivalent.

By drawing down these diverse but loosely-related associations, the poets could capitalize on their compelled quiescence or marginality, and emphasize the generosity—Nature's "ready wealth," for example—that enabled their spiritually productive acts of consciousness.

12. The concept of the organic fragment raises a contradiction, one that exposes the defensive and compensatory impulse of the larger figuration in which it participates: the refusal of "the mechanic" and all its implications. There are no fragments in the plant and animal kingdoms, or more to the point, nonaesthetic discourses on the organic do not represent phases or parts of organic wholes as fragments. A bud, for example, is not a fragment of a rose, nor are a paw and a puppy fragments of a dog. One may speak of bone fragments, or refer to the fragment of a leaf or twig, but inasmuch as these unnatural, traumatic partitions of organic material are, through their individuation, rendered lifeless, they are not, strictly speaking, organic fragments.

13. The RFP, while it collapses form and content, distinguishes text from poem. It is the latter one wants, of course, and which the early readers of Romantic fragments were accustomed to receiving *in* their texts. The RFP presents a text that facilitates a poem, a poem which is time-place-and-reader specific and therefore pointedly partial with respect to the infinite number of poems able to be derived from that text. The fragment thus arouses the reader's desire not just for more text but for more poem—or for a fuller, more inclusive, more authoritative reading. In this as in so many of its effects, the RFP was an unusually frustrating and thus controlling form.

14. Lawrence Goldstein, *Ruins and Empire: The Evolution of a Theme in Augustan and Romantic Literature* (Pittsburgh: University of Pittsburgh Press, 1977), p. 35.

15. Pierre-Simon Ballanche, quoted in Roland Mortier, *La Poétique des Ruines* (Geneva: Librairie Droz, 1974), pp. 163, 165.

16. R. L. Brett and A. R. Jones, eds., *Lyrical Ballads: Wordsworth and Coleridge* (London: Methuen, 1963), p. 301.

17. "Time, which destroys the beauty and use of the story of particular facts, stript of the poetry which should invest them, augments that of Poetry, and for ever develops new and wonderful applications of the eternal Truth which it contains" (Shelley, *Defence of Poetry*).

Wordsworth's fragment poem suggests that time itself has lyricized and made eternally autonomous the tragic narrative, just as it has sublimed the living creature, the boy, into a living spirit.

18. Moreover, by subverting narrative form, the RFP implicitly effected several denials. It denied the irreversibility of history; it repudiated causality; it offered an escape from the crisis-ridden contingency of life as it felt to the early nineteenth-century intellectual. The spatial fragment shifts the poetic center of gravity from event to the feeling and responses of a poet-hero who stands apart from history and is as a repository of eternal visions and values.

19. This might seem a curious motivation and effect, for the fragment can easily recommend itself as a friendly form, one that throws off the authority of conclusive statement and purport and invites the reader to share in the act of textual construction. The poet's sincerity—his neglect of all those technical, formal, and thematic defenses that finish the poem and force the reader into the position of passive admirer—might well be construed as an impulse toward communion with the reader rather than withdrawal from him.

The two interests are not mutually exclusive. First, because the fragment's realization depends upon the reader's active engagement with the text, textual critique must include self-criticism. The fragment formally demonstrates that "we murder to dissect"; by dramatizing the fact that critical "violence" wounds the critic as well as the text (insofar as the critic's involvement with the text half-constitutes it a poem), the fragment communicates its message with unusual force.

Second, by uniting poet and reader as equal participants in a corporate enterprise—the making of meaning—the fragment poem made available to the poet an experience (or hypothesis) of social cooperation and familial exchange. The RFP could thus come to the reader with its hands outstretched, to echo Keats, not plunged in its pockets and proudly indifferent to reception.

20. Friedrich Schlegel, *Dialogue on Poetry and Literary Aphorisms*, trans. Ernst Behler and Roman Struc (University Park, Pa.: Pennsylvania State University Press, 1968), p. 125; from Selected Aphorisms from the Lyceum, no. 37.

21. David Luke, "Keats's Letters: Fragments of an Aesthetics of Fragments," *Genre* 2 (Summer 1978):208–26.

22. From a modern perspective, the RFP looks like a strikingly use-oriented form in that its openness encourages literary *bricolage*, or creative adaptation of object to interest. I emphasize, however, the modernity of this outlook; in its own

day, the RFP's apparent failure to achieve its effect and thus to define its meaning or use to the reader presented an "anti" rather than "non" utilitarian aspect.

23. Before sketching the political environment of the Romantic poet, let me reiterate, there was no such "typical" and representative figure. In that my argument in the following pages rests on the premise that English poets of the early nineteenth century suffered an awesome loss of corporate identity, a loss that precipitated consistently defensive postures, I can hardly refer to these writers by way of a collective and reductive designation. The tremendous diversity and contradiction evident in the most cursory study of the English Romantics is, nonetheless, contained by a single, though complex ideology. It is that structure of predispositions, motivations, and values that I denote when I allude to "the Romantic poet."

24. Gerald Graff, *Literature Against Itself: Literary Ideas in Modern Society* (Chicago: University of Chicago Press, 1979). Jerome McGann, *The Romantic Ideology: A Critical Investigation* (Chicago: University of Chicago Press, 1983).

25. DeQuincy's inversion is itself symptomatic of the artist's unease and of his defensively idealistic response to that anxiety.

26. Karl Kroeber, *Romantic Landscape Vision: Constable and Wordsworth* (Madison: University of Wisconsin Press, 1975), p. 95.

27. Macherey, *Theory of Literary Production*, p. 19.

28. Ibid., p. 71.

29. Ibid., p. 19.

30. Robert Tucker, ed., *The Marx-Engels Reader* (New York: W. W. Norton and Co., 1972), p. 236.

31. McGann, *Romantic Ideology*, pp. 47–48.

32. Macherey, *Theory of Literary Production*, p. 84.

Chapter 13

1. This thought recurs in Wordsworth's "Hart-Leap Well."

> "She [Nature] leaves these objects to a slow decay,
> That what we are, and have been, may be known;
> But at the coming of a milder day,
> These monuments shall all be overgrown."

This statement makes sense only if we grasp the narrator's respect for "quiet being" as opposed to noisy meaning. As evocative and as morally useful as the historical monument is, its highest state will be, so the poem argues, one of sheer presence, undiluted by reference.

2. Tennyson's Mariana is the inheritor of Margaret's vigil. Mariana is "waiting" made active and heroic.

3. Roland Mortier, *La Poétique des Ruines* (Geneva: Librairie Droz, 1974), p. 131. "History, confronted by the ruin, seems like a cyclical procession in which the instant dissolves in duration, where there is no conqueror or victim, but a

derisive alternation" (my translation). See Michael Fisher, "Marxism and English Romanticism: The Persistence of the Romantic Movement," *Romanticism Past and Present* 6 (1982):27–46. The antiempiricist character of some dominant twentieth-century critical ideologies may be read as a more elaborate and radical defense against the conditions that precipitated the Romantic ideology.

4. Jerome McGann, *The Romantic Ideology: A Critical Investigation* (Chicago: University of Chicago Press, 1983), pp. 82–86.

5. Mortier, *Poétique des Ruines*, p. 99.

6. Larzer Ziff, *Literary Democracy: The Declaration of Cultural Independence in America* (New York: Viking Press, 1981), p. 252.

INDEX

. . . .